ANALYSES OF MUSICAL CLASSICS

Book I

By the same author

A GRADED MUSIC COURSE FOR SCHOOLS

Book One
Book Two
Book Three

SCORE READING, FORM AND HISTORY

Being Book Four of *A Graded Music Cours for Schools*

HARMONY

MELODY WRITING AND ANALYSIS

ADDITIONAL SIGHTSINGING EXERCISES

For use with *A Graded Music Course for Schools*

READ, SING AND PLAY—Teacher's and Pupils' Books

Book One
Book Two

BASIC MUSIC KNOWLEDGE

ANALYSES OF MUSICAL CLASSICS

Book Two

Book Three

GRADED AURAL TESTS FOR ALL PURPOSES

ANALYSES OF MUSICAL CLASSICS

Book I

Annie O. Warburton

LONGMAN

LONGMAN GROUP LIMITED
London

Associated companies, branches and representatives throughout the world

First published 1963
Latest impression 1978

ISBN 0 582 32484 x

Printed in Hong Kong by
Yu Luen Offset Printing Factory Ltd

Contents

Preface

This book is intended for music lovers of all ages who wish to analyse the compositions of the great composers in order to understand how they work. There is no better way of getting an appreciative insight into their music.

Such music lovers may be students working on their own, school boys and girls preparing for examinations such as the General Certificate of Education, or teachers who wish to study the works before passing their knowledge on to their pupils.

The book is planned on a chronological basis. Each chapter is concerned with a particular type of composition by a composer or a group of contemporary composers. It contains general comments on the period and the kind of works being written at the time, and then it goes on to analyse a number of representative compositions.

Most of the compositions chosen are works which have recently been prescribed for O Level in the General Certificate of Education by the various Examining Boards of England and Wales. They have previously been analysed in articles in the *Music Teacher*, and acknowledgment is gratefully made to Evans Brothers Ltd., who publish this magazine.

These analyses are intended for detailed study, with the copy of the music in front of the student, so there is no need for quotations in music type. Instead there are frequent references to bar numbers, so the student should have no difficulty in finding his way about.

The student who is working on his own should read the general comments at the beginning of a particular chapter, and then follow the analysis of one of the works in detail with the copy in front of him. After this he should try to analyse another of the given works by himself before looking at the analysis given in the book.

It does not follow that, if his analysis is different, it is wrong. There is often more than one way of analysing a movement, and two ways are quite frequently suggested here. The student who finds his analysis is different should think of arguments for and against the differing analyses, and thus clarify his own outlook on the music.

The more works that are analysed in this way the better. It will help the student to realize that no two works are alike, and that the great composers rarely produce a work which follows the text books on musical form in every particular. He will develop an appreciative understanding of how each composer adapted the various forms to suit his purpose. And thus he will gradually become competent to analyse an unprepared work, which may be a requirement for a diploma examination or for the Advanced Level or Special paper of the General Certificate of Education.

The O Level music candidate, however, cannot usually devote sufficient time to this kind of study. He may be able to do little more than read the general comment at the beginning of the chapter concerned and then study the particular work he needs for the examination. The Examining Boards tend to repeat their prescribed works, partly so as to save expense for the schools which have to buy the copies, and partly because certain works are particularly suitable for the student at this stage or are great classics which he ought to know. So a set of copies of this book in the school music library would probably come in useful every year: the general comments, and the analysis of a similar work would be of value even if a particular prescribed work was not included in the book.

There are other books of analyses which the student should find useful, notably the great series of volumes *Essays in Musical Analysis* by Tovey, published by the Oxford University Press, and the Pelican books on the Symphony, the Concerto and Chamber Music. These books fulfil a different purpose, however, as they are more in the nature of programme notes, intended for the concert goer or the radio or gramophone listener rather than for the student who wants to make a detailed study from the copy; and they do not usually contain references to bar numbers. There is obviously room for both kinds of approach, and it is hoped that this book will fill a need that has often been expressed by both students and teachers.

It would be surprising if there were no errors in a book containing so many references to bar numbers and key changes. The author apologizes in advance for any such errors, and would be grateful to readers who would be kind enough to point out any that they happen to see.

I

The Study of a Musical Classic

No work of art can be fully appreciated without an understanding of the life and circumstances of the composer, of the period in which he lived, and of the forerunners and contemporaries who affected his work.

So the logical study of a classic should proceed from the general to the particular. First the general, historical background of the composer should be studied, so that the student can realize the kind of world into which he was born, both socially and musically.

Following this should come a study of the contemporary musical scene, which will therefore include his greater musical contemporaries and any musicians with whom he happened to have contact.

Then the life of the composer can be read, and as many of his works as possible should be heard. The period in which he wrote the particular work should be given more attention.

Finally the particular work should be studied. It may be necessary, at this stage, to spend some time in studying the score and the instruments used if it is a chamber or orchestral work, and also to study the musical forms found in the work if they are not already known. The student should become thoroughly familiar with the work by repeated hearings on the gramophone. If it is a work he can play or sing, by himself or with other students or friends, so much the better. A concert performance is the ideal culmination of the study.

Let us suppose that an O Level candidate for the General Certificate of Education has to study the following works for the examination: Handel's "Messiah" (or part of it); Mozart's G minor symphony; Beethoven's piano sonata, op. 2, no. 1; and Brahms' "Academic Festival" overture. Here is an outline course of study, which can be followed by a teacher with his class or by an individual student working alone. It is divided into stages, but the amount of time that can be spent at each stage will vary very much. A teacher who is preparing a class for the examination and who has not sufficient lesson time available may have to leave some stages for the students to study on their own, by reading or listening, as the case may be. Students will find the author's *Score Reading, Form and History* useful as a basis for the background knowledge.

1. The social and musical world into which Handel was born.

2. The life and works of Handel's greatest musical contemporary, Bach.

3. The life and works of Handel, stressing that he was primarily an opera composer, and showing how and why he turned to oratorio writing.

4. A brief history of the oratorio. Also reference to development of French and Italian overtures.

5. The "Messiah".

6. The musical changes that took place between the times of Bach and Handel and those of Haydn and Mozart.

7. Haydn and his development of the symphony, the quartet, and musical forms, particularly sonata form.

8. The life and works of Mozart, linking him up with Haydn. Particular reference to the three great symphonies written in 1788.

9. The orchestral score at this period, with particular reference to Mozart's use of the woodwind and to the composition of the woodwind in these three symphonies.

10. Mozart's G minor symphony.

11. The life and works of Beethoven, linking him with Haydn and Mozart and comparing their compositions. The developments he made in symphonies and sonatas. The social changes taking place in Europe and Beethoven's reactions to them.

12. Beethoven's sonata, op. 2, no. 2, noting the passages which are in the style of Haydn and those which show signs of his future development.

13. Music in the first half of the nineteenth century, particularly in Germany. The development of romanticism. The new social world, and the concert-going public.

14. The life and works of Brahms. His links with both classicists and romanticists, and with Vienna, the home also of Haydn, Mozart and Beethoven.

15. The enlargement of the orchestra, comparing the Mozart and Brahms scores. The development of the concert overture, and the free use of modified sonata form in this particular overture.

16. Brahms' "Academic Festival" overture.

Other students, who have no examination in mind, may use this book. They may wish to obtain a thorough knowledge of one particular work, either because they feel very attracted to it or because they are concerned in a performance of it. But although this book is meant for consultation rather than continuous reading it should be pointed out that it is better to study more than the one work concerned, as every work thoroughly known helps towards the better understanding of every other work. This kind of study can be undertaken by a student on his own. The piano student, perhaps preparing for a diploma, who knows only the particular sonata he is preparing for the examination is obviously less well equipped as a musician than the person who has become acquainted with other sonatas by the same composer. And what better method can there be of really getting an understanding of the musical thoughts of a composer than that of analysing his music and seeing his mind at work?

Whatever the student happens to be, a composer, a conductor, a performer, a teacher of others, or just a music-loving amateur, he will be the better equipped for having made a thorough study of some great musical classics.

2

The English Madrigal Composers

A student may wish to make a study of madrigals because he is a member of a madrigal group, because he has to compose in the madrigal style for examination purposes or because he is required to study some madrigals for a particular examination.

He is recommended to read *The English Madrigal Composers* by Dr Fellowes, published by the Oxford University Press, or the same author's *The English Madrigal School: a Guide to its Practical Use*, published by Stainer & Bell.

Madrigals were written more for the enjoyment of the singers than for a possible audience, and the best way for students to get to know them is by singing them. A class of students can usually get together and make some attempt at performance, though the madrigals may have to be transposed downwards, as they tend to be high. A lone student should make an effort to find some friends who will help him out, for nothing takes the place of performance as a means of acquiring a real understanding and appreciation of a madrigal.

Grove's dictionary defines a madrigal as "a form of secular composition for two or more voices practised originally in Northern Italy in the fourteenth century and revived in the sixteenth and early seventeenth centuries, during which period it assumed the style by which it is chiefly known and became popular over the greater part of Europe". In the fourteenth century it was customary for the chief part to be sung by the tenor (Latin, *tenere*, to hold), but in the course of time it was transferred to the top part. Yet the perpetual imitation of fragments of tune between all the parts makes the top part merely the first among equals. This can be a source of confusion to an inexperienced student who expects a main tune, probably in the top part, with subordinate parts underneath, and does not know how to listen to the interweaving of equally important parts. This is one of the main reasons why he should get to know a madrigal by singing it.

Netherlandish composers living in Italy, such as Arcadelt, Willaert and Lassus had much to do with the development of the madrigal, though Palestrina, Monteverdi and many minor Italian composers wrote madrigals too. They were intended to be sung by cultured people and were usually in five or six parts. They were mainly love songs, offering plenty of opportunity for emotional expression. The poem was usually short, rarely exceeding twelve lines, and there was frequent repetition of the words.

There are a few examples of English madrigals written before 1580, such as "In Going to my Lonely Bed" by Edwards which is in the style of Arcadelt. But it was Nicholas Yonge who, by publishing a volume of Italian madrigals called *Musica Transalpina* in 1588, started the spate of English madrigal writing which ran through the rest of Elizabeth I's reign and on into Stuart times.

The madrigals were published in separate part books, so that a singer had to sing his part without the help of seeing how it fitted with the other parts. This is how a string quartet is published today, but vocal music usually has all the parts in the one copy, and modern editions of madrigals are published in this way.

Madrigal singing was a favourite source of enjoyment in the homes of cultured people, and the story is well known of the young gentleman who came to the composer, Morley, for lessons because he had been so ashamed the previous evening that he could not sing his part in a madrigal at sight. But there must often have been occasions when there were not sufficient singers to perform all the parts of a madrigal and the performance was helped out by instrumental players. Hence the phrase sometimes seen "apt for voices or viols". So the students of today who cannot muster all the parts are quite justified in making use of the piano, when singing for their own enjoyment and understanding.

Bar lines were not used in the original editions, and they are only inserted in modern editions as guide posts for ease in reading. They do not imply an accent, for the position of the accent varied from part to part. This free rhythm is another source of confusion to an inexperienced student who is only acquainted with music which has a regularly recurring accent in all the parts.

Nor did the original editions have expression marks, these are always the additions of a modern editor.

In madrigals it was customary to treat the first line of words for some time, usually with imitative entries, and then go on to the next line of words, using another set of figures for imitation, and so on to the end of the madrigal. There was no thought of a return to the original theme, and this again seems strange to modern ears.

Madrigals were written in the old ecclesiastical modes. In their original form these contained no sharps or flats. The Ionian mode was from C to C, with C as its final (or tonic, as we should say to-day). The Dorian mode had D as its final, the Phrygian E, the Lydian F, the Mixolydian G, and the Aeolian A. There was no mode on B, because it did not have a perfect fifth from its final to its dominant.

Of these modes the Ionian (our major scale) was the least used, as it was thought to be vulgar. The Dorian and the Aeolian, with modifications, became our minor scale at a later date.

All these modes could be transposed a fourth higher, and then they had a B flat as a signature. But no other transposition was used, so if you find an Elizabethan madrigal in, say, A major, you know it has been transposed by a modern editor so as to be at an easier pitch for the singers.

The above summary of the modes is a simplified statement, though it is hoped it is enough for the purpose of this book. There are many features that make a madrigal difficult to appreciate by a student brought up on the nineteenth-century classics: the free rhythm, the contrapuntal texture, the lack of regular four-bar phrases, the lack of the unity that is created by repetition, as used in later musical forms. But the use of the old modes is perhaps more responsible than any other feature for the feeling of strangeness. The student is unconsciously missing the modern tonality, the use of the primary triads, the familiar perfect cadence or a modulation to the dominant.

However, familiarity will bring acceptance and later, it is hoped, full appreciation of the nuances made possible by the variety of modes. It is noteworthy that in most music heard today we have only two modes in normal use, the major and the minor, though each can be transposed to twelve different positions. The madrigalists had six modes, though only one transposition was available. Six different arrangements of the tones and semitones in relation to the tonic obviously produce more subtle tonal effects than do two. It was the development of harmony in the seventeenth century that narrowed the modes down to two, for the old modes did not lend themselves to the use of primary triads and modulation to related keys, which are the essence of modern tonality.

Canzonets for Two Voices: Morley

These canzonets are easier to sing than many madrigals, as only two parts are required. Some of the canzonets are rather high, but transposition should not worry any students except the few with absolute pitch. Two-part madrigals are rare—in fact, these are the only ones in Fellowes' "English Madrigal School" series—but it is remarkable how full and satisfying they sound.

Most of these canzonets are for equal voices, and are full of imitation, quite often at the same pitch. It was the custom to change the dynamics when a passage was repeated: for example, first time *f*, second time *p*; but gradual crescendos and diminuendos were unknown. No expression marks were in the original editions.

As with all madrigals, the first line of words is treated for some time, then a new figure appears with a new line of words, usually again with imitative entries, and so on to the last line of words.

Numbers 1–7 have the key-signature of one flat, (referred to above), so their modes are transposed a fourth higher than the original modes. Numbers 8–12 have no key-signature.

Numbers 1–4, with one flat in the signature, have F as the key note or "final", so they sound to our ears very much as if they are in the key of F major. They are, in fact, using the Ionian mode, which is like our modern major mode (C to C without accidentals; or F to F with a B flat in the transposed mode, as in this case). There are a number of B naturals and E flats in these first four canzonets. If they had been written in the original and not the transposed mode they would have been F sharp and B flat, the two accidentals that had been allowed by custom for a long time.

Numbers 5–7 are in the transposed Dorian mode. G is the final, which is ray or the supertonic in modern parlance, given the signature of one flat. If there were no signature this mode would be D to D without accidentals.

Numbers 8 and 9 have no signature and are in the mixolydian mode (G to G without accidentals). Numbers 10–12 are, like nos. 1–4, in the Ionian mode; but they have no signature, so they are in the original, not the transposed, mode, with C as the final.

The Silver Swan: Gibbons

"The Silver Swan" is issued by Stainer & Bell in the original arrangement for five mixed voices. But it is also available in a four-part female voice arrangement, published by Novello, which should be particularly helpful for girls' schools.

The original arrangement has a key-signature of one flat. It feels very much like our modern F major, with a modulation to the dominant at "reedy shore" and "close mine eyes", and perhaps this is why it is such a popular madrigal with people who are not used to the madrigal idiom. It is in the Ionian mode (C to C, white notes of the piano), transposed a fourth higher. It is also more modern in that it repeats the second page on p. 3 to different words, thus making a plan **A B B**. In Elizabethan times it was more usual to introduce a new idea with every new line of words.

It begins in a very harmonic style, but imitative entries occur at "leaning her breast" and "farewell all joys". However the style is so simple that it makes a very good introduction to both singing and listening to madrigals.

As Vesta was from Latmos Hill Descending: Weelkes

This madrigal begins and ends in the mixolydian mode (G to G, white notes of the piano), though there are frequent places where it moves to the Dorian or Ionian mode. The original edition is without key-signature but it is very high for all parts except the alto. A transposed edition is published by Oxford University Press.

The madrigal is one of the set "The Triumphs of Oriana", edited by Morley, but written by a number of different composers. They are all in praise of "Oriana", and older history books say this was a poetic name for Queen Elizabeth, for whom they were intended. But some people now think they were for Anne of Denmark, who might have become Queen of England. Certainly Elizabeth had died before they were published.

It is possible that the many repetitions of the words may prevent some pupils from grasping their meaning as a whole. They are concerned with Diana's nymphs and shepherds, who leave their goddess "all alone" in order to join the shepherds of Oriana's train in singing the praises of the maiden queen.

The madrigal follows the usual method of treating a line at a time, often with imitative entries, and then going on to another musical idea with the next line of words. It is full of imitative word painting: "descending"; "she spied"; "ascending"; "running down". Two voices enter at "two by two"; three at "three by three", all five at "together", and one voice only at "all alone". All the voices sing *ff* in block harmony at "then sang the shepherds and nymphs of Diana"; and the many imitative repetitions of "Long live fair Oriana" form a grand climax.

3

Corelli and Purcell

The seventeenth century was an experimental period in the history of music. Opera had its birth round about 1600, and it stimulated the development of instruments (which were needed for its accompaniment) and the growth of a harmonic style of writing (which was more suitable as a background to a solo singer on the stage than was the polyphonic style).

Gradually the old modes died out as major and minor tonalities took their place. The harpsichord began to be used as a background to supply the harmony in almost all kinds of vocal and instrumental composition. The harpsichordist played from a figured bass which was called the "*continuo*". In chamber and orchestral music the 'cello played the bass line at the same time as the harpsichordist played the complete chords.

The violin family, which had existed for some time by the side of the viol family, began to supersede it, as its instruments were less clumsy and offered greater opportunities for virtuosity. The Amati, Guarneri and Stradivari families made their wonderful violins during this period.

Corelli, the first great violinist, violin teacher and violin composer, was born in 1653. He travelled a good deal, and achieved fame throughout Europe. His first set of sonatas for two violins, 'cello and *continuo* were published in 1681. The two violins had equally important contrapuntal parts above the *continuo* part, which was played by the 'cello and the harpsichord.

Purcell wrote a number of fantasias for strings in 1680. But these had no *continuo* part, and were more on the lines of the fantasias written for viols fifty years earlier. Then in 1683 he wrote two sets of sonatas for two violins, 'cello and *continuo* in the new Italian style, though they are less violinistic than Corelli's. According to Grove's dictionary these sonatas "appealed to those who carry musical souls about them, but much less to those who carried violins about them". Purcell was not primarily a violinist, as was Corelli, yet even Corelli did not go beyond the third position.

Corelli was also the first great string writer of *concerti grossi*. These were written for a group of solo instruments (*concertino* or *concertante*), contrasted with a *tutti* of strings (*ripieno*). There was always a *continuo* part, shown only by figures under the bass, which was harmonized as an accompaniment by harpsichord or organ. A *concerto grosso* was often in three movements, with a long first movement in *ritornello* form, a slow second movement, and a quick finale, often a rondo. (For more about *ritornello* form see p. 32.)

Opera had developed slowly in England. A masque of Ben Jonson's was set in the style of an opera as early as 1617. But "The Siege of Rhodes" is usually considered to be the first English opera. It was written in 1656 by five different composers, but the music is lost.

Purcell wrote a tremendous quantity of music in his short life. Most of it was vocal, either for the Church or the stage. He was continually commissioned to write incidental music for the stage, and he often collaborated with his contemporary, Dryden. Dryden wrote the libretto of "King Arthur" and "The Indian Queen", plays to which Purcell set an unusually large amount of music. But he wrote only one true opera "Dido and Aeneas", and that was commissioned for a girls' school.

He also wrote a number of suites or "lessons" for harpsichord, which were intended for his pupils. The pieces are simpler than those of the great Elizabethan virginal composers, and give the impression that he was not particularly interested in this branch of composition.

The Christmas Concerto : Corelli

In addition to writing sixty sonatas, Corelli wrote twelve *concerti grossi*, eight being church concertos (*da chiesa*) and four being for the chamber (*da camera*). Number 8, known as the "Christmas Concerto" is *da chiesa* and is therefore in a more serious style than the *da camera* concertos. It is the best known of them all, perhaps because of the famous Pastorale with which it ends.

This particular *concerto grosso* is more broken up than many. It has a few bars of *vivace* introduction, followed by a short *grave* section. Then comes an *allegro* in binary form, in which the string soloists have rather more to do.

A change of key, from G minor to E flat major, brings in a lovely *adagio* with imitative entries for the soloists. An imperfect cadence leads to an *allegro*, but the *adagio* section soon returns, and this time it has four bars of coda, ending with a perfect cadence in E flat major.

A short *vivace* follows, now in the tonic key, G minor, again. It is in binary form and is rather dance-like. So also is the following *allegro*, which is again in binary form. But the second part contains a repetition of the opening bars at 157, which almost gives a hint of ternary form, and it ends with some contrasting *piano* and *forte* passages which may have an underlying programme, possibly preparing for the Pastorale.

The final movement, the famous *Pastorale*, is in the tonic major. It is unusual to end a concerto with a slow movement, as happens here. The Pastorale is one of several famous examples of the same style, such as the pastoral symphonies in Bach's "Christmas Oratorio" and Handel's "Messiah".

Dramatic pastoral plays were one of the forerunners of opera. The Musette and the Siciliana were pastoral tunes imitating the sound of the shepherd's pipe. They were always in compound time, and often had a drone bass. Such were the origins of the Pastorale or pastoral symphony, which came to be associated with the shepherds in the field on Christmas Eve.

This particular Pastorale is in $\frac{12}{8}$ time. It has a cadence in the dominant at bar 12 and then returns to the tonic, ending with a cadence in that key at 26. A section beginning in E minor follows, and it ends in B minor at 35. Then comes a return to the opening in the tonic key. A coda begins at 47, in which dominant and tonic pedals are prominent.

This movement is frequently performed without the rest of the concerto, and most school orchestras should be able to play it with enjoyment.

Four-Part Fantasias, nos. 1–4*: Purcell*

The first four of the four-part fantasias were all composed between 10 and 19 June 1680. They were originally written for a consort of viols, without a *continuo* part, in the polyphonic Elizabethan style. But this style was already becoming old-fashioned, and the fantasias were never published in Purcell's lifetime. They are now published in an arrangement for violin, viola and 'cello, and are more often played in this form today. They are written in equally important contrapuntal parts, and at times are remarkably dissonant.

They are each in one movement, though there are variations of speed. Students who have sung, played or heard Elizabethan music, either for voices or viols, will recognize the style. At the beginning of each fantasia, and whenever there is a change of speed, it is usual for the instruments to enter in imitation of each other. When they have come to the end of the treatment of one figure they usually start off with another, just as happens when fresh words occur in a madrigal.

The slow section of the first fantasia begins in a more harmonic style, as does also the slow section of the third. But contrapuntal imitations always enter before very long. The style is free and fantasia-like, and the tonality is constantly shifting. Look, for example, at the slow section of the first fantasia. It begins in B flat major (the relative major); but in the course of the next two or three bars there are sharpened Fs, Ds and As, then comes Ic V in F sharp minor followed by I in F sharp major. This mixture of minor and major is typical of Purcell.

Three Songs: Purcell

Purcell's songs were written nearly one hundred years later than Morley's canzonets, and their style is very different. The modes had practically died out, though there are relics here and there. The voice was now accompanied by a *continuo* part normally played by a harpsichord, and often by other instruments as well. The *continuo* part was originally written as a figured or unfigured bass, and students should realize that the piano part which they see in their copy is a modern arrangement, based on the *continuo* and any additional instrumental parts the song may have.

"Sound the Trumpet" is taken from an ode "Come ye Sons of Art away", written for Queen Mary's birthday, which uses quite a large orchestra, including trumpets and drums. "Music for awhile" is part of the incidental music to a play of Dryden's called *Oedipus* and "I attempt from Love's Sickness to fly" comes from an opera "The Indian Queen". The probability is, therefore, that all these songs originally had orchestral parts in addition to the *continuo*, though modern editions show only a piano accompaniment.

"*Sound the Trumpet*" is a joyful noise in *coloratura* style, and few works are more fun for a choir to sing. It is built on a ground bass, which is played eight times in the first section in the key of F, while the second section has it twice in C major, twice in D minor and three times in F major again. Over this there are a series of figures treated imitatively, a new figure for each set of new words, so that there is a similarity here with the style of Morley.

The bass of "*Music for awhile*" is very similar. It has the same continuous quaver movement, with the ground bass five times in the tonic F minor, twice in C minor and twice in E flat major before returning to the tonic, where it is heard five times more. In this case, however, there are a few short links between some of the repetitions. The mood is very different, too, being grave instead of joyous; and the opening figure recurs later in the song. The repetitions of "eased" and "drop" are word paintings of a kind that are found elsewhere in Purcell's works.

"*I attempt from Love's Sickness to fly*" is in a more modern, harmonic style, with a harmonic form, that of simple rondo. Notice how much the phrase-lengths vary. The introduction is 5 + 7 bars long, and the first stanza of words repeats this. **B** is 5 + 6 bars long, and **C** is 4 + 6.

Dido and Aeneas: Purcell

"Dido and Aeneas" was written in 1689, for a girls' school in Chelsea. The plot is based on Virgil's story, with the libretto written by Nahum Tate. It is highly dramatic, offering scope for choruses and dances of witches, sailors and courtiers, in addition to a number of solo parts. A female chorus edition is available, and the orchestral parts are not very difficult.

The opera is scored for strings and *continuo*. A second orchestra behind the scenes is used for the echo dance of the furies at the end of Act I, and the recitatives are accompanied by harpsichord and 'cello, as was customary.

The *overture* is in the "French" style, as was natural considering that Purcell had been trained by Pelham Humfrey who had been sent to France by Charles II to study the French methods of composition.

The *lento* section is built over a tonic pedal at first, followed by a slow-moving chromatic bass. It is very solemn. Notice the "false relation", from F sharp to F, in bar 9. These abrupt semitonal changes are a feature of Purcell's writing.

The *fugato* which follows is short and simple. It starts with two entries at the same pitch in C minor, followed by three entries in the dominant. Then entries occur in the tonic (18), the subdominant (19), the dominant (20) and the tonic (21). A few entries in other keys follow—in B flat (22), E flat (23) and F minor (24). This almost corresponds to the middle section of a fugue. But then the style becomes more free, and consists of a series of sequences, first descending, then ascending, all based on the original figure. They reach a climax at 35 and then descend to the cadence in C minor.

Act I begins in C minor, the same key as the overture, and the music has C as tonic, apart from short, subsidiary modulations, until the chorus "*Cupid only throws the dart*", which seems a long time without a change of key to a modern listener.

Belinda's opening solo is built entirely on a dotted rhythm, which is another feature of Purcell's style. The dotted notes in her first bar are presumably meant as *coloratura* on the word "shake". The solo is in ternary form, with the middle section starting at "Empire growing" in E flat major and ending in G minor.

The chorus then enters in C minor, and it is followed by the first of four ground basses in the opera. This is Dido's song "*Ah, Belinda*", and the bass is repeated twenty-one times. The music is on the plan **A A B C B**. **B** starts at "Peace and I are strangers grown". **C** starts at "I languish" and has two welcome statements of the ground bass in key G before returning to key C. The climax follows at "Yet would not", with the highest notes in the voice part and agitated semiquavers in the accompaniment. **B** recurs at "Peace and I", and the orchestra has twelve bars to itself at the end.

A short conversation in recitative between Belinda and Dido leads to another short chorus in harmonic style, "*When monarchs unite*". In the conversation which follows notice the amount of word painting, *coloratura*, on "storms", "valour", "soft", and "fierce".

Then follows the delightful minuet "*Fear no danger*", sung first by Belinda and the second woman and then repeated by the chorus. It is a clear, simple example of rondo form, and makes much use of the syncopated rhythm, crotchet minim in $\frac{3}{4}$ time, of which Purcell is so fond. The key has now changed from C minor to C major, and though the tonic is the same it certainly feels more cheerful.

Aeneas now appears, and his recitative acts as a modulatory link to E minor, a welcome change of key, in which the chorus sings "*Cupid only throws the dart*". It is more contrapuntal than the previous choruses and starts with imitative entries. A brief recitative by Aeneas leads to a mimed scene between the lovers during which Belinda sings "*Pursue thy conquest, Love*". This aria is on the plan **A A B A**, and it returns to C major, in which key the music stays to the end of the scene. The final chorus is quite long and is on the plan **A B B A B C**. It is simple harmonically, but there are again a good many dotted figures in section **B**.

The *Triumphing Dance* which ends scene I is on a ground bass which is used twelve times. The fourth and ninth appearances are in the dominant, and there are two bars between the seventh and eighth statements in which the bass is silent and there is a partial statement in the upper strings. The dotted rhythm appears very frequently in this dance.

Scene II is the effective scene in the witches' cave. It has a powerful orchestral introduction, with a few surprisingly modern discords. It begins in F minor, but the scene as a whole is mainly in F major and D minor. The Sorceress speaks in F minor, the other witches mainly in F major, and they sound quite blood-curdling.

In between the conversations there are short choruses. The first one "*Harm's our delight*" is in B flat; the second one "*Ho ho ho*" begins and ends in C major but has the signature of one flat; the third one, "*Ho ho ho*" is almost a repetition of the second one, but starting in F, not C.

After this two witches have a duet, which starts with a six-bar canon in D minor and is full of imitation and *coloratura*. The famous *Echo chorus* follows, in which a second chorus behind the scenes echoes the end of every phrase of the witches on the stage. It is in binary from and in F major.

Scene II ends with the *Echo dance* of the furies, which requires two orchestras, one being behind the scenes. The scales in imitation sound full of fury, and the movement is again in binary form and in F major.

Act II contains another ground bass "*Oft she visits*", in which the ground is played six times with the voice and then five times as a dance; and it includes a thunderstorm.

Act III introduces the sailors, both in chorus and in dance. Then the witches enter, and they sing the chorus "*Destruction's our delight*". After this, the witches and the sailors dance together. Later comes the famous "*When I am laid in earth*", with its ground bass in falling semitones. It also happens to be in binary form—a rather unusual combination. The opera ends with the beautiful chorus "*With drooping wings*".

Harpsichord Suites I and II: Purcell

Purcell wrote eight suites for harpsichord, and a number of short pieces, including minuets, airs (the one in D minor is well known), trumpet tunes (including the famous one in D major), and the popular Irish tune "Lilliburlero". The most elaborate harpsichord piece is a toccata in A major.

All the suites except no. 7 begin with a prelude. In the first suite it is only ten bars long, and is nothing more than a string of broken chords. The prelude in suite 2 is longer and more toccata-like. It begins in G minor, and the first part ends at bar 11 with a cadence in D minor. The next section continues in the same style, and modulates to F major. The third section begins in B flat major at bar 16 with a change of style, and ends in the same key at 20. A return to the opening style then occurs, and the music gradually returns to the tonic key. Do not try to force this piece into a form with a "label". There are four cadences as landmarks, making a little modulation scheme; otherwise, the style is improvisatory.

In both these suites an Almand in binary form comes next. The one in the second suite is again longer and more involved. Both suites then have a Corant in binary form. The first suite ends with the well-known Minuet in G. No movement in this suite is longer than twenty-two bars, and each dance modulates to the dominant at the end of the first half. The best known piece in the second suite is the Sarabande with which it ends. It is the shortest, most melodious, and most easily understood by present-day listeners; and, like the dances in the first suite, it has often been arranged for string orchestra.

introduces new words, but continues to use the same figures. It modulates from F minor, through E flat major to A flat major. The third section returns to the first words and is very similar to the first section except that it starts in F minor and ends in C minor, instead of starting in C minor and ending in G minor.

The second duet is again based on a number of rhythmic figures, though there are more of them than in the first duet. It is in *da capo aria* form. The middle section begins in the tonic key, B flat, but modulates rather freely, and even touches once on A flat major, which is not a closely-related key. It contains a number of new rhythmic figures and ends in G minor.

The Christmas Oratorio: Bach

This work is really a series of six cantatas, intended for the six festival days of Christmas—25, 26 and 27 December, 1 January, the Sunday after Christmas, and Epiphany, 6 January (or the twelfth day of Christmas). The work was written in 1733, and first performed at St. Thomas' Church, Leipzig in 1734.

The Lutheran version of the gospel is sung by a narrator, the Evangelist, interrupted by a solo or a chorus when speech occurs in the text. The Evangelist's recitative is *secco*, i.e. it is accompanied only by the *continuo*—organ or harpsichord—while the speakers' recitatives are accompanied by the orchestra. Chorales, whose words and tunes were known to the German congregations, occur quite frequently; and original verses provide a commentary on the story, sung sometimes by a solo voice and sometimes by the chorus.

The oratorio as a whole begins and ends in the key of D. Each separate cantata also ends in the key in which it begins, and this key is always closely related to key D. D major seems to be particularly suited to trumpets playing in jubilant vein, and the opening choruses of cantatas I, III and VI are good instances of this. Strings and *continuo* are, of course, the foundation of the score, but flutes, oboes, trumpets and drums are used very effectively for certain numbers of the work.

Three chorales are used more than once in the "Christmas" oratorio. The "Passion" chorale, which occurs so often in the "St. Matthew" passion, is used twice here (nos. 5 and 64), "Von Himmel Hoch" has three different treatments (nos. 9, 17 and 23); and nos. 7 and 28 are different versions of another chorale tune. "Luther's Hymn" is used for no. 59. All these chorale versions repay study.

Three arias and three choruses are analysed below.

Christians be Joyful, no. 1

This is a highly jubilant opening to the work, and makes good use of trumpets and drums in a majestic flourish at the beginning. Although students will probably study this work in a vocal edition they should hear it on records, or better still, at an actual performance, and they will certainly remember the bright effect of the trumpets and drums.

The chorus is in ternary form, with a *da capo*, a common vocal form at this period. It is constructed on a series of "figures", which is also usual with Bach. The long orchestral introduction summarizes the first section of the movement and is based on five figures: (*a*) bar 1 in the drums; (*b*) bar 2 in the trumpets; (*c*) bar 9; (*d*) bar 17; and (*e*) bar 21.

When the voices enter at bar 33, they have the drum figure (*a*), while the trumpets continue with (*b*). The first ten bars (33–43) are two bars longer than in the introduction, but are all based on the tonic chord. Then the voices enter with (*c*) at 43.

Bars 50–64 are an interpolation, as compared with the orchestral introduction. They consist of imitative counterpoint based on figure (*f*) at 50.

Bars 65–81 are the same as 17–33 of the orchestral introduction, making use of (*d*) in the sopranos at 65 and (*e*) in the orchestra at 69. But they are a fourth lower, so as to get to the dominant key instead of the tonic.

A few bars of orchestra alone (81–9), based on (*c*), lead to a repetition of the whole of the first vocal section, except that (*f*), at

106, is treated rather differently and leads to (*d*) at 121 a fourth higher than at 65. This means that it is in the same key as the orchestral introduction, and it continues similarly so that it ends in the tonic key.

Now comes the quieter middle section, without trumpets and drums. The orchestra is merely an accompaniment to the voices, whereas in the first section it was almost more important than they were. It starts in B minor (the relative minor) and the voices enter in imitation. They reach a cadence in the tonic key at 154, and then continue with entries of the same figure in this key, eventually leading to a cadence in B minor at 170.

Figure (*c*) is now interpolated in the orchestra between the two vocal halves of this middle section. The second half, starting at 186, is similar to the end of the first section (121–37), but it now leads to F sharp minor, the mediant minor.

Then follows the full *da capo* of bars 1–137.

Prepare Thyself, Zion, no. 4

This has many similarities to the opening chorus. It is again in ternary form with a complete *da capo*; the orchestral introduction is again a summary of the first part; and it is again based on small figures. It modulates quite freely, but keeps within the circle of the five most closely related keys, as is customary with Bach.

Figure (*a*) starts in A minor at bar 1, and figure (*b*) appears at bar 8. Then the voice enters with (*a*) at 16. At bar 26 the orchestra continues with (*b*), while the voice has little interjections (*c*).

Bar 36 starts a repetition from the beginning of the voice part; but at 45 the voice has a modified form of (*b*), which was in the orchestra before, and (*c*) is deferred till bar 53.

The first section might have ended at 52 but instead there is an interrupted cadence leading to a sequential extension passing through D minor (56), A minor with a *tierce de Picardie* (58), G major (60), F major (62) and D minor (64) before leading to a final cadence in the tonic at 72. The voice and the orchestra answer each other antiphonally from bars 57–64 using figure (*d*). Then (*b*) returns at 64 and continues to the end of the section. Finally the orchestra repeats the introduction as a coda.

The middle section starts at 58 in C major and moves at once to G major. Bars 95–8 are a sequence of 91–4 a tone higher in A minor. The music then moves to E minor, and a long extended phrase (103–14) with (*b*) in the orchestra, leads to a cadence in that key, and the end of the first half of the middle section.

An interpolation of the opening figure (*a*) of the first section now follows in the orchestra in E minor. As it reaches (*b*) at 122 the voice enters again, and returns to the tonic key. It passes through G major (126), E minor (130), and D minor (132), and ends in the relative major, C major, at 138.

The recapitulation of the first section then follows.

Mighty Lord and King most Glorious, no. 8

Part I, or the first cantata, tells the story of the birth of Jesus. The Evangelist recounts "And she brought forth her first-born Son" in no. 6; and the commentary which follows (no. 7) takes the form of an unusual chorale, in which the soprano voices of the chorus sing the chorale melody, interspersed with interjections by the bass soloist in recitative and with orchestral interludes.

Then follows "Mighty Lord and King most Glorious", no. 8. It contrasts the greatness of Christ with His lowly birth in a manger. It is in D major, the prevailing key of the first cantata as of the whole oratorio, and is in ternary form. The steady moving bass is typical of that of many of Bach's works, and helps to give the feeling of grandeur.

There is an orchestral introduction of fourteen bars which is an ornamented version of the first section of the voice part. Notice particularly the first two bars of the voice part when it enters, as this chordal figure is frequently used. It starts the next section at bar 29, though now it is based on the dominant chord; and it appears again on the tonic chord at 33, proceeding to move, momentarily, to the subdominant key. Then, at 41, a syncopated version of it is used, imitated by the orchestra. This section comes to an end at bar 50 in the tonic key, and one might have thought that it was going to be the end of the **A** part of the ternary form, but the opening section recurs at 51. It again modulates to the subdominant and again uses syncopation, but the voice part finally comes to an end at 66. The orchestra has another fourteen bars, however, before coming to the final cadence.

The middle **B** part of the aria begins at 81 in the relative minor, though it immediately modulates to E minor and then to A major. In fact this section modulates every few bars, but always to keys closely related to the tonic. It introduces a new melodic figure, in which syncopation is a feature. After eight bars orchestral interlude, starting at 97, it reverts to the opening figure of bar 81 again, though this time it starts a fifth higher. This section ends in the dominant key at 121, and then the whole of **A** is repeated.

The first cantata then comes to an end with another chorale "Ah, dearest Jesus, holy Child", the melody of which is used again in nos. 17 and 23.

Slumber Beloved, no. 19

Part II, the second cantata, starts with the pastoral symphony, and then tells the story of the angels appearing to the shepherds in the field. Number 17 is the chorale "Within yon gloomy manger lies", and is followed by an accompanied bass recitative "O haste ye then, ye shepherds go". Then follows the cradle song of the Madonna "O slumber beloved", no. 19, one of the most beautiful contralto arias ever written. It was originally part of a cantata "The Choice of Hercules", written for the Prince of Saxony in 1733. Bach transferred it to this oratorio, written in the following year. There are other instances of his using the same material in a later work. It saved labour and was quite a common practice in those days.

"Slumber beloved" is in the usual ternary or *aria* form, with the first section **A** divided into two parts, the first part starting in G major, and the second part starting in the dominant key, D major, at 69. The second section, **B**, starts at 113 in the relative minor and ends in that key. It is followed by a complete *da capo* of **A**.

The aria is really a duet between contralto and orchestra, and is based, as is usual, on a number of short figures which recur frequently in different combinations. They can be labelled thus: (*a*) bar 1; (*b*) 5; (*c*) 9, which has an affinity with a figure much used in the pastoral symphony (see the bass of bar 1 and the melody of bars 9, 11, 13, etc.); (*d*) 13; (*e*) 16; (*f*) 20. All of these are heard in the orchestra alone before the voice enters, and then they continue against soothing, long notes in the vocal part. Notice the frequent use of the flattened leading note, as for example in bars 1 and 3, and in the voice part, bar 32. It has a soothing effect, as has also the tonic pedal which is heard in bars 1–12 and again at 41–52.

At bar 40 the singer begins to use some of the figures that have been played by the orchestra, for example, (*c*) at 41, (*a*) at 45. She reaches the dominant key at 56 and the orchestra ends the first part of **A** with fourteen bars alone, based on (*e*) (inverted at 56 and in its original form at 58) and (*f*) (60 onwards).

The second half of **A** starts at 69 in the dominant key, and is based on the same figures. It returns to the tonic key at 73, and the singer ends in that key at 96. **A** is rounded off by a return to the opening sixteen bars in the orchestra.

B starts at 113 in E minor. Notice the *coloratura* on "Exultation". This section as a whole is quicker than **A**, so one is glad of the return to the serene first section at the *da capo* sign.

Glory to God in the Highest, no. 21

Number 20 is a recitative, in which the Evangelist sings "And suddenly there was with the angel a multitude of the heavenly host praising God and saying". Then follows the chorus "Glory to God in the highest", no. 21. It is longer than most of the choral interjections which occur in the passions. The many imitative entries give the impression of a host of angels.

There are three distinct sections in this movement. Section I, bars 1–24, is based on two figures. Figure (*a*) is first heard in the sopranos and altos in bar 1, and is used in all voices imitatively throughout the section. Notice its use in diminution in the alto in bar 5. Figure (*b*) is the continuous quavers heard in bar 1 in the tenor and bass voices, and in the orchestral accompaniment throughout. Notice that the wind and the upper strings take the quavers antiphonally in pairs.

Section I ends in B minor in bar 24, and is followed by section II, which provides a contrast with the words "And peace on earth". There are again imitative entries, but this time they are over semibreve and reiterated crotchet bass notes, which give an impression of peace. There are some remarkable harmonic clashes in bars 27 and 29.

Section II is very short, and is followed by a *fugato*, section III. All the entries are in pairs, so it is convenient to label them as subject and answer, though the key relationships of a fugue are not kept. "S" and "A" enter in soprano and alto in bar 31 in G major, and are followed by the tenor and bass in bar 33. The dominant key is reached in bar 35, when two more entries, "S" in alto and "A" in tenor, return to the tonic. Then, at 37, "S" in the bass in the dominant is answered by "A" in the soprano in B minor. Bar 39 introduces "S" and "A" in the tonic key in alto and tenor voices.

The next pair of entries occur in bars 42 and 43, "S" in dominant in the bass and "A" in tonic in the soprano. The last pair occur in bar 46, "S" in E minor in the alto and "A" in C major in the soprano, and the section ends in bar 49 in C major. The orchestral parts are not independent but double the voice parts throughout the *fugato*.

Then follows a return to section I, but this time all the voices have figure (*a*), leaving (*b*) to the orchestral parts. The section starts in C major but returns to the tonic key at the end of 51. The diminution of (*a*) occurs again, this time in the soprano at 53.

Section I is much shorter than before, and is followed by section

II at 57, based entirely on a tonic pedal. Then, at 61, the *fugato* section, III, returns for the last four bars.

After a short recitative, no. 22, this second cantata ends with the grand version of the chorale "With all Thy Hosts, O Lord, we sing". It is accompanied by the pastoral symphony in the orchestra, thus unifying the cantata by letting it begin and end with the same musical theme.

Come and Thank Him, no. 36

The prevailing key of Part I of the oratorio is D major, of Part II is G major, and of Part III D major again. These are all bright keys. But Part IV has F major as its key centre, and is more devotional in style.

"Come and thank Him", no. 36, is in ternary form, but is not a *da capo* chorus because the return to the first section is modified and therefore written out. **A** begins in F major and ends in the dominant key, C major, at 96. An orchestral interlude (80–96) ends this section.

B starting at 96, modulates to G minor. It is not very different from **A**, though it contains several long sequences. It is in two parts, the first part ending in D minor at 120, and the second part starting with the same idea in C major at 137, and ending in A minor at 160. The two parts are separated by an orchestral interlude, 120–36, whch is based on **A**.

There is no orchestral interlude between the end of **B** and the return of **A** at 161, though the orchestra interpolates two bars at 163 and again at 167, a feature which did not occur in the first **A**. The section as a whole is also considerably modified. Bar 205 stays in the tonic key, whereas it modulated to the dominant at 61, the equivalent place in the first **A**. The orchestra has a coda of sixteen bars, based on the main theme of **A**.

Notice the pedals in this chorus: F in the bass (25–38); C in the tenor (64–70); C in the soprano (173–81); and F in the alto (210–17), all of which come in the **A** section. They give a feeling of tranquility. The **B** section has rather more movement.

My Heart ever Faithful: Bach

The original version of this aria was in a secular hunting cantata written by Bach in 1716 to commemorate the birthday of Duke Christian of Saxe-Weissenfels, whom he was visiting with his master, the Duke of Weimar. Bach transferred it, about twenty years later, to the church cantata "God so loved the World". In both versions it is in the key of F, which make it rather uncomfortably high for a soprano. It was marked *presto* by Bach himself, and should sound happy and gay. There is an *obbligato* part for a *violoncello piccolo*, a small 'cello, now obsolete, in addition to the *continuo* part.

If the Novello edition of this aria is compared with that published by Oxford University Press, the student will realize that, though the vocal part and the chord scheme are the same, the "realization" of the 'cello and the *continuo* parts for the piano is quite different, and depends a good deal upon the editor. Dr Whittaker, who edited the Oxford version, has often put the 'cello piccolo part an octave higher, partly because it was a lighter instrument than a 'cello, and partly because the whole aria is transposed a third lower than the original and the 'cello semiquavers sound very heavy at the lower octave.

By comparing the two editions one realizes that the 'cello piccolo *obbligato's* part starts in the alto in quavers in bar 1 of the Novello edition. This figure can be called (*a*), and its continuation in semiquavers, written in the tenor in bar 3, can be called (*b*). One of these two figures is always present in the *obbligato* part, though the key is changed and (*b*) is sometimes extended.

The voice enters at bar 5 with a figure which can be called (*c*). It breaks off after two bars, while the 'cello continues with (*b*). Then it repeats itself in bar 9 and, this time, it continues until it reaches the dominant key at 16. Notice the change in the voice part at bar 13, which falls a fifth instead of a semitone at "faithful".

Bars 17–20 are the same as 1–4, except that they are in the dominant key. Then the voice enters again, this time with a falling sixth.

This figure can be called (*d*)—but notice that (*b*) still continues in the 'cello, and this time it goes on for four bars, passing through the subdominant major (22) and the relative minor (24). Notice also the rising sevenths in the voice part at 23, the leaps giving the impression of happiness. The voice continues until it reaches a cadence in the relative minor at 28, while (*a*) and (*b*) are heard in the 'cello at 25 and 27 respectively.

Then follows another 'cello interlude, consisting of (*a*) and (*b*) in the relative minor, and it leads to another vocal section starting at 33 which can be labelled (*e*). It passes through the subdominant major and leads to an imperfect cadence in the tonic key at 36, at which moment a recapitulation of bar 5 onwards starts.

This recapitulation is the same up to bar 45, when vocal interjections occur. Bar 49 corresponds to 13, but the music changes at 51 so as to end in the tonic key. Notice the unusual major seventh between the last two notes in the vocal part.

Flocks in Pastures Green Abiding: Bach

This aria is taken from the same secular cantata as "My Heart ever faithful". It is scored for two flutes and *continuo*, and sounds very lovely in this form, though it is often heard in arrangements. The flute parts are based on two figures: (*a*) in bar 1, and (*b*) in bar 3. The *continuo* is in quavers throughout, and the simple *cantabile* vocal part, with its clearly-defined cadences, can be more easily grasped by people today than some of Bach's more complex melodies: hence its popularity.

It is in ternary form. The vocal melody of **A** is 4 + 6 bars with a three-bar extension. **B** is 6 + 11, and the vocal melody becomes more elaborate in the last section of **B**.

But the flutes and *continuo* enter before the voice starts with **A**, there is a four-bar interlude between **A** and **B**, and another one between the two halves of **B**. The flutes play mainly in thirds or sixths and there are many reiterated bass notes in the *continuo* part (which was, of course, written merely as a figured bass).

Notice the tonic pedal in the first two bars, and the descending bass which follows. When the voice enters it is accompanied by the *continuo* part alone at first, but the flutes enter at bar 9 and again at bar 14.

The middle section is similarly treated—*continuo* alone at 21, flutes entering at 26. This section starts in the relative minor and ends in the dominant.

Et Exultavit: Bach

"Et exultavit" is an elaborate aria, taken from the "Magnificat" which was probably written in 1723. The "Magnificat" was usually sung in German in the Lutheran Church in Bach's day but, on special occasions, it was sung in Latin, together with other items of concerted music performed at Vespers after the sermon.

"Et exultavit" is in binary form. The first part ends at 51 in the relative minor. A connecting orchestral passage, also ending in B minor, leads to the second section starting at 59. This is based on the same material as the first half, and eventually returns to the tonic. Bars 81–92 are a repetition of the orchestral introduction (1–12). There are frequent transitory modulations to the five most closely related keys throughout the aria.

The material is based on three figures: (*a*) the figure starting in crotchets in bar 1; (*b*) the quaver figure starting in bar 3; and (*c*) the bass figure in bar 2. One or other of these figures is present throughout, though (*c*) is confined to the orchestral part. The tune in bar 5 is a filled-in version of (*a*). It is repeated a note higher in its plain form in 7, then in its decorated form in 9. Bar 12 is a development of (*c*).

The voice part starts at 13 with (*a*) followed by (*b*). Then, as so often happens, it breaks off, while the orchestra continues for four bars, before starting again at 21. This time it continues, rising higher at 25, developing into a *coloratura* run at 30, based on (*b*). It reaches a cadence in the dominant key at 36, but immediately returns to the tonic. There is further *coloratura* at 40–6, developed in sequence.

The orchestral interlude (51–9) consists of modified sequences of (*a*). The second section, starting at 59, moves to G major, but soon returns to the tonic at 64. Notice the leap of the major seventh at 75–6, a feature which was also found at the end of "My heart ever faithful". Bach treats the singer as if he were an instrumentalist, and expects him to be able to sing any interval he considers musically appropriate.

Acis and Galatea: Handel

Handel wrote three versions of "Acis and Galatea". The first, called "Acis, Galatea e Polifermo" was a serenata written in 1708, while Handel was in Italy, and was intended for the marriage of the Duca D'Alvito. The second was written in 1720, after Handel's arrival in England, when he was in the service of the Duke of Chandos, for whom he wrote the Chandos Anthems. Handel was living in the ducal court at Canons, near Edgeware, and the work was performed by the Duke's chorus and orchestra. Gay, of "Beggar's Opera" fame, wrote the words; and the work, now called a masque, was probably given only one performance.

In 1743 Handel produced his first oratorio, "Esther". It was based on the music of an earlier masque written for Canons; and its success made musical pirates wonder whether they could make money by resurrecting and performing other old works by Handel. A furniture-maker and undertaker, Arne, father of the composer of "Rule Britannia", produced the Canons version of "Acis and Galatea" at the little theatre in London, without Handel's permission. He even used Handel's cook, Herr Waltz, in the cast! Composers did not then have the copyright protection they enjoy today; and the only way Handel could combat this was to produce his own version at the King's Theatre.

For this third production he used a mixture of the Naples and Canons versions. It was a hurried makeshift, and Handel was apparently content to let the songs from the Naples version be sung in Italian while those from the Canons version were sung in English! There was a stage setting showing a country scene, with rocks and groves and shepherds, but as there was neither costume nor action the result was neither an opera nor an oratorio. Its unusual character created interest, however, and the public flocked to hear it. It was a triumph and made nearly £4,000 for the composer.

This work, which Grove lists under "secular choral works", largely consists of a string of arias in the popular Italian ternary form. It contains very few choruses, as compared with the oratorios in which the chorus is such a prominent feature.

Wretched Lovers

This is the opening chorus of Part II and is a contrast to the chorus "Happy We" at the end of Part I. It tells of the coming of Polyphemus to spoil the happiness of Acis and Galatea; and it is the most elaborately constructed movement in the work. The first section consists of a series of imitative entries in five parts. The second section "Behold the monster Polypheme" brings in a quicker theme, which is soon effectively combined with that of the first section. Sopranos are divided for a few bars, thus making six vocal parts. The third section "See what ample strides he takes", strides along in staccato chords; and at "the mountain nods, the forest shakes" there is further descriptive writing. The runs on "frightened" and "roars" are particularly effective.

O Ruddier than the Cherry

This grotesque song is sung by the giant Polyphemus in clumsy praise of the nymph Galatea. It has many more leaps than Handel normally uses in a vocal part, and is presumably intended to portray the enormous size of the giant. As a result, it is one of Handel's most difficult bass solos. The vocal part is in unison with the bass accompaniment, as often happens in Handel's bass arias, and most of the time there is only one contrapuntal part above it. Notice the *coloratura* runs on "merry" and "bluster". The form is clearly ternary, with the middle section starting in the relative major and ending in the dominant minor.

Messiah: Handel

In the summer of 1741 Handel stayed at the country house of a Leicestershire squire called Charles Jennens. Jennens arranged the text of "Messiah", probably with the help of suggestions by Handel. The libretto is in three parts. Part I consists of prophecies from the Old Testament of the coming of the Messiah and of an account of His birth as given in the New Testament; Part II concerns His sufferings and death, though again it largely consists of prophecies from the Old Testament; Part III relates to His second coming and concludes with "Worthy is the Lamb that was slain".

Handel began the composition on 22 August 1741, and finished it in twenty-four days. He was inspired by the words, and his style was less theatrical than in his other oratorios, though he used material from some of his earlier compositions.

"Messiah" received its first public performance in Dublin in 1742, for the benefit of the poor prisoners of the city. While Handel was waiting for the boat at Bangor, however, a trial run-through was made. It received its first performance a year later at Covent Garden Theatre, but was not well received. In 1750 the Foundling Hospital started to give yearly performances and then the work became very popular. Handel left the Foundling Hospital a fair copy of the score in his will, and in twenty-seven years, the hospital had benefited by performances to the amount of £10,293.

Although Handel called "Messiah" an oratorio, it was not conceived as church music, and the earliest performances took place in theatres, concert rooms and even taverns. It was originally scored for strings and *continuo*, with trumpets in four numbers and drums in two. Handel added parts for oboes and bassoons later, but they are not independent parts: they usually double the string parts or the vocal parts in the choruses. Mozart re-scored the work in 1789, using a typical Mozart orchestra, and his version is usually played today. But occasionally performances with the original scoring and a small choir are given. Performances are also often given by churches or small towns with few resources, and then maybe the only accompaniment is that of the organ. Students should realize that this is not the original version, however, though "Messiah" is such a great work that it can stand many kinds of modifications and arrangements. For example, a girls' school that has no opportunity of a production with male voices can get a good deal of enjoyment as well as understanding of the work by singing the choruses in a female voice version.

Part I

Although Handel was so much indebted to Italy for his operatic style he preferred to use the French, rather than the Italian style of overture in his oratorios. This consisted of a slow introductory movement, often making a feature of dotted notes, as in the "Messiah" overture, followed by a quick, fugal movement, and sometimes, as in "Samson", concluding with one or more stately dances. The "Messiah" overture consists of a *grave* introduction and a fugal movement only.

The introduction is based on a frequently-repeated dotted crotchet and quaver figure in E minor, and is very solemn. It is played twice, the first time loudly and the second time softly, as is usual with short repetitions in this period; and it ends on the dominant chord of E minor.

The fugue subject consists of two figures: (*a*) bars 1–3, and (*b*) bars 4–5, and both are used frequently in imitation in later stages of the fugue. The answer, starting in the second violin in bar 5, is tonal; then the subject returns in the 'cello in bar 9. A codetta starts in 13 and is based at first on (*b*), in imitation. Then (*a*) is used in imitation at 19, and this leads to the last entry of the subject in the exposition in the dominant key at 23—therefore called the answer.

The middle section starts at 27 with an episode, which begins with (*b*) in sequence. It passes through D major (28) and E minor (30), on its way to G major, in which key a dominant pedal starts at 34. Over this pedal (*a*) appears in imitation. A middle entry in key G starts at 38.

Another episode starts at 42, in which both (*a*) and (*b*) are used in various related keys. This leads to a dominant pedal of the tonic key starting at 57, over which imitative entries of (*a*) continue to appear. More partial entries of (*a*) lead into the final section, which starts at 74.

This contains only one full entry of the subject in the tonic key, and it merges into a coda at 78, which ends with three solemn bars, *adagio*.

The first section of Part I consists of prophecies of the coming of Christ, from Isaiah and other parts of the Old Testament.

"*Comfort Ye*", *no. 2*, is a recitative. The many recitatives in "Messiah" are both *secco* and *stromentato*. *Recitativo secco*, or dry recitative is accompanied by *continuo* only, and consists of little more than punctuating chords, originally written in figured bass. Quite frequently it begins and ends in different keys, acting as a modulatory link from one key to another. Intervals such as augmented fourths and diminished sevenths occur in recitative much more frequently than in arias, being used for dramatic effect. The singer is free to sing an apparently equal string of quavers in the natural rhythm of the words. *Recitativo stromentato* is accompanied by the orchestra. The singer must now sing in strict time, in order to fit with the accompanying string figures.

The first part of "Comfort Ye" is *stromentato*, but the end, "the voice of him that crieth in the wilderness" is *secco*, though the chords are played by the strings as well as by the *continuo*.

"*Every Valley*", *no. 3*, is in binary form. Most of the arias in Handel's other oratorios were in the conventional ternary form, but "Messiah" has considerably more formal freedom in the arias, some of which are quite irregular. "Every Valley" is scored for strings only, in Handel's original version, though Mozart's version of "Messiah", which contains many instrumental additions, is often performed today. The melody of "Every Valley" is based on two figures: (*a*) to the words "Every valley", and (*b*) to the words "the crooked straight". Notice the *coloratura* on "exaltation" and "plain".

"*And the Glory of the Lord*", *no.* 4, like most of the other choruses, is built on a series of figures, linked with their own words: (*a*) "And the glory"; (*b*) shall be revealed"; (*c*) "and all flesh shall see it together"; and (*d*) "for the mouth of the Lord". The voice parts start with imitative entries of (*a*) and (*b*), then go on to (*c*) and (*d*), and finally combine all four. Notice how often the bass has the main theme in the *tuttis*. The chorus ends with a grand plagal cadence.

"*Thus saith the Lord*", *no.* 5 is another recitative which starts *stromentato* and ends *secco*. The *coloratura* on "shake" is highly dramatic. It leads to the bass aria "*But who may abide*", no. 6, which is very far removed from the conventional ternary form. The words must have inspired Handel to be so irregular. The *prestissimo* at "For He is like a refiner's fire", with an excitingly dramatic string *tremolo* accompaniment, occurs twice with a short return to the first section in between. The first time it starts in F major, the relative major, but the second time, which is longer, it starts in the tonic key, and has a different melodic line, though it is in the same style. Notice the leaps in the voice part at "He shall stand".

"*And He shall purify*", *no.* 7 is difficult to sing and is not as popular as some numbers, so it is often omitted in performance. It is a very irregular fugue, with a subject that has two sections to it, almost producing a kind of double fugue. The first section, (*a*) comes in bars 1 and 2, and the second section, (*b*) which is used much more than the first, comes in 3–5.

In the exposition the voices enter in an unusual order: subject, treble (bar 1); answer, bass (5); answer, alto (9), with the (*b*) section transferred to the tenor at 11; subject, alto (*b*) only (13); subject, treble (*b*) only (15); answer, bass (*b*) only (16); subject, tenor (*b*) only (18). A syncopated figure which first occurs in the tenor at "Sons of Levi" (12–15) occurs often enough later in the fugue to become almost a countersubject.

The middle section starts at 20 in C minor, with an episode in a more harmonic style. A middle entry of (*b*) occurs in the bass at 28 in C minor, while another one in F minor is divided between altos and trebles in 29–31. Then the treble has (*a*) in B flat major at 34, followed by (*b*) in *stretto* between bass, treble and tenor.

The final section starts at 38, with (*a*) and (*b*) interrupting each other in *stretto*, combined with the countersubject theme. A coda starts at 51, in harmonic style.

"*Behold! a Virgin shall conceive*", *no. 8*, is a short *secco* recitative leading to the aria and chorus "*O Thou that Tellest*", *no. 9*. This is again based on rhythmic figures, four of the six of which come in the orchestral introduction. They are: (*a*) bar 1; (*b*) bar 3; (*c*) end of bar 4 onwards; and (*d*) bar 9. The two other figures which are used later are: (*e*) bar 31, the sequence on "mountains"; and (*f*) which occurs at the end of the eighth bar of the chorus at "arise". Figure (*a*) starts each section of the work; (*b*) consists of sequential figures, which are so common in Handel; and (*c*) consists of imitative entries, though this is not so obvious in the piano arrangement. Apart from (*a*) the figures occur more often in the orchestral than in the vocal parts. When the chorus enters it is with imitative entries of (*a*).

"*For behold, darkness*", *no. 10*, is *recitative stromentato*, starting with a sighing figure in the strings which is extraordinarily suggestive. The figure stops at "But the Lord shall arise", and the music changes to the major key, with rising sequences on "arise".

In "*The People that Walked in Darkness*", *no. 11*, Handel deliberately uses awkward intervals to give a groping effect. A bass solo always creates a problem in harmony: it is mostly too low to treat as a melody with a bass below it. Handel often solves the problem, as here, by having the orchestra play in unison with the voice, both having the "real bass". The aria is in binary form with a short orchestral interlude between the two halves. Notice the sudden change to the major again at "have seen a great light".

"*For unto us a child is born*", *no. 12*, is another prophecy from the Old Testament, but it can also be considered to be the beginning of the Christmas music. Handel scored it for strings, trumpets and drums. Two main ideas alternate throughout, and the key plan is roughly tonic, dominant, tonic, subdominant, tonic. The opening is a *fugato*, with exciting *coloratura* on the word "born". The second idea is the dotted figure starting at "and the government". This works up to the magnificent unanimity of "wonderful, counsellor", where the voices enter together for the first time. Against their block chords the strings run round in exciting semiquavers. Towards the end the three upper voices enter together on "For unto us", and treble and alto have the semiquaver *coloratura* at the same time, which makes it more exciting than ever.

"*The Pastoral Symphony*", *no. 13*, was written for strings only, though later arrangements, such as Mozart's, add wind. The middle section was an afterthought, but is built on the same idea as the opening section, beginning and ending in the dominant key. An exact repetition of the opening section then follows. Notice the effective use of pedals in this number. Handel was imitating the *piffero*, an Italian bagpipe with a drone bass. Alessandro Scarlatti, Corelli and Bach all wrote similar Christmas Pastoral Symphonies in $\frac{12}{8}$ time. "Symphony", in this period, meant no more than that a piece was played and not sung.

Now follow three recitatives, to St. Luke's words. "*There were Shepherds*", *no. 14*, starts *secco*, but changes to *stromentato* at "And lo! the angel of the Lord", with violin arpeggios effectively representing the sound of the angel's wings. "*And the Angel said unto them*", *no. 15*, is again *secco*, but the angelic accompaniment returns even more excitingly at "*And suddenly there was with the angel*", *no. 16*, and this time the semiquavers are *staccato*.

The recitative runs straight into the chorus "*Glory to God*", *no. 17*, which makes a most effective climax. It is again scored for strings, trumpets and drums, and is built on three figures, each associated with their own words: (*a*) "Glory to God"; (*b*) "and peace on earth"; and (*c*) "goodwill towards men". The exciting semiquavers of the previous recitative continue as accompaniment to (*a*), but stop abruptly at "and peace on earth". Imitative entries are used at (*c*).

"*Rejoice greatly*", *no. 18*, is a famous florid aria for treble. It is in a rather modern style of ternary form, the last section having a resemblance to the first without being an exact repetition, and therefore being written out. Handel scored the aria for violins and *continuo* only, but other instruments are always added when it is played today. The singer "rejoices" a note higher each time in the first phrase, and follows this with a *coloratura* falling sequence. There are frequent *coloratura* runs on "rejoice" except in the middle section, which is quieter and contains no semiquaver runs.

"*Then shall the eyes of the blind*", *no. 19*, is a short *secco* recitative. It is followed by "*He shall feed His flock*", *no. 20*, which was originally written for treble in key B flat, as older editions show. But more modern editions have the first part written for alto in F, and then repeated by the treble in B flat. The melody is in binary form but the phrasing is irregular. **A** consists of five bars repeated, and **B** of seven bars, which is repeated by the treble but not by the alto.

The final chorus in part I is "*His Yoke is Easy*", *no. 21*. It contains two ideas: (*a*) "His Yoke is easy", and (*b*) "His burthen is light". At first all the voices enter separately with (*a*) followed by (*b*), the end of one entry overlapping with the beginning of the next, and all in the tonic key. Then (*b*) occurs alone for a few bars, at 11. This is followed by entries of (*a*) and (*b*) in the dominant key in bass (15) and treble (17); then by tenor in D minor (19), treble in C minor (21), alto in C minor (23) and bass in F (24). A few more bars of (*b*) by itself lead to *stretto* entries of (*a*) in treble and bass (31). Finally all the voices come in together with (*a*) in the tonic key at 41, and this is followed by a short coda.

Part II

Part II is divided into two sections. The first section is often called the "Passion Music", and is performed by itself at Easter time. Like Part I it is concerned more with prophecies and Old Testament texts than with telling the story as related in the gospels. It ends with no. 36 "Thou art gone up on high", and is followed by the second section which is concerned with the spreading of the gospel.

"*Behold the Lamb of God*", *no. 22*, acts as a noble introduction to Part II. It starts with a dotted descending figure in imitation, which, at bar 9, and again at bar 13, is heard in ascending form. Bar 18 starts a new figure in the alto; but the dotted quaver and semiquaver rhythm continues almost throughout.

Then follow a series of prophecies from Isaiah, nos. 23–6. "*He was despised*" is a much-loved contralto aria. The first section is in binary form, with the first half of it ending in the dominant key at bar 21. Notice the effective plaintive G flat on the word "grief" at 18. This bar is in B flat minor instead of B flat major, and admirably suits the words. The second part, starting at 25, modulates through F minor (25), G minor (26) and F minor again (28) before returning to the tonic key. But 30 and 31 move temporarily into the tonic minor, just as 18 moved to the dominant minor. A coda starts at 34. The second section of this aria is completely different, and is often omitted in performance. It begins in C minor and ends in G minor, and has a dotted rhythm in the accompaniment throughout.

The dotted rhythm continues in no. 24 "*Surely He hath borne our griefs*". At first all the voice parts have the same rhythm; and "surely" is very effective treated in this way. At "He was wounded" the style changes, though the dotted rhythm comes back in the accompaniment at "the chastisement". This is quite a short chorus.

It is followed by a fugue "*And with His stripes*", *no. 25*. Notice the diminished seventh from D flat to E natural in the fugue subject, a characteristic interval which is easily recognized whenever it comes. Fugue subjects often have a distinguishing feature of this kind; and this diminished seventh may remind some students of its use in Mozart's "Requiem", in the "Kyrie Eleison".

This fugue is quite a regular one. The answer is tonal, and there is a regular countersubject, starting in the soprano at bar 7. There is a redundant entry in the soprano at 25 and the middle section starts at 31 with an entry in the tenor in B flat minor. Further middle entries follow: in the bass at 37 in the tonic key, in the alto at 48 in E flat major, and in the soprano at 55 in A flat major. The final section starts at 63, with the subject in the soprano in the tonic, answered by the bass in 67. Soprano and bass have further entries at 79 and 83 respectively, but the alto and tenor have no entries of the subject in the final section.

"*All we like Sheep*", *no. 26*, is a most effective piece of word painting which choirs enjoy singing. It is based on four figures: the crotchet chords at "all we like sheep"; the quaver runs at "astray"; the semiquaver runs at "turned"; and the octave leaps at "we have turned". All but the first are treated imitatively, and the effect is extraordinarily like scurrying sheep. The sudden *adagio* at "and the Lord hath laid on Him", with its solemn minim chords, makes a wonderful contrast. Handel took the first part of this chorus from an earlier work, a set of Italian duets he wrote in 1741.

Then follows a series of settings of the Psalms, nos. 27–9. "*All they that see Him*" is accompanied recitative, with the strings representing the scornful laugh. It is followed by the highly dramatic chorus "*He trusted in God*", which is another fugue. As with the previous fugue the answer is tonal, but this time there is no regular countersubject. There is however an episode to the words "let Him deliver Him", which occurs four times with very similar treatment: (*a*) at the end of the exposition (bar 19); (*b*) at the end of the middle section (bar 33); (*c*) between the bass and soprano entries in the final section (bar 45); and (*d*) after the sorpano entry in bar 54. Middle entries occur in the alto at bar 23 in B flat major and the soprano at bar 29 in E flat major, and there are also a few partial entries. The entries in the final section are in the bass (42), soprano

(50) and bass (57), thus again keeping to the outside voices as in "And with His stripes".

The tenor soloist follows with another recitative, a wonderfully descriptive one, "*Thy rubuke has broken His Heart*". It is *secco*, but the vocal line is so poignant, with its unusual intervals and its remarkable changes of key that it is one of the finest recitatives in existence.

The tenor now goes on to sing a very short aria "*Behold and See*", and he is followed by the soprano singing a *secco* recitative, "*He was cut off*", and an aria "*But Thou didst not leave his Soul in Hell*". These two are sometimes sung by the tenor soloist—the tenor clef is used in the original score—and sometimes they are omitted. The aria is in binary form.

"*Lift up your Heads*", *no. 33*, is the only chorus in more than four parts in the whole of "Messiah". The female voices are divided into three parts at the beginning so as to give fuller harmony when singing antiphonally against the men. Later the altos join the men to make three-part harmony. When the antiphonal singing ceases, the voice parts revert to four-part harmony. The music gradually becomes more contrapuntal and more ornate, with frequent imitations at "The Lord of Hosts".

The next three numbers are often omitted in performance, perhaps because, "Lift up your heads" makes a better ending to the passion music. After a short tenor *secco* recitative, no. 34, the chorus sings "*Let all the Angels of God*". This is a very irregular fugue, in which the subject is frequently in diminution at the same time as in its original form. The subject is first heard in the strings in bar 4 in both forms, then the answer is heard in both forms in soprano and alto voices in bar 6, and then the bass enters with the subject in bar 7. All the entries are in the tonic and dominant keys except for the bass entry in G major in bar 12, but the two rhythmic forms are most intricately interwoven.

"*Thou art gone up on High*", *no. 36*, is a bass solo. It consists of two musical themes to the words "Thou art gone up on high" and "that the Lord God might dwell among them". The first theme modulates from D minor to F major and is followed by the second in A minor. Then the first returns in A minor and modulates to G minor, in which key the second theme returns and, after considerable extension, ends in the tonic key.

When "Messiah" is performed as a whole with only one interval, the second half usually starts with "*The Lord gave the Word*", *no. 37*. It begins in declamatory unison in tenors and basses, and this figure is repeated by the sopranos and altos in bars 9 and 10. Otherwise it consists of an *allegro* in which the four parts keep closely together, with *coloratura* runs on "company" in each part in turn. "*How beautiful are the feet*", *no. 38*, is well known. Like "He shall feed His flock" and the "pastoral" symphony, it is in $\frac{12}{8}$ time and has a simple pastoral style. It is quite short and is in binary form. The first section modulates to the relative major, and the second section starts with the opening theme in C minor (the subdominant minor) before returning to the tonic key.

"*Their Sound is gone out into all Lands*", *no. 39*, consists of two ideas, both of which are treated imitatively. The first, to the words "Their sound is gone out" has imitations at the unison or octave, but the second is in *fugato* style with the subject in dominant and tonic keys. Both ideas then recur.

Now we come to the famous bass aria "*Why do the Nations*", *no. 40*, in which the voice and the orchestra vie with each other in furiously raging together. When a bass has quick *coloratura* passages it is always exciting. Unlike many quick bass arias the voice part is an independent melody over the orchestral bass part. It starts by leaping up the tonic chord and then runs down the scale; and these two ideas, together with the runs on "rage" and "imagine" are the outstanding features of the first section. This section is in binary form, with the first part modulating to the dominant key and the second part returning to the tonic. The middle section "The kings of the earth rise up" is in the relative minor, and it is usual to return to the first section after it, though it is doubtful if Handel intended this.

"*Let us break their Bonds asunder*", *no. 41*, is in *fugato* style. The soprano enters a beat later than the tenor, an octave higher; and two bars later the bass and alto enter in the same way, but a fifth lower. They modulate to the dominant key, in which key all the four voices enter again. Then a new figure enters to the words "And cast away their yokes from us", and this is also treated in *fugato* style, but with the entries further apart. This section is in G major, and the answers are in the dominant, the alto providing a real answer (12), and the bass a tonal one (18). The first figure returns at 23 with the entries even closer together. This is followed by a return to the second figure at 35, in *stretto* in tenor and soprano. Yet another *stretto* of "Let us break their bonds", at 45, is even closer, with all four parts entering within two bars; and it is followed immediately by an equally close *stretto* of "And cast away" at 47. The last vocal *stretto*, at 54, is on the first figure again, and is followed by orchestral *stretti* of both figures as a kind of coda. This chorus is a wonderful example of the cumulative effect of increasingly tightening *stretti*.

After a short recitative the tenor has a solo "*Thou shalt break them*". This has a violin part which is quite as important as the voice part. It consists of a curious little semiquaver mordent figure followed by big quaver leaps. Against this the voice begins in stern crotchets, though later on it breaks into *coloratura*. Notice the bass line. It is a very free treatment of a chromatic ground bass, four bars long, with occasional connecting bars from one repetition to the next. The seventh time it appears, at bar 30, it is in the relative major; and the ninth and twelfth times, at 44 and 65, it rises instead of falls.

"*The Hallelujah chorus*", *no. 44*, so inspired Handel in the writing of it that he exclaimed "I did think I did see all Heaven before me, and the great God Himself". It so moved George II, when he first heard it, that he rose to his feet, and English audiences have stood for it ever since. Perhaps it is its very simplicity that makes so wide an appeal. The opening "Hallelujah" is in simple chordal harmony based on the primary triads. "For the Lord God omnipotent reigneth", at 13 and 17, is in unison, and alternates with more chordal "Hallelujahs". In bars 22–32 the two ideas are combined. Then follows the simple chordal setting of "The kingdom of this world" with its *p* and *f*, low and high contrasts.

Bars 40–51 are a complete fugal exposition to the words "And He shall reign for ever and ever", with tonal answers in the tenor and the soprano. It looks as if this is going to be the beginning of a normal fugue, but it breaks off at 51 with the wonderfully simple "King of Kings and Lord of Lords" in the sopranos, the reiterations rising from A to top G, while the lower voice parts interject "For ever" and "Hallelujah". At bar 69 the fugue subject returns in the basses, answered by the sopranos two bars later with subsidiary accompanying figures. Then follows a coda based on previous material, with a grand plagal "Hallelujah" at the end.

7

Haydn and Mozart: Piano Sonatas

It is easier to study a piano sonata on two staves than a chamber or orchestral work with a larger number of staves to read and with varieties of scoring to be considered, so Haydn's and Mozart's piano sonatas are discussed before their other works in this book. Students who intend to study more than one kind of work are advised to follow the order given here.

Haydn should be thought of as an experimental composer. He experimented with all the musical forms that are found in sonatas and symphonies, with the use of the string quartet, and with the scoring of a symphony orchestra. But he lived such a comparatively long life and had such an influence on other composers that, by the end of his life, his experiments had become established as a foundation upon which others could build.

Mozart's life was much shorter and he was considerably influenced by his friend, Haydn. On the whole he was content to accept the forms that Haydn used, and the quartet as he found it. But he was very interested in the question of orchestral colour, and his scoring is more delicate and imaginative than that of Haydn. So Haydn, at the end of his life, learnt something about scoring from hearing the orchestral works of the then deceased Mozart.

Although one thinks of Haydn's and Mozart's sonatas as having been written for the piano it must not be forgotten that the harpsichord and clavichord were still in regular use, particularly in Haydn's early days, and these "clavier" sonatas could well have been played on the earlier keyboard instruments. Also the sustaining pedal had not yet been invented, the range was much smaller than that of the present-day piano, and the touch was lighter.

Haydn and Mozart tended to write their sonatas in three movements rather than the four more commonly found in Corelli, Bach and Handel. And they usually had a first movement in sonata form, followed by a slow movement and a rondo as finale. But there are many exceptions to this. Sometimes the second movement was a minuet, and occasionally there were only two movements. A theme with variations might also appear as one of the movements.

Sonata form was evolved from the older binary form. Some of J. S. Bach's longer and more elaborate movements in binary form show signs of an embryo sonata form. The first half ends with a distinct cadence figure in the dominant or relative major key, while the second half ends with the same figure in the tonic. This cadence figure was further extended by his sons C. P. E. and J. C. Bach and their contemporaries, until, in the hands of Haydn, it emerged as a definite second subject.

Also, the second part of such a highly developed binary movement was considerably longer than the first, and began to modulate freely into other keys. This modulatory part later became the development section of sonata form.

After this tonal digression it began to be felt that a return to the opening bars in the tonic key was necessary, and this marks what we now call the recapitulation. In other words, the second part of the binary movement split up into the development and recapitulation of sonata form.

It will thus be seen that sonata form, which seems to us today to be clearly in three parts grew from the binary form of Bach's day. It evolved gradually, and many varieties of growth can be seen in the period between J. S. Bach and Haydn, though music of this experimental period is not often heard today.

Haydn studied the sonatas of C. P. E. Bach as a young man and learnt much from them. But he continued to experiment; and the student who expects a Haydn movement in sonata form to conform always to a textbook plan has a quite false idea. Haydn is more inclined to "irregularities" than either Mozart or Beethoven, though all three felt that musical form was their servant, not their master. It is only the second-rate composer who slavishly follows a plan in every detail.

So the student should not be surprised at finding Haydn using the same theme for both first and second subjects, or Mozart introducing the first subject in the subdominant key in the recapitulation, in order that the key relationship between the first and second subjects can be the same in exposition and recapitulation. For example, keys C and G in the exposition can become F and C in the recapitulation.

It is unfortunate that there is a great variety of terminology with regard to musical form. Sonata form is also called first movement form or even extended binary form. None of these terms is ideal. Sonata form is not the form of a sonata, but only of one movement of it; the form does not only occur in first movements; and, whatever its derivation, the form does not seem to us, today, to fall into two parts.

A movement which is in sonata form without a development section is said to be in modified sonata form by some, abridged sonata form by others.

A slow movement which falls into three main sections with the first and third the same, or nearly so, is sometimes said to be in ternary form, sometimes episodic or episodical form and sometimes in aria or song form.

Similarly sonata-rondo is also called rondo-sonata and modern rondo form.

But the greatest difference is over the use of the words binary and ternary, and this includes a real difference of opinion as well as of terminology. There are some movements which are clearly in binary form, such as a typical movement of a classical suite. There are others, rather more rare in instrumental music, in which the form is clearly **A B A**, as may be found perhaps in a short nineteenth-century piano piece. But a form that is frequently found in a Haydn or Mozart minuet is **A**:||:**B A**:||, and this is called both binary and ternary by different schools of thought. Some authorities always call this plan binary, because it divides into two sections, with each section repeated; others always call it ternary, because of the return to **A** in the plan. Professor Tovey calls it binary in some cases and ternary in others. If the first **A** ends with a finished cadence in the tonic key he calls it ternary; but where the first **A** is not complete in itself, because it ends with an imperfect cadence or modulates to another key, he calls it binary. Others call the form binary if **B** is a continuation of the same idea as **A**, and ternary if **B** is new material. Extended binary and hybrid binary-and-ternary form are terms which are also used for this very common form. It should be pointed out, however, that what the listener hears is **A A B A B A**, which does not divide into either two or three parts.

The student should adopt one terminology and keep to it. And he may derive some comfort from the thought that, if he is preparing for an examination, any reasonable terminology will, perforce, be accepted. Fortunately it is possible to describe the form of such a movement quite clearly without giving it a title at all; and an understanding of the structure is all that really matters.

Apart from differences in terminology a movement may often be analysed in more than one way. Again, it hardly matters what method a student adopts, as long as he knows the alternatives, is consistent, thinks his own analysis is the best, and is prepared to defend it in an examination room, if necessary. Sometimes an alternative method of analysis is suggested for some movements in this and the following chapters. It does not follow that, because a student analyses a certain movement differently from the way it is analysed in this book, he is necessarily wrong. But he should think about his reasoning again, and hear the movement several times until he is convinced that his analysis makes musical sense. We do not know how the composer thought of the structure of his work, and all we can do is to hear it often enough to feel that we have really got inside his thoughts.

Sonata in D: Haydn

(Augener, no. 7; Collected Edition, no. 37)

The *first movement* is in sonata form, and, apart from some possible differences of opinion over the transition, it presents no problems.

The first subject leads to a definite perfect cadence in the tonic key at bar 8. This could be called the end of the first subject, in which case bars 9–16 would be called the transition. Bars 9–16 feel transitory, consisting, as they do, of "passage" work; and this is perhaps the best definition of the section. But it stays in the tonic key, and the corresponding passage in the recapitulation (74–9) is very similar, though shorter, and ends with the same chord in the same key. So it is possible to consider that it is a second section of the first subject, and that there is no transition in this movement. Here is a legitimate difference of opinion.

This section, whatever it is called, ends on the dominant chord of the tonic key, and the chord is then repeated as the first chord of the second subject, being now the tonic chord of the dominant key.

The second subject is in two sections, the second section starting at 22. But this bar is also the last bar of the first section, so the two sections overlap. Bars 33–5 end the second section with a perfect cadence in the dominant key, and they are followed by a short codetta.

The development section starts at 41, with the first subject in the dominant key (as so often happened in this period), but with the parts inverted. Bar 42 is a development of bar 9. These two bars are then repeated in B minor. Bars 45–6 are a modified sequence of 44. Then follows a few bars of passage work, in which syncopation is a feature. Bar 53 is derived from bar 30. Bar 58 seems about to resolve into B minor but does not do so. Instead it leads into the recapitula tion in the tonic at 61.

The recapitulation starts like the exposition but it is extended at 67, so that there is no perfect cadence as at bar 8. Bars 74–9 corres-pond to 9–16, and can be called a second section of the first subject or a transition, as before. But the first two bars (9–10) are omitted, so that it starts an octave higher, as at bar 11; and there are variants in 77 and 78. However, 79 gets to the same chord as bar 16, so the alterations in the recapitulation are due to Haydn's exuberance rather than to any need to get to a different key.

This time, however, the dominant chord of the tonic key at 79 stays in the tonic key, and resolves on to the tonic chord at 80 for the beginning of the second subject. The harmonies are varied but the figuration is the same. The second section (85–98) is as before, except for 93–4 and the change of key. The codetta (98–103) is also the same except that it is now in the tonic key.

The *second movement*, which is very short and in binary form, is in the tonic minor. Notice that the first half is nine bars long, because the second phrase is extended to five bars. This half ends, as expected, in its relative major, F major; and the second half modulates to G minor at 11 before returning to the tonic at 12. Notice the unex-pected chord at 16. The movement ends on the dominant chord, so as to lead straight into the tonic chord of the next movement.

The *finale* is in rondo form. The first section, **A**, is a complete little piece in binary form, with the first part ending in the dominant key. The second part contains a return to bar 1 at 13, but changes at 17 so as to end in the tonic key. Some people might say this was in a hybrid form, a mixture of binary and ternary. But it can hardly be called ternary, because it is divided so definitely into two parts, each repeated, and because the first part is not complete in itself, as it does not end in the tonic key.

Section **B** is another little piece in binary form. It begins in D minor, the tonic minor, and modulates to its relative major, F major, at the end of the first half. The second half moves to G minor before returning to D minor; and when it does return at 35 the two hands are in imitation.

A[2] (41–60) is exactly as before.

C (61–80) is again in binary (or hybrid) form. Its main key is the subdominant major, G major, and the first half ends in the tonic key. The return to the opening occurs at 73, and is exactly as before. Some people might say that **C** was in ternary form.

Bars 81–93 form a link, which is rather like **B**.

A[3] (94–end) has the repeat of each half written out. The first half needs to be written out because the repetition has broken chords; but the second half, which continues the broken chords, is exactly the same the second time except for the addition of two more chords at the end.

Sonata in F, K. 280: Mozart

The *first movement* is a very regular example of sonata form, the only unusual feature being that the first subject is more melodious than the second.

The first subject could have ended at 10 but the cadence is withheld, bar 10 repeating bar 7, so that the subject comes to an end with the perfect cadence in the tonic, bars 12–13.

The transition is built on broken chord triplets. Notice the bass descending in semitones from 18 to 22. These bars are very chromatic, but they finally lead to Ic V in the dominant key at 26.

The second subject, which is in the usual dominant key, starts with crotchets in the bass at 27, answered by semiquavers above it. Triplets return at 35, and the exposition could have ended with the perfect cadence in the dominant key at 42–3. However, there is a codetta, which says nothing very much, but repeats itself an octave lower at 48. The last three bars (54–6) are an extended cadence.

The development is very short. It begins in the dominant key by using triplets in the bass in the form first heard at 35, and this is answered by a new dotted figure in the treble. Then, at 67, there is a reference to the second subject starting in D minor. However, bars 81–2 lead back to the tonic key, and the recapitulation starts at 83.

The first subject is exactly as before. The transition, which starts at 95, changes at 101 and gets to Ic V in the tonic key, instead of the dominant, at 108.

The second subject is the same as before for the first eight bars, except for the change of key. But bars 117–23 are an interpolation in which the bass crotchets from the first bar of the second subject are developed antiphonally between treble and bass. Bar 123 corresponds to 35, and from there to the end of the movement the music is the same as in the exposition except that it is in the tonic key. There is no coda.

The *slow movement* is also in sonata form. The first subject ends in bar 8, and after a pause the second subject enters at bar 9 in the relative major. There is a short codetta (21–4).

The development section starts with the first subject in the relative major, and then leads to B flat minor at 29, where a few bars of new material are interpolated before there is another reference to the first subject at 33, this time in C minor.

The recapitulation starts at 37, and the first subject is shorter than before, though it ends in exactly the same way. After the pause the second subject starts in the tonic key at 43, though the tune is different in the first four bars. Bar 47 corresponds to 13; but by bar 53 the recapitulation is different again. The codetta (57–end) is, however, very similar.

The *third movement* is yet again in sonata form. Notice how often, in this movement, Mozart says the same thing twice over, perhaps with slight variations. Bars 9–16 begin by repeating 1–8 an octave lower, though the endings are different, as 7–8 make an imperfect cadence and 15–16 a perfect one.

Bar 17 starts the transition over a tonic pedal, and leads to the dominant of the dominant key at 37.

After a pause the second subject starts in the dominant key. It starts on *fah*, which is unusual, and may possibly make some students think it is still in F major. But the first four bars are really implying dominant harmony in C major. An imperfect cadence is reached at 48–9, and then these twelve bars are repeated in a fuller, decorated version, ending with a perfect cadence at 61–2. Then the last four bars are repeated an octave lower. Bars 66–77 are a codetta, which begins with an augmentation of the opening bars.

The development starts with a reference to the second subject in G minor. Bars 86–93 are a sequence a tone lower, leading back to the tonic. Then the last four bars are repeated in sequence in D minor. Bars 98–106 are a development of the codetta at 72. (But notice that the passages beginning at 25, 59, 72 and 98 all resemble each other.)

The recapitulation starts at 107, and the first subject is exactly as before. The transition (124–48) starts as before, but four extra bars are interpolated at 136–9, so that 140 corresponds to 29, except that it is a fourth higher so as to lead to the tonic key.

The second subject (149–77) is almost identical with the second subject in the exposition, except for key: and the codetta (177–90) is the same except that the final cadence is extended. There is no coda.

Sonata in C, K. 309: Mozart

The *first movement* is a straightforward one, about which there can be little or no difference of opinion. It is in sonata form, and the first subject ends on the first beat of bar 21. This subject is perhaps unusually long, and it might have been thought to end at bar 8 if it had not been for the following facts: that bar 9 begins a repetition; that there is no real moving away from the tonic key; and that there is a definite perfect cadence in the tonic key at 20–1.

Bars 21–32 are the transition or bridge passage. The chief points about this section are that it *does* move away from the tonic, and that it ends with the dominant chord of the dominant key, ready to lead into the second subject. It also feels rather unimportant and transitory, being little more than a series of decorated chords linking one key with the other. But subordinate character is not an essential feature of a transition. There are cases in which the transition has a really important theme which is much used later in the movement. The essential function of a transition is its movement away from the tonic to the key of the second subject.

The second subject is from 32 to 58, and again there can be no difference of opinion. It begins with two bars of accompaniment, then it has a four-bar tune which is repeated, with a slight change at the end. Mozart, like Browning's thrush, often sings his song twice over. A second idea occurs at 43, and again there is a repetition (at 46), but this time the theme is decorated. The subject ends with a perfect cadence in the dominant at 53–4, and is followed by a short codetta, which again says the same thing twice.

The development is founded on the first two bars of the first subject, a new figure which first occurs in 63–6, and the codetta. After two bars of the first subject in G minor, the last bar is repeated twice, in the form of echoes. The new figure then occurs in D minor (63–4); is decorated in 65–6; and is followed by the first subject, also in D minor. The idea of 63–6 is then used in A minor in 69–73, leads into the first subject figure in A minor in 73–4, and is followed by a sequence in G minor (75–6). The last bar is again used, echo-like, in 77 and 78; and a diminished seventh (79–81) leads to a perfect cadence in A minor. The four bars of the codetta are then exactly repeated in A minor, and lead to the first subject in A minor, with its second bar repeated as before. These four bars are then repeated over the dominant chord of the tonic key, and lead into the recapitulation.

There are several interesting points about the recapitulation. The repetition of the first subject which occurred at 8–21 now begins in the tonic minor at 101, though by 110 it is the same as 15. The two transitions begin in the same way, but there is no equivalent of 27–8 in the recapitulation; the idea of 29–30 is extended to three bars; and it ends with the dominant of the tonic key instead of that of the dominant.

The beginning of the second subject is also interesting, as the right and left hands of the exposition are inverted in the recapitulation. However, by 135, it becomes the same as the exposition except for the obvious change of key. After the codetta, there is a short coda, starting at 152, based on the first subject.

The plan of the *slow movement* is basically as follows: **A** :|| :**B**, link, **A** :|| Coda. But the student may not immediately realize this, because there are no convenient double-bar lines and repeat marks. The repeats are written out because each repetition contains further melodic decoration.

A is from bars 1–16, with its decorated repetition at 17–32. **B** is from 33 to 40, and it is followed by a short transition or link (40–4) and a return of **A** (45–52). Bars 53–72 are a decorated repetition of 33–52. Bars 72–9 form a short coda, ending with three repetitions of a perfect cadence.

This is therefore the hybrid binary-ternary form discussed earlier in this chapter. **A** ends every time with a perfect cadence in the tonic, so that Professor Tovey would consider it to be in ternary form, as would most other people. But others might say that **A** :|| :**B A** :|| is always binary form. And there is so much decoration that others might say it was in variation form, perhaps combined with binary or ternary form.

Although there are many chromatic notes in this movement they are decorations only, and the only modulation is to the dominant key in **B**. Notice the frequent use of feminine endings, which suit the graceful style of the melody.

Everyone would agree about the form of the *last movement*, though there are alternative names for it, sonata-rondo, rondo-sonata, and modern rondo being the most common. This form seems to cause more trouble to students than any other, and anyone who is not quite sure about it should study it carefully from a textbook. Unfortunately Mozart adds to the difficulties in this case by writing a long and complicated movement, and by producing an irregularity, that of re-introducing the second subject before the first in the recapitulation.

The first subject ends at 19, and is followed by a long transition (19–39) which leads to the dominant key. Both the first subject and the transition consist of an idea which is repeated and then extended. The second subject starts in the dominant key at 39, and has two distinct sections, the second one starting at 53. The figure first heard at bar 58 should be noticed, as it is much used later. This second section of the second subject ends with a perfect cadence in the dominant key at 76–7, and is followed by a short codetta (77–85) and a link back to the first subject (86–92). The first subject, which returns at 93, is varied at 101, and becomes quite different at 108. Bars 111–16 form a link based on the figure first heard at 58.

The middle section is very short, and consists of an episode in F major (116–23) which is repeated an octave lower (124–31). A transition (132–42) leads to the dominant of the tonic key and to the recapitulation.

Now we come to the irregularity. Mozart does not start his recapitulation with the first subject, but immediately introduces his second subject in the tonic key. Perhaps he felt the movement was getting too long, perhaps he thought the first subject was occurring too often—who knows? Play it once with the first subject inserted here, and see what you feel about it. Bar 143 feels recapitulatory, however, partly because of the passage work leading into it, and partly because of the return to the tonic key with a previously heard idea, so the balance is satisfactory.

The first section of the second subject is slightly longer than in the exposition, and the second section begins just as before, apart from the change of key. But it continues for longer, the codetta is omitted, and it merges into the return to the first subject at 189. This is shortened and decorated, and ends at 207.

The coda which follows makes use of a number of previously heard themes, and is almost like a little development section. It refers to the codetta at 211; to the figure from bar 58 at 221; to the transition at 234, and finally to the first subject, over a tonic pedal, at 245.

Sonata in A Minor, K.310: Mozart

The *first movement* is in sonata form. The first subject is built on a tonic pedal, and ends with a perfect cadence in bars 8–9, which overlaps with the beginning of the transition. The transition starts with a decorated version of the first subject, but soon modulates to F major. It reaches a dominant pedal of key C at 16, and the dotted rhythm from bar 1 continues over the top. Bars 20–2 form a cadence extension (I V five times over) which is typical of Mozart. But notice that bars 16–22 are in C *minor*, though the second subject, when it enters at 23, is in C *major*, the relative major. There are almost continuous semiquavers from here to the end of the exposition, and the music is often sequential. A second section of the second subject starts at 35, but there is little more than cadence repetition from here to the double bar. Notice that 40 repeats 35 in invertible counterpoint. Bars 45–9 form a codetta based on the dotted figure from bar 1.

The development starts with the first subject in the relative major and leads to a dominant pedal on B at 58. Over this the rhythms of bar 1 (58) and bar 8 (59–61) appear. The pedal resolves itself on to the tonic chord of E major at 62; and bars 58–61 are repeated sequentially: a fourth higher in key A (62–5) and a fourth higher again in D minor (66–9). Bars 70–2 develop bar 42 in falling sequences; and the same figure appears in the left hand in 74–8. Bar 79 reaches the dominant chord of the tonic key and leads to the recapitulation at 80.

In the recapitulation the transition (88–103) begins differently, with the first subject theme in the bass; but 94 onwards corresponds to 14 onwards, except for the usual change of key. The second subject, now in the tonic key, and minor instead of the original major, corresponds to the second subject in the exposition, except for slight changes, and three extra bars, inserted at 126, which make a climax before the introduction of the codetta.

The *slow movement* is also in sonata form, and is in the submediant major. The transition (8–14) does not modulate, but ends with an imperfect cadence which leads naturally into the dominant key for the second subject at 15. The R.H. figure at 15 appears in L.H. at 17. A codetta starting at 22 is little more than a cadence extension repeated three times over.

The development section begins with a free version of the first subject in the dominant major. Bars 37–8 introduce a new rhythmic figure which is derived harmonically from the transition. This is transferred to the bass at 43, and descends in sequences, finally reaching the dominant of the tonic key at 51, thus leading into the recapitulation at 53.

In the recapitulation the first subject is as before; but the transition, though based on the same idea, is differently treated and modulates twice, to B flat at 63 and G minor at 65, whereas before it did not modulate at all. It is the same length as before and ends with the same chord, so the changes are purely for the sake of variety. The second subject has a few slight changes also, in addition to being now in the tonic key. As in the first movement, there is no coda.

The *finale* is the only movement in the sonata which might cause differences of opinion. It is certainly in a free kind of sonata-rondo form, and it is certainly irregular. It is as well to remember that the textbook kind of sonata-rondo only began to appear regularly in Beethoven's works.

The first subject consists of five phrases, and certainly comes to an end at 20. Bars 21–63 may be thought of as transition leading to the second subject in the dominant minor at 64. Or it may be thought that the second subject starts immediately in the relative major at 21. The difficulty is that there is no real contrast of themes in the exposition—or, indeed, throughout the movement. Bar 21 is based on the same rhythm as the first subject; bar 29 returns to the first subject in C minor, while the following phrase (33) reverts to C major; the phrase starting at 37 uses the figure from bar 1, repeating it down the scale; and 64 uses the first subject theme in the bass, now in the dominant key. If one compares 21–87 with 195–245 in the recapitulation one finds the same material in a different order.

Bar 195 corresponds to 20; 203 to 64; 211 to 37; 219 to 72; 266 to 56; and 233 to 37. Bars 21 and 195 seem to be transitional; while 64 and 203 seem more like a second subject (mainly because 64 establishes the dominant and 203 the tonic key) in spite of the fact that the theme is the same as the first subject.

Bars 86–7 end with a perfect cadence in the dominant; and a link leads to the return of the first subject at 107, thus bringing the exposition to an end at 142.

The episode (143–74) is a complete little piece in binary form with repeats. But neither the key nor the theme forms a real contrast, as they would in a Beethoven sonata-rondo movement. The key is the tonic major; the first bar (143) uses the rhythm of bar 1; and the phrase beginning at 147 has a resemblance to that beginning at 37. The first section is built largely on a tonic pedal.

The recapitulation starts with an exact repetition of the first subject at 175. Bars 195–245 have already been discussed. After this there is no return to the first subject in its original form, probably because 204 onwards has already made so much reference to the first subject in the tonic. Bars 245–52 form a short coda.

8

Haydn and Mozart: Chamber Works

Chamber music is music for a room (*da camera*), in contrast to a theatre or church (*da chiesa*). The term originally included vocal as well as instrumental music, and music for a small orchestra. Cantatas, sonatas, and concertos *da camera* were all species of chamber music.

Gradually the term was narrowed down to apply to instrumental music for groups of solo performers. But even as late as Haydn, the distinction between chamber and orchestral music was not as clearly defined as it is today. We are not sure whether some of Haydn's very early string works were intended for quartet or small orchestra.

The fundamental difference between chamber music of the Corelli–Bach period and that of Haydn is that the *continuo* was an essential feature of all chamber works of the former period, while Haydn and later composers ceased to use it. Each instrument became equally important, and no background was required.

It is well known how Haydn's visit to Weinzierl, when he was twenty-three, resulted in the writing of his first string quartets, as he happened to find two violinists, a violist and a 'cellist available. In his earliest string quartets the violins usually have the most interesting parts, with the viola and 'cello taking the supporting harmonies that, in the sonatas of Corelli, had been given to harpsichord and 'cello *continuo*. But gradually Haydn realized that the viola and 'cello could take their turn with the tunes, and in his later quartets all four instruments have equally interesting melodic parts.

C. P. E. Bach's sonatas, which influenced Haydn in composing his string quartets, consisted of three movements, quick, slow, quick, none of them being dance movements. But Haydn liked the minuet so much that, from the beginning, he began to add it to his chamber and orchestral works. Many of his first quartets were in five movements, with two minuets, but eventually he established a four-movement scheme, with a minuet for the third movement.

Mozart wrote a number of string quartets, which certainly owe something to the influence of Haydn. But he was interested in using other instruments in his chamber combinations. The oboe quartet and the piano quartet in G minor are both analysed in this chapter. When he discovered the lovely tone quality of the new instrument, the clarinet, and found a good player, Stadler, available, he lost no time in writing a clarinet trio and a clarinet quintet, which are also both included in this chapter. Stadler was very fond of the deep tones of the chalumeau register, and Mozart gave him scope to use this register in these works. Notice also the use of widespreading arpeggios and large leaps in the clarinet part, both of these devices being particularly effective on the instrument.

The student should read from paragraph six onwards in the previous chapter for comments about musical form which apply to this chapter.

String Quartet in F, op. 3, no. 5: Haydn

This early quartet by Haydn is a very straightforward one to analyse. The *first movement* is in sonata form. The transition starts at bar 17, and modulates to the dominant, where the second subject begins at 28. Another section, still in the dominant, starts at 42. It is so tuneful, and there is such a pronounced cadence just before it enters, that some people may prefer to consider that this marks the beginning of the second subject. But bar 28 is clearly in the dominant key, and the corresponding place in the recapitulation (162) is just as clearly in the tonic, so this passage must be considered as second subject and not as transition.

The tuneful theme which starts at 42 continues for some time. It might have stopped at 65, but an extension occurs instead, and again at 69 and 73. Alternatively, 69 and 73 can be considered as separate sections of the second subject. A short codetta, based on the transition, begins at 84, and rounds off the exposition.

The development section begins with a reference to the first subject in the dominant key; and a decorated version of it begins in D minor at bar 99. Extensions begin at 107 in G minor, and pass through G minor (114), C major (118), F major (120), B flat major (122) and G minor (124), finally leading to a dominant pedal of the tonic key at 126, which heralds the recapitulation.

The recapitulation starts at 138, with slight modifications of the first bar each time it occurs. The transition which begins at 154 starts in the subdominant key, and passes sequentially through the dominant, finally arriving at the second subject in the tonic at 162. From there to the end of the movement the music is almost the same as in the exposition, except for the obvious change of key.

The *second movement* is the very popular Serenade. It is, in effect, a solo for the first violin, with the other three instruments playing a broken chord, *pizzicato* accompaniment throughout. One has only to compare it with the equally well-known slow movement of the "Emperor" quartet, op. 76, to realize how far Haydn had travelled during the intervening years in his use of the four instruments as equal partners.

This movement is a clear example of how sonata form grew out of binary form, because not only is each section repeated (as also in the first movement) but the second section begins with the first theme in the dominant and returns to the tonic, as is usual in binary form.

The transition starts at bar 12, and the second subject at 20, with a codetta at 28. The development, which is based entirely on the second subject, only lasts from 34 to 41. The recapitulation starts at 42 with a shortened first subject; and the transition, which starts at 48, is different. But it leads to the second subject in the tonic at 59, and the music proceeds tranquilly to its expected end.

The opening rhythm of the *minuet* is unusual, because the semiquavers come in unexpected places. It is in the hybrid form that some people call binary and others ternary; but the divisions are clear enough. The first section ends in the dominant key, and is followed by a short development of the opening bars before it repeats them at bar 15. The ending of the two sections are different because 5–10 modulates to the dominant, while 19–24 moves back to the tonic.

The trio is very slight, and is entirely in one key, with an imperfect cadence at the first double bar and a perfect cadence at the end. The form is very similar to that of the minuet, with the second part developing the theme slightly for four bars, and then repeating it with a twist at the end, so as to finish with a perfect cadence. Although, in both minuet and trio, there is an obvious return to the opening theme, perhaps it is preferable to call the form binary in each case, though there is a good deal to be said for avoiding the use of either term.

The *finale*, which is of the folk dance variety, is again in a simple sonata form. The transition starts at bar 9, and the second subject at 21. The latter has a second section at 29, and a jolly repetitive ending. Bars 29–45 are entirely on the dominant and tonic chords of the tonic key.

The development grows out of the first subject, and leads into the recapitulation at 62. The first subject modulates to the subdominant at 69 and merges into the transition; but by 72 it corresponds to 13 a fifth lower, and so leads to the second subject in the tonic at 80.

String Quartet in D, op. 64, no. 5 ("The Lark"): Haydn

This quartet contains more irregularities than the previous quartet analysed above. But Haydn's intentions are always quite clear, and the result "comes off" because balance of theme and key is musically satisfying.

The *first movement* conforms in all essentials to sonata form, though there is the usual Haydnesque diversity of detail, and a surprising addition at the end of the movement. The lower strings begin with a *staccato* theme which marks the pulse. Over this the first violin enters with a counter-theme at bar 8. It starts quite high, and after four repeated notes leaps a sixth higher, hence the nickname "Lark" given to the quartet. The first subject comes to an end at bar 20, and a transition leads to the second subject in the normal dominant at bar 36. (The transition reaches the dominant key at 27, but continues with the first subject themes a little longer, more particularly with the *staccato* crotchets and with bar 17.)

The first section of the second subject starts at 36 with syncopated chords, and the second section starts at 50 with scales in triplets. A short codetta at 56 refers again to bar 17.

The development begins with a complete statement of the first subject, as it first occurred in bars 8–20, but in the subdominant key. Bar 73 refers to the second section of the second subject, and passes through E minor and F sharp minor. It is followed by a development of the first section of the second subject at 89, and of the second section again at 96.

The recapitulation begins at 105, though it omits bars 2–7 of the exposition. The transition and the first section of the second subject are also omitted, and Haydn goes straight into the second section at 117. This is extended and combined with the syncopated first section at 131. After a pause at 141 there is a surprising return to the first subject. This can be thought of as the beginning of a rather long coda or of a condensed repeated recapitulation. It is followed by the first section of the second subject at 155 and the second section at 169; and bar 17 is repeated four times at the end of the movement. Haydn was not in the habit of writing a long coda, or of repeating a recapitulation, so this is certainly a surprising addition.

The *second movement* consists of a simple song-like melody which, after its first statement, is followed by a development in the tonic minor key (35), and then by a variation in the tonic major (51) which is exactly the same as the original, apart from the extra decoration. The form could be called ternary, though the middle section contains no contrast of theme; and it also has a link with variation form. But there is no need to give the form a title. Haydn wrote several movements on a similar plan.

The divisions of the *third movement* are shown, as always, by repeat marks. But there is the usual difficulty of deciding whether to say the minuet is in binary form because the first section ends in the dominant and is therefore incomplete, or ternary because the opening bars return at bar 17. This difficulty can be overcome by avoiding the use of either term. Notice that the second section starts by developing the opening bars, and that the return is extended three times, at bars 21, 27 and 32.

The trio is in the tonic minor, and modulates to its relative major at the end of the first section. When the first section returns at 61 it is in invertible counterpoint, with the original violin part in the 'cello, and the viola part in the violin. It is also shortened and modified so as to end in D minor.

The *finale* is a breathless movement in continuous semiquavers. The first section of the movement is divided into two parts with each part repeated. But the first part ends in the tonic key, and there is a complete return at 21, so that many people would say this first section was in ternary form. It is certainly **A**:||:**BA**:||, whether one prefers the term "binary" or "ternary". The middle section, beginning at 29, changes to the tonic minor key and introduces a new theme in the first violin over the continuous semiquavers in the second violin. This new theme is then taken up by the second violin, the 'cello and the viola in turn; and quite an elaborate *fugato* is built up, with the semiquaver movement still running on continuously. Eventually, at bar 76, the semiquavers run into a complete return of the first section, but without the repeats. At bar 95 the first violin jumps an octave higher, and the semiquaver movement is extended to all the instruments. Finally, at 103, the semiquavers run into the coda.

String Quartet in C, op. 74, no. 1: Haydn

The *first movement* is in sonata form, but like a number of other Haydn movements, such as the first movement of the well-known

"London" symphony, it is built mainly on one theme, instead of two contrasting ones.

After two bars of introduction the first subject is stated in bars 3–10. There is a second sentence (bars 11–18) which might be thought of as transition, because it begins to modulate. But the modulation (to F, at 13) is only momentary, and it returns to another perfect cadence in the tonic at 18. The transition then begins, with imitative entries in quavers. It reaches the dominant key at 26, and runs into the second subject in the dominant at 31.

Bar 31 quite clearly establishes the dominant key and begins another division of the movement; but the first few bars are a restatement of the first subject. Contrast of key is even more essential than contrast of subject for the second part of an exposition; and Haydn obviously thought it was more important. It was Beethoven who developed the idea of a complete contrast of mood and theme for a second subject. However, after four bars of first subject Haydn goes on to some new material, "passage work" using quavers and semiquavers, which starts at 35. The second section of the second subject starts at 42, and uses both the first subject theme and passage work.

The development begins with the first subject passing through E flat to B flat major, in which key a new theme appears at 61. It has grown out of the first subject, and it then proceeds to combine with it. Bar 75 introduces the quaver and semiquaver figures from 35. The first subject returns in A minor at 84; and after some more passage work on a dominant pedal, the recapitulation is reached at 97.

This begins with a restatement of the first subject in bars 1–10, and then has a short *fugato* on it. It merges into the transition at 111, over a dominant pedal. The second "subject" starts at 119. The first three bars are modified, and the music then proceeds as at 35, apart from the change of key. The second section starts at 128 (compare 42). It is extended, so that 142 corresponds to 45. Bars 149–53 are an interpolation, and they lead to a cadential extension corresponding to 52–5.

The *second movement* is in sonata form. The transition starts at 14, and modulates to E minor (24) on its way to the dominant, in which key the second subject starts at 38. Bars 51–7 form a short codetta.

The development modulates to E flat, in which key the first subject appears at 63. There is a reference to the second subject in A minor at 80, and it is repeated sequentially in G major before reaching a dominant pedal at 89, which leads into the recapitulation.

This starts at 94 with a decorated version of the first subject. The transition (107) begins as in the exposition, but the passage from 22–32 is omitted, and 115 corresponds to 33 a fourth higher, thus leading to the second subject in the tonic at 120. Bars 120–33 are the same as 38–51 apart from the change of key.

The movement has quite a long coda. It starts at 133, with imitative entries of the first subject, which are repeated in ornamented form at 141. They reach the unexpected key of C sharp minor at 147–8, but a clever twist brings the music back to the tonic at 155–6. A reference to the transition then follows, and the last seven bars of the movement are the same as the exposition, but in the tonic key.

Both the *minuet* and the *trio* are on the plan **A** :|| :**BA** :||, with the first **A** ending in the dominant. In other words they are built on a very usual plan, that some call binary and others ternary. The minuet ends with a long extension, built partly over dominant and tonic pedals. The trio is in A major, an unexpected key in relation to C major, and one that foreshadows Schubert. Bars 97–112 form a link back to the minuet, but they do not lead back to C major, as one would expect. They are built on the dominant chord of A, and end *pp*. The note E, *soh* in A major, is held alone in the first violin for two bars, *pp*, and then becomes *me* in C major, as the *fz* of the minuet returns—another Schubertian touch.

The *finale* is in sonata form, but, like the first movement, it is built mainly on one subject. The "second subject", which starts at

50, consists of the first subject in the dominant key plus a semiquaver counter-theme which is made much use of later. There is a codetta on a double pedal, starting at 91.

The development takes the theme and counter-theme as they appeared in the second subject and builds a *fugato* on them. This leads to a dominant pedal of A minor at 132, which resolves itself on to the tonic chord at 148. The bass then slips down to the dominant of key C, and the recapitulation glides in at 155. The first subject is shortened, and the second subject is modified and lengthened as compared with the exposition. But it ends with the same codetta on a double pedal, now in the tonic key.

String Quartet in D Minor, K. 421: Mozart

The *first movement* is in sonata form. The first subject is in two sections, with the second section starting at bar 9; and it ends with a prolonged dominant chord, bars 12^3–14^2.

The transition starts in the middle of bar 14 with a *forte* chord, and begins to modulate. It reaches the relative major, F major, at 17. Notice the figure starting in the 'cello on the last beat of bar 18, which is imitated in the viola. Another figure starts in the 'cello at 20, beginning with an octave leap, and this is imitated by all the instruments in turn. The transition ends with a perfect cadence in the relative major in bar 24.

The second subject starts in the first violin at bar 25, but notice the accompaniment figure which starts in the second violin and viola half-a-bar earlier, as this appears in triplet form at 35, and is later used for the development section. A decorative repetition starts at 29.

The codetta starts in the middle of bar 33. First there is a six-beat cadential figure in the second violin which is imitated by the first violin. Then there is a second figure which is accompanied by triplets based on the figure first heard in bar 24. It appears in the first violin and is then repeated an octave lower in the second violin.

Finally, at 39, the triplets continue and form a link into the return of the exposition or on to the development section.

The development starts by using bars 1 and 2 of the first subject beginning in E flat major and then modulating. The second bar of this figure is then developed in imitation. At bar 53 the first two bars have a *fugato* on all the instruments. At bar 59 the triplets from 35 are combined with a hint of the second subject, heard in imitation between the two violins. At 66 a dominant pedal of the tonic key starts, over which are heard the triplet figure and a hint of the 'cello figure first heard in the transition in bar 18. The pedal leads into the recapitulation.

In the recapitulation the first subject is the same as in the exposition. The transition uses the same idea but is differently treated. Notice the half-beat syncopation at 84 and the quarter-beat syncopation at 86. The tonic key is reached at 86. At bar 88 the figure which was first heard in the 'cello now appears in the viola. By bar 90 the music corresponds to bar 20, except that it is a third lower and in the tonic key. Notice that the figure at 84 is half-a-bar longer and this makes all the music from here half-a-bar "out", so that the second subject starts at the half-bar instead of at the beginning of a bar. But this is more of a visual than an aural effect.

The second subject starts in the middle of bar 94, with a decorated version occurring as before at 98. The codetta starts at 102. The first figure is now eight beats long instead of six. It is imitated at 104, as before. The second figure starts at 106 in the first violin, and is repeated by the second violin an octave lower as before. Then, at 110, the triplets continue as a link, on to the repetition or to the coda.

Notice that the development and the recapitulation are repeated as a unit, thus showing that Mozart was still thinking of sonata form as being fundamentally a development of binary form.

The form of the *second movement* can clearly be perceived, but it does not come into any category with a label. It is in the relative major.

I. Bars 1–26 form a complete little piece, **A**:||:**B A**:||. **A** is bars 1–8, ending in the dominant key and is repeated. **B** is 9–14 and modulates through C minor (10) and G minor (11) before returning to the tonic key. **A** returns in 15–26, but modulates to the subdominant instead of the dominant at 20 and returns to the tonic key at 24. The cadence is then repeated twice. Bars 9–26 are then repeated.

II. Bars 27–34 form a short episode in the tonic minor—what Haydn often designated as "minore". It modulates to C minor at 33.

I. Bars 35–42 are a variation of I in A flat major.

II. Bars 43–52 return to II in the tonic minor, as before. But the music reaches C major, not C minor at 47, which leads better into the return of I in the tonic key.

I. Bars 53–77 are exactly as the first I, except that there are no repeats. Bars 78 to the end form a coda, based on the end of I.

The *third movement* is the usual minuet and trio and is in the tonic key. The minuet is in the hybrid form **A**:||:**B A**:||, as is the first part of the second movement. But in this case **A** ends in the tonic key, so it might be called ternary, while the first section of the second movement might be called binary. **B**, starting at bar 11, modulates to A minor. Bars 22–6 are a series of sevenths resolving on to one another, and establishing B flat in 27. Bar 28 is an augmented sixth chord, resolving on to V in the tonic key in 29. Bars 30–9 are an exact repetition of the first **A**, there being no need for modification, as the first **A** ended in the tonic key.

The trio is in the tonic major. **C** (bars 40–7) has the theme in the first violin, with a *pizzicato* accompaniment below. **D** (48–55) starts with V I in the tonic key followed by V I in the dominant key. I in the dominant key then becomes V in the tonic, ready for the return to C major. **C** returns at 56 and continues to the end.

The *fourth movement* is in variation form and is in the tonic key. The theme (bars 1–24) is in binary form. **A** consists of eight bars in the tonic key, repeated. **B** consists of eight bars in the relative major followed by eight bars in the tonic, repeated.

Variation I (25–48) has continuous semiquavers in the first violin. The third bar is based on VI instead of I, otherwise the harmonies are the same.

Variation II (49–72) is built on the same chord scheme except for bars 69–70. Viola and 'cello mark the rhythm against two different cross-rhythms in violin I and violin II, both syncopated. Violin I is, in effect, in $\frac{3}{4}$ time for the first three bars. By bar 53 the rhythm is straightforward again but with semiquaver triplets in violin II. Cross-rhythm starts again after the double bar.

Variation III (73–96) is a duet between viola and violin I, who have four bars of the theme alternately. But the chord scheme remains the same.

Variation IV (97–112) is in the tonic major key. The tune is back, in simpler form. The second half is eight bars long instead of sixteen, and it is on a different chord scheme, because it has to modulate to the dominant (being major) instead of the relative major.

The coda (113–end) returns to the minor key. The first eight bars are nearly identical with the original theme, but the second eight bars are different, and are over a dominant pedal. An interrupted cadence is reached at 130; and bars 136 to the end are a cadence extension.

Oboe Quartet in F, K. 370: Mozart

Mozart's oboe quartet was written in 1781, when the composer was just twenty-five, and is one of the earliest of his chamber works using wind instruments, the delightful flute quartets being the only earlier ones. The famous clarinet quintet came eight years later, only two years before his death. The oboe quartet was written for his friend Ramm, who was a famous oboist, and it belongs to the short period Mozart spent in Munich, where he wrote his first important opera, "Idomeneo". He was still officially in the service of the Archbishop of Saltzburg, but left later that year, and settled in Vienna for the rest of his life.

Like the flute quartets, the oboe quartet is a comparatively slight work, but it was customary to treat chamber music involving wind instruments in a lighter vein than that of the string quartet. It contains only three movements, and the second movement is very short. Its style is a mixture of the *concertante* and the "chamber music" style, with the oboist's part sometimes being treated like that of a soloist in a concerto. There is even a place for a cadenza in the slow movement at bar 31; and at bars 95–108 of the finale the oboist goes off on an excursion of his own in $\frac{4}{4}$ time against the string players' $\frac{6}{8}$!

The *first movement* is in sonata form, and has a typically graceful Mozartian first subject. Its second sentence, beginning at bar 9, has a feature of minim *appoggiaturas* in the oboe part a semitone below the chord note. The violin has two bars of melody at 15–16 before the oboe comes in again to lead to a perfect cadence in the tonic at 19–20 and the end of the first subject.

The transition, which starts at 20, begins by decoratively restating V I in the tonic key twice, before proceeding to modulate to the dominant at 28. The oboe part becomes more ornate, passing from triplets to semiquavers as it leads to a concerto-like cadence.

The second subject starts at 37 with the first subject theme in the dominant key. It states the first four bars twice in the violin, with a new reply in the oboe. Then comes a second section, starting at 45, which is completely different. Its second sentence, starting at 50, is stated first without the oboe and then repeated with it.

A codetta begins at 57 in which the strings have a theme starting with minims against quaver decorations in the oboe.

At the beginning of the development section the minim theme from bar 57 is treated with imitative entries by all the instruments in turn. It leads to a series of sequences at 68, in which the oboe has decorative semiquavers and the violin has syncopated minims. These two ideas, of imitation and sequence, are then repeated at 72–8 but, this time, the semiquavers continue in imitation between oboe, violin and viola.

The next few bars appear to be leading to a cadence, but several times this is foiled, until finally Ic V in the tonic key is reached at 96, and this leads to the recapitulation.

In the recapitulation the first subject is treated more elaborately than before. The violas have the counter-theme that was first heard in the second subject version at 37, while the violin imitates the oboe at two-bars' distance. This happens twice, before the music settles down at 106 to an exact repetition of the exposition. But it is shortened at 112, the two bars in the violin (15–16) being left out, and the cadence at 112–13 being imperfect instead of perfect.

The transition includes references to bar 1 in the violin at 113, 115 and 117, in addition to the original semiquaver figure.

The second subject starts at 119 with the equivalent of 45; that is, the first section, with its reference to the first subject, is omitted. This is natural, as it has just been heard in the tonic. At 124 the violin and 'cello change round, as compared with 50, and the theme is developed, but the oboe takes it up at 127 as before.

The codetta starts at 131 but the oboe figuration is different. The tonic pedal, which was three bars long at 61–4, now lasts from 135–40, and it is followed by two statements of a perfect cadence.

The *second movement* is a short, simple *adagio* in ternary form. **A** begins in D minor, but at bars 7–8, where a perfect cadence in the tonic might have occurred, there is an interrupted cadence instead, and an extension leads to a perfect cadence in B flat major in bar 12.

B starts in bar 12. Notice the little rhythmic figure in violin and viola, which they play five times, and which also starts the oboe theme. This section ends with Ic V in the tonic key at bar 20.

A returns at 21. The oboe enters two bars earlier than before, and its long note is shortened. But it now stays in D minor, and ends with a perfect cadence at 27–8.

Now follows a coda, which begins with the rhythmic figure which was the feature of **B**. It leads to Ic in the tonic key, and the pause is an indication that the oboist can now improvise a cadenza. He resolves it on to a trill implying V, as is usual, and the strings take up the **B** rhythmic figure again, while the oboe has a last reference to the **B** theme.

Mozart calls the delightful *finale* a "Rondeau", but it is really a mixture of sonata and sonata-rondo form. The first subject is stated by the oboe and then repeated by the violin at bar 9. The oboe joins in again at 13, and the phrase is extended and then repeated again by the violin. The first subject ends with a perfect cadence in the tonic at 21–2.

A transition starts at 23 and passes from F major through C major (24), D minor (25–6), C major (27–8) and G major (31–2), before reaching the dominant key and the second subject at 35.

The second subject starts with semiquaver figuration, and the oboe leads to a perfect cadence in the dominant key at 50–1. An attractive codetta figure starts at 52 and ends with imitative semiquavers between oboe and violin which act as a link to the return of the first subject at 65. This is exactly as before and ends at 86. So far this is a typical exposition in sonata-rondo form, as one would find it in movements by Beethoven.

Bars 86–9 form a short and rather obvious modulatory link to B flat major. Then follows a development section based mainly on the first subject. It is first developed in B flat major in the oboe, with the figure rising each bar. Then follows the extraordinary passage where the strings continue with a rather pedestrian accompaniment in $\frac{6}{8}$ time while the oboe freely embroiders over the top in $\frac{4}{4}$ time. It is most unusual for Mozart to experiment with cross-rhythm in this way.

This passage comes momentarily to rest in D minor at 102 and then modulates back to the tonic key, in which key it returns to the fold of $\frac{6}{8}$ at 108. The dominant chord of the tonic key is reached at 112 and from here it leads naturally to the recapitulation.

The recapitulation starts at 118. The first subject is exactly as before and ends at 139. There is no transition, so the second subject starts in the tonic key at 139. It is modified, and shortened to thirteen bars instead of seventeen, reaching its cadence at 151. But then it is repeated in the violin, with embellishments in the oboe, reaching its cadence at 164. The codetta follows as before, but there is no return to the first subject. Instead, the imitative semiquaver figure between violin and oboe is extended to lead to the final cadence.

To sum up, the exposition is like an exposition in sonata-rondo form; but the middle section (which is mainly development), and the recapitulation (which does not end with a final return to the first subject) follow the lines of sonata form. Yet the first subject occurs often enough for the movement to feel rondo-like, and to justify Mozart's title of "Rondeau".

Piano Quartet in G Minor, K. 478: Mozart

The piano quartet in G minor is one of two. It was written in 1785, and the one in E flat, K. 493, was written a year later. The publisher of the G minor quartet complained that it was too difficult and the public would not buy it, so Mozart transferred the second quartet to another publisher. The combination of piano with string trio was quite unusual in 1785, and the interweaving of the strings, each of them having the theme in turn, would prove difficult to the amateur string players of the time. The piano is usually set in contrast to the strings, and is sometimes quite concerto-like in style.

This quartet is unusually passionate and earnest for the period. Mozart used the key of G minor for such moods—think of the deep feeling in the lovely G minor symphony.

The *first movement* is in sonata form, with the development and recapitulation repeated as a unit in addition to the repetition of the exposition. This was usual in Mozart's day, and clearly shows how sonata form was thought of as growing out of binary rather than ternary form.

The first subject consists of an assertive unison figure played *tutti*, followed by a more florid reply in the piano. It is based on the tonic chord leading to the dominant, and is followed by another similar statement on the dominant chord leading to the tonic. This completes the first subject.

Bar 9 starts the transition with a flowing figure in the violin answered by the piano in the following bar. This is repeated and is followed by another unison *tutti* leading to a perfect cadence in the tonic. At bar 17 the first subject figure returns in a harmonized form in the strings and is answered by the piano in C minor. The antiphonal treatment continues, with the subject in the strings in F major, and in the piano in B flat major in bar 23.

Now follows a long section in the relative major (the usual key for the second subject), but it is all based on the first subject and does not feel at all like a second subject. Bars 23–57 are very simple harmonically, being largely based on reiterations of the primary triads. Bar 32 introduces a new tune growing out of the first subject figure, while yet another version starts at 37. The theme appears in *stretto* between left and right hands of the piano at 45, with accompanying contrapuntal figures in all three string parts. Eventually this section comes to rest with a conventional trill over the dominant chord leading to a perfect cadence in the relative major at 57. Bars 23–37 may be simple and conventional as far as the harmony is concerned, but melodically and contrapuntally they are a complete little development of the first subject enclosed within the transition between the first and second subjects.

The second subject begins in the relative major at 57, and has a peculiar cross-rhythm which makes it easily recognizable. It is stated first by the piano, then by the strings. Mozart is fond of saying things twice, and the contrast between the piano and the strings in this work makes this device very effective. It happens again in the second section of the second subject, which is stated in the strings at 65 and then in the piano at 74, though this time the violin imitates the piano a bar later. An extended cadence, starting at 82 and ending with the conventional trill, leads to the third section at 88, in which the strings have the figure twice and then the piano has it twice with the second time in a decorated version. After an inverted cadence in the relative major at 98 there are two modulatory bars returning to the tonic. The first time they lead to the repeat of the exposition, but the second time they lead to an interrupted cadence which starts the development section.

This middle section, which starts at 100, should perhaps be called a free fantasia rather than a development, though the descending fourth of the main figure, starting at 104, is an augmentation of the first two notes of the first subject. The first few bars (100–4) modulate from G minor through E flat major to C minor by means of two interrupted cadences. The main theme which follows has two "limbs" to it, starting at bars 104 and 108, both being stated first by the piano. Then the first limb appears antiphonally as a duet between viola and violin, starting in E flat at 112 and modulating through F minor (116), G minor (120) and D minor (124). When the 'cello joins in with the figure at 126 the violin proceeds to the second limb containing the ascending semiquaver scale. This is imitated two bars later by the viola, and two bars later again, at 130, by the 'cello, by which time the first limb has disappeared. Imitation of the second limb between 'cello, viola, violin and piano at one bar's distance leads to a version of the first subject at 134 in the strings. The semiquaver scale continues in the piano while the strings descend by steps with the first subject figure to the tonic key and the recapitulation at 141.

At first the recapitulation is identical with the exposition, but an interrupted cadence at 148 leads to an extension of the quaver figure and merges into the transition. There is no equivalent of bars 9–31, but 152 is the equivalent of bar 32, now in the tonic key. There is no further change until 165, when an interrupted cadence leads to the submediant major key for a time; but it returns to the tonic at 173.

The second subject starts in the tonic key at 178, and is almost identical, apart from the change of key.

The coda starts after the second double bar at 224, and is based entirely on the first subject. In bars 224–39 the treatment is very similar to that at the beginning of the recapitulation, but with the quaver figure extended: it is used eight times instead of three. From bar 239 to the end the strings are in unison. At first they are accompanied by broken chords in the piano, but at 237 the piano joins in with the unison, to make a very emphatic ending.

The *second movement* is in the relative major and is in modified sonata form. The first subject, stated in the piano and then repeated at 9 with the addition of the strings, is extended by cadential repetition up to bar 19.

Bar 20 starts the transition. Notice that at 24 the piano and string parts change over. A new figure appears in the piano at 62 which is to prove significant later. By bar 31 the dominant chord of the dominant key has been reached, ready for the entry of the second subject.

The second subject starts at 35 in the dominant key. The first phrase is announced by the strings only, then the answer appears in the piano at 39. This is all then repeated (43–50) with the instrumentation changed round.

Bar 51 starts the second section of the second subject, but notice that it is based on the figure first heard in bar 26 in the transition, though now it starts in the dominant key. At bar 59 this section is also repeated, with the piano and the strings changed round.

Bars 66–74 form a short link returning to the recapitulation and the tonic key.

There are few changes in the recapitulation. Bars 83–7 have a more ornate bass than before; and there is the usual change at 103 so as to lead to the second subject in the tonic instead of the dominant key. There are no more changes until 138, when an inverted cadence leads into a short coda, which is little more than a series of cadential extensions.

This quartet has only three movements, and the *finale* is in a rather irregular sonata-rondo form. It is quite common for a large-scale work to fall off towards the end, but this one certainly does not do so.

One lovely tune after another comes pouring out in the last movement.

The movement is in the tonic *major*, and is very sunny compared with the rest of the work. Mozart used the opening theme later for a rondo for the piano, so he must have been particularly fond of it. It is played first by the piano, then repeated by the strings in bar 9. The second stanza starts in the piano in bar 17, and it, too, is repeated in the strings.

An extended cadence, bars 39–43, leads to another tuneful theme in the tonic at 43. This theme modulates to the dominant in bars 58–9, thus leading to the second subject, and it therefore acts as a transition. But some people may prefer to call it a second theme of the first subject, partly because it is so tuneful, and partly because of its treatment in the recapitulation—of which more later. Like so many themes in this quartet, it, too, is stated twice, first by the piano and then by the strings.

The second subject, which starts in the dominant key at 60, contains no fewer than four distinct and tuneful sections, and the second section contains a number of subordinate melodies, so that the second subject seems to be full of new tunes. The first section starts in the piano at 60, and the second section begins in the strings at 70. Notice the viola figure at 79, imitated by the violin at 80, as this is developed into another tune at 87. Bar 83 has an attractive figure in the piano too; and the violin has yet another tune at 95, which has a resemblance to 87, though the 'cello continues with the figure from the previous bars. So this second section, though it hangs together as one, contains five memorable and tuneful figures.

The third section of the second subject, 101–11, is shorter and little more than passage work linking the second to the fourth section which starts at 112. This fourth section starts with a gay melody in the violin which is repeated by the piano at 120. Cadence repetitions lead to a pause on the dominant seventh of the tonic key at 135, and a return to the first subject.

This follows its normal course up to 166, where it begins to change key and to lead to the middle section.

The middle section starts at 170. The rhythm of the piano part bears a resemblance to that of 102–4 in the piano and 105–7 in the violin and viola, and the resemblance becomes more marked when the figure begins to be developed at 179. The opening figure at 170–1 is answered by a string figure at 171–3, which is rather like the quaver figuration of the first subject. Both these resemblances are probably quite unconscious on Mozart's part, but this middle section does not feel like a completely contrasted episode, either in material or key.

Bar 180 starts a series of imitations between the bass of the piano and unison strings. This is followed by a few bars of rather chromatic harmony, 187–92, leading to a return of the opening bars of the middle section, in which the parts for strings and piano change round. Then, at 200, the second figure is treated antiphonally in the violin and piano. A hint of the first subject appears at 209, in imitation between the upper strings and 'cello, and this leads to the dominant chord of the tonic key at 217. A conventional passage in the piano leads into the recapitulation in the tonic key at 225.

But *not* into the first subject! Mozart starts with the transition first heard in bar 44. Perhaps he felt that the first subject was going to be heard too often, or that the movement was getting too long. Certainly this gives an additional argument to those who think this theme is part of the first subject and not merely a transition.

At bar 233 the theme moves into the tonic minor, and it then leads into the second subject, now in the tonic.

But again the first theme is left out! Bar 250 starts with the second section, and the first section does not appear again at all. It does not stay in one's memory as much as does the second, and perhaps Mozart was again trying to shorten this long movement. But these two omissions make the form rather unusual.

After this, the second subject is the same as in the exposition, apart from the change of key, until it reaches 307, where it is extended by descending sequences. At 311 a long trill in the piano acts as an upper dominant pedal, under which hints of the first subject appear in the strings, eventually leading to a full appearance of the first stanza of the first subject at 322. The second stanza is omitted; but the extended cadence of 39–43 is repeated at 338–42, though this time it ends with an interrupted cadence which starts the coda.

The coda is based on the opening bar of the first subject used antiphonally in strings and piano, followed by a conventional extended cadence, over which the figure is heard for the last time.

Clarinet Trio in E Flat, K. 498: Mozart

The trio was originally published for "clavicembalo or forte piano with an accompaniment for violin and viola". There was an addendum stating that "the part for violin can also be played on the clarinet". It was probably worded thus because violinists were more common than clarinettists, so the reference to violin would command a better sale. But the work was actually written for Francisca Jacquin, a pianist friend of Mozart's, and Anton Stadler, the clarinettist, with Mozart himself playing the viola. The "violin–clarinet" part was obviously written with the clarinet in mind. The broken chords in bars 72–5 and the *arpeggi* in bars 119 and 127 of the last movement are far more effective on a clarinet than on a violin.

The *first movement* is in sonata form, but the exposition does not end with a perfect cadence in the dominant, and the usual double bar line with a repeat is also lacking. There are also several other little "irregularities". The student who has been trying to make an analysis of this movement, and has been worried by it, will find it helpful to look at the general harmonic scheme rather than at small changes of melodic detail, as the harmonies are quite clear and easy to follow.

Notice the melodic feature of the "turn" which first occurs in the viola in bar 1. It is used frequently, rather as Brahms sometimes uses an opening figure as a "motto". One associates the "turn" with the early Wagner operas, but the treatment here is quite different. The first subject might have come to an end at bar 12, but an interrupted cadence occurs instead, and the subject continues for another four bars.

The transition starts at bar 16. It still uses the "turn" figure, and begins rather like a codetta to the first subject; but by bar 24 it has reached an imperfect cadence in the dominant key, ready for the second subject.

The second subject starts in B flat major at bar 25, with the melody in the clarinet. The second section starts at 35 with a decorated version of the same melody in the piano. The "turn" figure makes a reappearance, and the music reaches a perfect cadence in the dominant at 47. A short codetta follows, based on the transition; and it ends with what appears to be a dominant seventh about to lead into the key of F, which is a most unusual ending for an exposition.

After a pause the discord resolves unexpectedly on to a chord of A flat, and a short development section follows. It begins with the second subject theme in the clarinet, in the key of A flat major. After touching on C minor at 62–3, it moves to G major at 64, where the viola and the piano play in imitation, using the "turn" figure of bar 1. Gradually the chords move to a dominant seventh of the tonic key; and bar 74 brings in the recapitulation.

The recapitulation begins with all three instruments bringing in the "turn" figure in imitation of each other; and there are other differences as compared with the exposition, though the harmonic scheme is unchanged. The first subject comes to an end at 85, however, and is four bars shorter than the similar passage in the exposition, because the interrupted cadence of bar 12 and the four-bar extension are omitted.

The transition starts at 86, and it begins by repeating the previous four bars a fourth higher, in the key of A flat. This corresponds to the repetition which occurred after the interrupted cadence at bar

12; but as it is moving away from the tonic key, it feels here as if it marks the beginning of the transition, rather than the end of the first subject. Bars 86–97 are the same as 13–24 a fourth higher, and they lead to the second subject in the tonic at 98.

Notice that the viola has the melody which was in the clarinet before. In fact, apart from a slight change in the clarinet in 104–5, the viola and clarinet parts have interchanged, and can be said to be in double counterpoint from 98–107 as compared with 25–34. The cadence at 112–13 corresponds to that at 56–7. Bars 114–17 are a shortened version of the codetta; and the coda, which starts at 117, is based on the "turn" figure from bar 1.

This work has only three movements, and the *second movement* is a minuet. It is in the dominant key—later composers might have chosen a more remote key, as there has been a good deal of dominant in the first movement. The first section ends at bar 12 in the key of F major, the dominant of B flat; and the second section modulates to C minor (16) and E flat major (18) before a dominant pedal (22–6) leads to a varied return of the first section at 28. The minuet ends with a short codetta (37–41).

The trio is in G minor, and the three instruments have very independent parts. The first section ends in the usual dominant key at 62. In the second section the piano takes over the crotchet clarinet figure and the viola triplets, while the viola and clarinet play crotchets together. The return to the first section starts at 73, but it changes at 78, when the three instruments play the crotchet figure in imitation, and the section is extended.

Bars 95–102 form a link into the return of the minuet, which is then repeated exactly. A coda starts at 144. The first four bars are based on the minuet and the remainder on the trio.

The *third movement* is called a rondo, and its analysis may cause difficulty because it is neither a short clear example of old rondo form nor the more modern sonata-rondo. Students should try to analyse it themselves before they read this. And if they should have reached different conclusions or used different terminology for the sectional divisions, it does not follow that they are wrong. Examiners will accept any analysis that makes sense.

This, then, is a very elaborate example of the old rondo form, with a number of long transitions that bear evidence of the influence of the newer sonata form. The general plan is as follows:

A. Bars 1–16. Tonic key. Bars 9–16 are a repetition of 1–8, with varied instrumentation.

B. 17–43. Dominant key. This is in two sections (17–24 and 36–43) with a link (24–36) mainly consisting of passage work on the piano.

Transition. 43–57, again mainly passage-work, and returning to the tonic key.

A². 58–65 Tonic key.

C. 66–89. Relative minor. This is a complete little section in binary form, with repeats. The first section ends at 75 in the relative major of the key for this episode. The second section begins with four bars for the piano modulating back to the minor, followed by a return to the opening of **C** in the viola at bar 80. The ending is modified so as to end in the tonic key for this section, C minor.

Transition. 90–107.

A³. 107–14. Tonic key.

D. 115–52. Subdominant major. Another complete little piece in binary form. The first section (115–22) ends with an imperfect cadence, and is then repeated (122–30) with different scoring, and modified so as to end in E flat major. The second section, beginning at 131, touches on A flat minor before returning to the opening of **D** at 145.

Transition. 153–67.

A. 167–91. Tonic key. This uses **A** twice, 167–74 and 184–91, divided by a link of passage work, with a dominant pedal from 179 to 183.

Coda. 191–end. This has a tonic pedal from 191 to 197, which is repeated with different scoring from 200 to 206; and the remainder is mainly an extended cadence.

Clarinet Quintet in A, K. 581: Mozart

The *first movement* is in sonata form, with the second subject starting at bar 42 in the exposition in the dominant key, and at 148 in the recapitulation in the tonic. The student may think that the transition between the two subjects starts at bar 26 in the exposition or at bar 19. Here is an opportunity for him to think out reasons for either alternative, and—even more important—to *feel* which is right, after repeated hearings. Arguments for bar 19 are (*a*) that there is a distinct perfect cadence in the tonic key at 18–19, whereas 25–6 is much less cadential; (*b*) that 19 starts a new idea which is merely repeated at 26 with the parts changed round; and (*c*) that, in the recapitulation, the change takes place at 130, which corresponds to 23. A change is much more likely to occur in the transition than in the first subject.

The development section is largely built on the quaver and semi-quaver arpeggios which first occurred in bars 7 and 8, with imitative entries in each instrument in turn. By bar 99, both types of arpeggios are occurring together, and a good time is had by all! The recapitulation starts at 118, with the violin and clarinet parts changed round.

The *second movement* is short, and in an unusual shape which cannot be given a name. It contains very little modulation, and the second theme, at bar 20, is, most surprisingly, in the same key as the first. The plan is: **A**, tonic key, 1–20; **B**, tonic, 20–30; a development of **B**, modulating through the relative minor to the dominant key, 30–45; a short link, returning to **A** exactly as before, 51–70; **B**, as before, except that triplets are used instead of duplets towards the end, 70–80; short coda over tonic pedal, 80–end.

The *third movement* contains two trios, thus making a longer movement. The first trio gives the clarinet player a welcome rest, and the middle section of the second trio is entirely based on a dominant pedal.

The *finale* is a series of five variations on a very simple theme in binary form. The chord scheme and the phrase shape are the same in each variation. Variation 1 begins with the first violin playing the theme, while the clarinet adds a counterpoint above it. In variation 2 the first violin has a new tune against triplets in the second violin and viola. Variation 3 changes to the tonic minor, and nothing remains of the original theme except the chord scheme and phrase shape. Variation 4 returns to the major and the tune comes back again, with decorative semiquavers over it. Bars 81–4 form a short link to the fifth variation, which consists of yet another variant over the original chord scheme. Another link (101–5) leads to the coda, which begins very like the original theme, and then develops the first four bars of it from 114 to the end.

9

Haydn and Mozart: Orchestral Works

If one compares an orchestral work by Bach or Handel with one by Haydn or Mozart the most obvious difference is that the latter composers have ceased to use a harpsichord *continuo* part throughout. A second difference is that Bach and Handel often wrote for strings and *continuo* only. If they added other instruments they varied according to what they had available for a particular performance. And, having chosen their instruments, they used them all for most of the time, instead of bringing in a solo instrument for occasional tonal contrast, as did the later composers. The most common additions to a string orchestra were oboes, bassoons, horns, trumpets and drums, though they also used some instruments which are now obsolete. But all the instruments that Haydn and Mozart used are still in use today. Their earliest works were usually for oboes, bassoons and strings only, but later they added other instruments, so that, by the time that Haydn wrote his second set of London symphonies, the so-called "classical" orchestra of two flutes, two oboes, two clarinets, two bassoons, two horns, two trumpets, two drums and strings was established.

The third difference is in the development of the various forms associated with the new kind of sonata and symphony, and more particularly with sonata form. For more comments about these forms see the introductory paragraphs of chapter 7.

Haydn was appointed as second *Kapellmeister* to Prince Esterhazy in 1761, when he was twenty-nine, and he stayed in the Esterhazy service for the rest of his life. It was fortunate that the Esterhazys were not only very wealthy but extremely musical and they kept a large musical establishment. This gave Haydn a wonderful opportunity for experimenting with musical forms and with scoring for a symphony orchestra, as rehearsals took place every day. His fame spread rapidly and his symphonies, cassations and *divertimenti* were soon being played all over Europe.

Haydn wrote 104 symphonies, though the earliest ones are mostly slight. The "Farewell" symphony is well known because of the story attached to it. The later symphonies are longer and more elaborate. Some of the earliest that are still heard today are the six composed in 1785–6 for the Concert Spirituel in Paris. But the best known and the greatest are the two sets of six symphonies he wrote for Salomon in London between 1791 and 1795. The first set are written for one or two flutes, two oboes, two bassoons and strings, but five of the second set of six also include parts for two clarinets. Two of these last symphonies are analysed later in the chapter.

Although Haydn wrote a large number of other orchestral works, such as *divertimenti*, cassations, overtures, marches and concertos, very few of them are heard today. The D major 'cello concerto and the trumpet concerto are perhaps the best known of the many concertos, but his piano concertos cannot compare with those by Mozart.

Mozart wrote forty-one symphonies. Most of the earlier ones were written for two oboes, two horns and strings. But flutes, bassoons, trumpets and drums appear in the later symphonies. The "Paris" symphony, written in 1778, is the earliest to include two clarinets. The "Haffner" symphony also uses clarinets. Of the last three great symphonies, written in three months in 1788, the E flat uses clarinets; the G minor exists in two versions, the first without and the second with clarinets; but the Jupiter, the last one, has no clarinet parts. Mozart loved the clarinet, which he had first heard in the Mannheim orchestra, and he wrote for it whenever there was a clarinet player available. But he still tended to think of clarinets as alternative to oboes, not fully realizing, as did Beethoven a generation later, that the two instruments could be effectively used in contrast to each other in a symphony orchestra. A complete analysis of the G minor symphony, no. 40 is given later in the chapter.

But whereas Mozart was, on the whole, content to follow Haydn's ideas in the composition of his symphonies, he was much more adventurous in his concertos. Just as Haydn can be called the father of the modern symphony, so Mozart can be called the father of the modern concerto. He was the first great composer to realize how effectively a solo performer could be contrasted with the orchestra. His greatest contribution to the art-form was the twenty-five piano concertos he wrote at various periods of his life. His violin concertos are all early works, but he also wrote concertos for flute, oboe, clarinet, bassoon, and horn, as well as several for more than one instrument. The bassoon concerto is the earliest of the wind concertos, written when he was only eighteen, and it is analysed in this chapter.

Mozart's operas are discussed in the next chapter, but an analysis of "The Magic Flute" overture is included in this one, as it is an orchestral work which is often heard on its own.

The Farewell Symphony: Haydn

This is a comparatively early symphony by Haydn, written when he was forty, and the circumstances of its composition and first performance are well known. Probably it would be no better known than any of his other early symphonies if it had not been for the title and the story connected with it. It is scored for the typical small orchestra for which he wrote in his early days: two oboes, two horns and strings. But a bassoon appears in the last movement—perhaps the player was in the castle, and was therefore brought in for the final denouement.

The *first movement* is in sonata form. It has a concise first subject ending at 16, and is followed by a transition based on the first subject but modulating through A major, 23; E major, 26; and returning to A major, 29.

A second subject starts in the relative major at 29, with a one-bar imitative figure alternating in violin and 'cello. But it is soon interrupted by a return to the first subject in the tonic minor at 38. The second subject figure reappears in the violin at 49 and is transferred to the 'cello at 50. It breaks off with an interrupted cadence at 54–5 and a second section of the second subject starts in C sharp minor (the dominant) at 56 and ends in that key at 69.

The development section starts with the first subject in the relative major. It passes through E major at 92, B minor at 96, E minor at 98 and reaches B minor again at 102, in which bar there is a reference to the second section of the second subject, ending with a pause at 107.

Now follows quite a long episode in D major. It reaches a perfect cadence in D at 130–1, and then the figure starts again, but this time modulating back to the tonic key, and ending poised on a discord at 140.

The recapitulation starts at 142 after a rest, but almost immediately it begins to change, merging into the transition. It reaches a dominant pedal at 157 and then modulates to B minor at 169. This leads into the first section of the second subject in the tonic minor at 179, and the second section follows at 195, still in the tonic.

The *second movement* is also in sonata form and is in the relative major. The first subject is a graceful theme for strings only and ends at 16. A transition starts at 17 (notice the rhythm in the violins which is used later). It modulates to the dominant, in which key the second subject starts at 29, with the oboe joining in with the tune. Notice the sudden change to minor at 31, and the syncopation which starts at 35 and which is a feature of the rest of the exposition. The second section of the second subject starts at 46 and ends at 71. The next five bars are a codetta, based on bar 17, the transition.

The development starts with the same dotted figure, now in the bass, which merges into a development of the second section of the second subject at 90. The dotted figure returns at 99, followed by the syncopated theme again, which ends on a pause at 109. A reference to the first section of the second subject starts in C sharp minor at 110, finally leading by means of the first violins into the recapitulation.

This starts at 137, but the horns are playing now, in addition to the strings. It is much shorter than before and the second subject enters in the tonic key at 135. From here to the end is a repetition of the exposition except for the change of key.

The *third movement* is a minuet and trio in F sharp major on the following plan: Minuet **A**, 1–12:||: **B**, 13–24; **A**, extended, 24–40:||. Trio **C**, 41–52, starting with the theme in the horns, and ending in the dominant key:||: **D**, 53–70, returning to the tonic key, first major, then minor; **C**, 71–6, tonic:||. The minuet is then repeated.

The *finale* is in a regular sonata form until it breaks off with its unusual ending. The first subject, which is stated twice, ends at 16, and four bars of transition lead to the second subject in the relative major at 21. This begins with imitations between the violins and the 'cello, and they alternate for some time. The music works up to a climax on a diminished seventh at 36 and then falls to a perfect cadence in the relative major at 44–5. Bars 45–56 form a codetta.

The development section starts with the first subject in the relative major and continues to develop it for some time, passing through B minor (62) and C sharp minor (64–80). The rest of the development section consists of a series of cadences: C sharp minor (80–3); B minor (84–5); A major (86–7); D major (88–9); and finally F sharp minor, the tonic (90–97).

The recapitulation starts at 98. The first subject begins the same, but alters at 111 so as to get to the second subject in the tonic at 117. Changes in the second subject are only slight apart from the obvious change of key. But the codetta which starts at 138 is different, and it reaches a dominant pedal at 144 and finally comes to a halt on the dominant at 150, followed by a pause.

Then follows an *adagio* which is still part of the finale, though the Eulenberg edition begins to number the bars from bar 1 again as if it were a fresh movement. It does, however, consist of new material, and it starts in A major, not in the tonic key. The first section ends with a perfect cadence in A major at bar 10, and the second section modulates to E major, the dominant, and ends at 25. The cadence is then repeated up to 31.

Up to this moment the orchestration has been unusually full, and everyone is playing at 31. But now the first oboe and the second horn stop playing, and we are told that they blew out their candles at the first performance and stole out of the room.

The rest of the orchestra begins to modulate back to the tonic key for the return of the first section at 42. At 47, the bassoon, who appears to have been brought into this symphony specially for this purpose, as he does not play until this movement, also stops playing and goes out. At 54 the second oboe and the first horn similarly stop playing, so that now only the strings are left. But they have come to the end of their statement of the first section, and now they seem to be marking time. The double bass has the most to say in this extension, perhaps so that it will be more obvious when he, too, stops and retires at 67.

The orchestra has now returned to the tonic key, but in the major mode, and the remaining strings proceed to play the first theme again in F sharp major, but the 'cellist stops at 77. Then the third and fourth violins stop at 85, leaving only two muted violins and a viola.

Lastly the viola departs at 93, leaving the two violins to fade away into a *pp* ending. We are told that Prince Esterhazy took the hint, and gave the orchestra the holiday they desired.

The Clock Symphony: Haydn

The "Clock" symphony is one of the "London" symphonies, and has been given its name because of the tick-tock accompaniment to the second movement. It is scored for two flutes, two oboes, two clarinets, two bassoons, two horns, two trumpets, two drums and strings—what has since come to be called "the classical orchestra".

The clarinets only take part in the *tutti* sections however, as the instrument was so new, and players were unreliable. The other wind instruments all have a tune at some stage, but not the clarinets.

Haydn was rather fond of slow introductions, more so than Mozart or Beethoven. The introduction to this symphony starts with a rising scale figure in crotchets, which is later used for the opening notes of the *presto*. In bar 4 it is answered by descending crotchets, and the music flows gently on till it reaches the dominant chord at bar 22.

The *presto* which follows is a gay sparkling movement. The transition starts at 34 with the rising quaver first subject figure over a tonic pedal; and when it starts with the figure yet again at 49, it begins to move away from the tonic key, first into E minor, then, after a brief return to the tonic, into A major, the dominant, which it reaches at 61. This unusually long transition is based entirely on the first subject.

The second subject, in the usual dominant, which is, by now, clearly established, begins at 81. It is not very different from the first subject: compound time never offers as much rhythmic variety as does simple time, and is probably chosen less frequently for first movements for this reason. It appears to be coming to an end about 98, but a series of extensions hold back the main cadence until 116. Notice that the ascending chromatic movement in 92–5 is inverted in 110–15. The short codetta (116–26) consists of dominant tonic harmony followed by an inversion of the ascending first subject figure, which leads naturally into the repeat of the exposition.

The development begins with the strings using the second subject figure in imitation. It passes through B minor at 130, F sharp minor at 136, B minor again at 144, and then surprisingly reaches C major, an unrelated key, at 150. At this point, Haydn begins to develop the first subject by inversion, and uses the full orchestra once more. The music passes through D minor (164), E minor (170) and reaches a dominant pedal of B minor at 174, though it finally resolves itself into G major at 184. A sudden *pp* at 197 in B minor in the strings brings in the second subject figure again, violin and flute having it in turn. This works up to a *tutti crescendo*, ending with a dominant seventh in the tonic key (213–17), ready for the recapitulation.

The recapitulation starts at 218, and the short first subject is identical with its presentation in the exposition. The transition (228) begins in the same way, too, but at 235 a minor chord occurs instead of a major; and by 241 the music has reached a dominant pedal, over which hints of the second subject are heard, finally ending in a unison *fortissimo* at 248. The transition is much shorter than in the exposition as well as being considerably modified.

The second subject begins in the tonic at 250, and it is considerably changed and extended. It is treated imitatively at first, in the strings, and the chromatic figure of 92–5 is extended in 269–77. Further development of the second subject figure occurs at 281; and a dominant pedal at 294, followed by a tonic at 300, seems to be leading to a close; but Haydn has still more to say. Bars 309–13 are similar to 111–14, but they lead to an interrupted cadence at 314. A few *pp* bars bring in a complete return of the first subject in the tonic at 324, and this marks the beginning of the coda. Bars 334 to the end repeat the last two bars over dominant and tonic harmonies.

This is a most highly evolved movement. Haydn had come a long way since his first short symphonies in his early Esterhazy days.

The "tick-tock" at the beginning of the *second movement* is produced by two bassoons and lower *pizzicato* strings. Over this the violins have a simple melody on the plan **A** :‖ : **B A** :‖. The first **A**, as well as the second, ends in the tonic key, so most people would say this section was in ternary form.

The key signature then changes to the tonic minor, and a new section begins, based on the dotted rhythm from bar 4. There is a syncopated "tick-tock" in bars 40–4, combined with a more lively demi-semiquaver movement. The latter combines with the dotted rhythm for the rest of this section, but it quietens down again into a return to the first section at 64, with the "tick-tock" now in flutes and bassoons.

At 98 there is an abrupt change of key to E flat major, and a further variation of the original theme occurs, in which the second bar is developed. Bar 112 brings a return to the tonic key, and another decorated version of the original theme in its entirety appears. Bars 144 to the end form a short coda.

The divisions of the sections and the changes of key make this movement appear rather like a rondo. On the other hand, the sections beginning in G minor and E flat major are not episodes in the sense that they consist of new material; and it could just as reasonably be argued that the movement is in variation form. Haydn has, in fact, cleverly combined the two.

The *minuet* is planned as follows: **A**, bars 1–28, ending in dominant :||:**B**, 29–49; **A**, 49–80, ending in tonic :||. This is a very common plan, and it is unfortunate that some people call it binary and others ternary. It might be as well to avoid both terms in an examination.

The trio, while not confining itself to three instruments, as the name originally implied, is much slighter in texture. It contains a flute solo, and a charming little duet between flute and bassoon; and it is built on the same plan as the minuet.

The *finale* is in rondo form. The opening theme is, like the minuet, **A**:||:**BA**:||; but both **A** sections end in the tonic, and the second one is an exact repetition of the first, so the form may legitimately be called ternary.

A long transition beginning at bar 28 leads to the first episode at bar 62 in the dominant key. It does not provide a complete contrast, however, as it is based on a development of the first three notes of the main theme. It ends at 94, and is followed by a short transition based on the crotchets of the first theme. This leads into a decorated return of the first section in the tonic key.

Bar 138 starts an episode in the tonic minor. At first, it is completely new material, but at 156 it refers to the first episode. The first theme returns again at 189, but now the first three bars are treated fugally for some time. They enter *ff tutti* at 233. A coda begins at

250. The strings have the first theme alone at first, but it soon leads to the conventional noisy *tutti* that marks the end of all symphonies of this period.

Notice how the episodes in this rondo each contain some development of the original theme, so that the movement is more of an organic unity than is the conventional rondo of the earlier composers, and is truly symphonic in conception. A symphony like this prepared the way for the young Beethoven.

The Drum Roll Symphony: Haydn

Haydn's symphony in E flat, known as the "Drum Roll" is one of the second set of six symphonies, commissioned by Saloman for London. It is next to the last symphony he wrote, the famous so-called "London" symphony being the last.

It is scored for what had, by 1795, become the standard symphony orchestra, i.e. two flutes, two oboes, two clarinets, two bassoons, two horns, two trumpets, two drums and strings.

The *first movement* starts with a drum roll on E flat, hence its name. It is followed by quite a long *adagio* introduction, starting with a twelve-bar theme in unison in the lower strings. Then the first six bars of the theme (notice the six-bar phrases) are repeated in the first violins, harmonized by the second violins in syncopation. But the answering phrase is different and longer. The *adagio* ends with a mysterious reiterated A flat G, which seems to be leading into C minor.

But suddenly the A flat and G are gaily repeated in E flat major as the beginning of the first subject of the *allegro*. It is a four-bar theme in the strings, repeated an octave lower, and reaching a perfect cadence in the tonic at bar 48.

The *tutti* which follows is the beginning of the transition. It makes a joyful noise without saying anything very much, until it reaches an imperfect cadence in the tonic at 59. Then the oboe, which follows, begins to change key, first to C minor, then to B flat major.

At 64, therefore, we have reached the dominant key. Is the second subject to follow? What comes next is a reference to the first subject again, but now in the dominant key. Haydn has been known to start the second subject with the first subject theme in the dominant, as for example, in the first movement of the "London" symphony, so perhaps this really is the beginning of the second subject? But the reference to the first subject is only brief, and he soon moves away again from the dominant key (into C minor at 69). There is a distinct second-subject theme later (at 80), and (perhaps the most important point of all) bars 60–80 simply do not appear in the recapitulation. So most listeners will surely feel that bar 80 marks the beginning of the second subject.

Before Haydn gets to bar 80, however, he has another surprise in store for us. At 74 he brings in the theme from the introduction, now completely transformed, its sombre mood changed to gaiety. This, too, is in the dominant key.

It would be quite reasonable to state that the second subject starts at 64 and includes a reference to the first subject and to the introduction before introducing new material at 80; and that the equivalent of 60–80 was omitted in the recapitulation.

However, the new theme at 80 arrives at last, with oboe and violin having the gay waltz-like tune. The extended cadence, starting at 88, brings in the whole orchestra.

The development section is unusually long and intricate for Haydn, with unexpected touches of drama. It starts with imitative entries of the first bar of the first subject, which lead, at 104, to a fuller statement in A flat major, This builds up to a *tutti* climax in C minor, ending with a pause at 112.

Then a reference to the introduction creeps in, in the lower strings, starting in the tonic key. It still sounds rather gloomy and mysterious, in spite of the quicker speed. After building up to another *tutti* it dies down again to a *piano* reference of the first bar of the first subject in F minor at 130. After another pause it is repeated over the dominant seventh of key D flat, but instead of resolving on to the tonic chord of D flat the bass slides up to Ic V in the original tonic key of E flat. The same figure is then heard again, in E flat major at 140, C minor at 141, A flat major at 142 and F minor at 143.

This leads to an entry of the second subject at 144 in the remote key of D flat major. It builds up to another climax, passing through E flat minor (151) and F minor (153), and reaching the tonic key at 154, in which key it ends with a dominant seventh at 159, followed by a pause.

In the recapitulation which follows, the first subject (160–6) is exactly as before. The transition begins as before but changes at 177 so as to stay in the tonic key. This is only four bars away from the second subject, whereas there were another twenty-two bars in the equivalent place in the exposition.

The second subject starts at 180 in the tonic key. It builds up to a *ff tutti* at 189 over a pedal on A flat, and gradually dies down again, ending with a pause on a diminished seventh at 201.

Then the opening drum roll dramatically reappears, followed by the first twelve bars of the introduction at their original speed. We have got used to dramatic references to *adagio* introductions in the work of later composers such as Beethoven and Franck, but at this period it must have seemed a remarkable innovation.

However, as Tovey says, it is dismissed with laughter at 214, when it is heard in diminution, *allegro con spirito*. A reference to the first subject is introduced by the horn in 220, imitated by woodwind and then strings. The third bar of the second subject is then heard in the bass at 223, and it brings the movement to an end.

The *second movement* is in variation form, and is based on two themes. Haydn was a master of this form, and he was particularly fond of writing variations on two themes, often contrasted minor and major, as here. Some pupils may know his "Andante and Variations in F" for piano.

The first, minor theme begins in two-part harmony, and after rising to a climax reaches the relative major at the end of its first section, **A**. The last two notes become the starting figure for the second section, **B**, which is mainly in three-part harmony at first. It passes through F minor (12) and leads to dominant harmony of the tonic key, and to the return of the first section, **A**, in the lower strings at 17, against a continuation of **B** in the upper strings. The lower strings change at 21 so as to end in the tonic key. The shape is thus **A** :|| : **B A** :||, the hybrid form which is unfortunately called both binary and ternary by different people.

The second, major, theme is also the same shape, so that it might be labelled **C** :|| : **D C** :||. Being in the major key, **C** moves to the dominant on its first appearance, and again changes on its return, at 47, so as to end in the tonic. **D** also grows out of the cadence of **C**, just as **B** grew out of the cadence of **A**. **C** is built over a tonic pedal for the first six bars, until it moves to the dominant key.

Notice that the opening figure of the major theme is very similar to the opening figure of the minor theme, and even more like bar 3 of that theme. Also notice that the minor theme is confined to strings while the major theme introduces wind.

The first variation of the minor theme is nearly identical with the original in the strings, but wind interjections are added. The repeat of the first section is written out because more wind instruments are used. The second section is not repeated, and when **A** returns it is given to the viola and bassoon instead of to the viola and 'cello.

A variation of the major theme follows at 85. This is based on the same harmonic scheme as the original, but a solo violin has a decorated variant of the melody.

Then comes the second variation of the minor theme. In the first section the melody of **A** is an octave higher in the first violins and is doubled by flute and oboe, while the bassoon and lower strings play a semiquaver accompaniment. In **B** the violins often use demi-semiquavers to decorate the theme, but the return to **A** at 125, is in the lower strings, as before.

Finally there is another variation of the major theme. In section **C** the oboes have the tune, while the flute makes interjections over a *pizzicato* string accompaniment. This section is not repeated. In **D** at 143, the strings join the oboes, while at 147 flute and violins have demi-semiquaver decorations. When **C** returns, at 151, the tune is in all the upper wind and string instruments, while in the extended cadence (157–60) the strings are silent.

Bar 160 begins a coda. It starts by repeating the previous phrase, and then gradually dies away. Then it makes an abrupt modulation to E flat major, and fragments of bar 1 of **C** appear in the flute and oboe. Finally the music returns to C major at 187 and repeats 151–60.

The *minuet* returns to the tonic key. The rhythmic "snap" first heard in bar 2 is a feature found in many folk tune , such as those of Scotland and Hungary. It occurs at the end of the sentence in the violin at bar 8, and is then comically imitated, first in the bassoons and horns, then in the flutes and oboes. So **A** ends inconclusively and up in the air.

At the beginning of **B** the violin takes up the same interval of a fifth, but now in quavers, having lost its "snap", and modulates to E flat minor and then to G flat major, introducing a more flowing tune at the same time.

A development of **A** occurs at 19, with imitation between upper and lower strings. This is in E flat minor, and is full of *sforzandos*. Eventually it dies down to first violins only and leads, at 32, to a return of **A** in the tonic major. This breaks off with an interrupted cadence at 39, and an extension brings the minuet to an end.

The trio consists mainly of gracefully flowing quavers. It is very simple in style. The first section **C** ends with a perfect cadence in the tonic key and returns exactly the same as before at 73. So the trio could reasonably be said to be in ternary form, in spite of its apparent division into two repeated sections.

The *finale* is based on one theme, and hardly a bar is without it. Contrast is obtained by key rather than by theme, with the tonic key recurring in between the different modulating sections. In fact, if one lettered the music according to contrast of key rather than of theme, one would have **A**, **B**, **A²**, **C**, **A³**, coda, which makes a kind of a rondo form. **B** starts in the dominant at 107; **A²** starts at 158; **C** starts in D flat major at 217; **A³** starts at 264, and the coda starts at 316.

The theme itself is said to be a Croatian folk song, and it is preceded and accompanied in the first few bars by a horn call. The opening figure of the tune consists of four repeated notes, the fourth carrying the accent, followed by a step downwards. But, in later repetitions, this last note is frequently changed. Notice, for example, bar 36, where it drops a fifth, and 58 where it rises a second.

At bar 73 the tune is heard *forte* in clarinet, bassoon, viola and 'cello, against a development of the horn call in the flutes, oboes and violins.

The first **A** ends with a tumultuous climax in the dominant key at 107, and then **B** (i.e. **A** in the dominant) enters quietly in the 'cellos. It moves to B flat minor at 121, but returns to the major at 133, and this section ends with a noisy *tutti* at 146.

The next twelve bars form a link to the return of **A**. Notice the imitation between the violins: violin I rising at 147, and violin II falling at 148.

Although **A²** starts in the tonic key it does not stay there. It moves, for example, to C minor at 182, and imitative entries continue. It again leads to a *ff* climax, this time in D flat major at 217, where the stage is set for **C**.

C includes entries in F minor, starting at 228, but returns to D flat at 247. Its climax ends, this time, on a reiterated chord of G (259–63), which appears to be about to lead to key C.

But after a pause **A** returns once more. **A³** ends like the first **A** (compare bars 99–107 with 308–16), except that it is now in the tonic instead of the dominant key.

The coda starts quietly in the tonic key, but the trumpets suddenly interrupt at 342 with the opening horn call in augmentation. After this the strings continue quietly again, but soon all the instruments have entered for the final *ff* climax, starting at 368.

Symphony no. 40, in G Minor: Mozart

Mozart originally scored this symphony without clarinets. Then, presumably because two clarinettists became available, he wrote another version with two clarinet parts added. It is interesting to compare the two versions, and to see what parts Mozart has left to the oboes, what parts he has transferred to the clarinets, and where he uses both. The symphony is usually performed with clarinets today and it is this version which is referred to in this analysis.

Another noteworthy point about the scoring of this symphony is that it contains no trumpets or drums. Yet it is quite a sonorous work. The horns are in two different keys, B flat and G (B in German is B flat in English). By this means Mozart could obtain the notes of the tonic chord: G B flat and D; and also of the tonic chord of the relative major key: B flat, D and F. If both horns had been in G, he would have had a harmonic series based on G *major*: G B natural D, so the tonic chord of G minor would not have been available.

Mozart has written some lovely music in G minor. The piano quintet in G minor is another example. It becomes a peculiarly poignant key in his compositions. The delicacy and beauty of the first movement in this symphony and the mixture of gay and sad intensity in the last movement make it a much-loved work with musicians.

There is no introduction to the *first movement*. The lower strings start a chordal accompaniment over which the first and second violins play a beautifully-curved melody in octaves. As it comes to an end, the woodwind enter with a two-bar continuation in three octaves, and then the whole orchestra plays the cadence chords five times.

The transition starts at bar 20. It begins by repeating the first subject figure, but the second phrase modulates into the relative major and leads to a vigorous *tutti* in that key at 28. Notice the *sforzando* chords in 34–7. They lead to five bars of dominant pedal, followed by a bar's rest, all of which helps to mark the entry of the second subject at 44.

This second subject begins in the relative major, as expected. Notice its use of chromatic semitones in bars 44–5 and 48–9, which make the theme pathetically beautiful. Mozart often uses semitones most effectively in this way.

Notice also the division of the theme between strings and wind, and that, when the phrase is repeated, the string and wind parts change round. The second time does not, however, finish with a perfect cadence, as it did the first time at 50–1. Instead it moves (at 58) to a dominant seventh in the key of A flat, and starts an extension, which does not get to a perfect cadence until 65–6, when it reaches key B flat. Then follows a six-bar phrase, in which unison strings have the chromatic movement of 48–50 in an ascending instead of descending form. This can be considered to be a second section of the second subject.

There is quite a long codetta starting at 73. It refers to the opening figure of the first subject, tossing it from clarinet to bassoon twice, and then asserting it strongly in the first violin. The whole of this is repeated at 80–8, except that, this time, the bassoon enters first. Bars 88–99 are a cadence-extension, in which the cadence is repeated so often that no one is in any doubt that the end of the exposition has been reached. Bar 100 is a dominant seventh of the tonic key, leading back to the repeat of the exposition or on to the development section.

The development section is based entirely on the opening figure of the first subject. It appears first in the remote key of F sharp minor—the student with sufficient knowledge of harmony should work out how Mozart has got there. The four-bar phrase occurs three times in the violins, using chromatic harmony.

Then, when it is about to resolve itself into E minor, it is interrupted, *forte*, by the violas and 'cellos at 115, using the same figure in E minor. Against it, the violins have a new quaver counter-theme; and from 115–34 upper and lower strings alternate with the two main themes, passing through E minor (115), A minor (118), D minor (120), G minor (122), C major (124), F major (126), and B flat major (128). It will be realized that up to this point the keys make a sequence of rising fourths. But at this stage the shape and the harmonies change so that G minor is reached by 133. However, this use of the tonic key is only momentary, as it leads to a dominant pedal in the key of D minor at 134.

From 134 to the recapitulation at 165 there is a series of pedals, over which the first subject figure is tossed between woodwind and upper and lower strings. It is a wonderful passage, staying poised in the air until it glides into the recapitulation. Bars 134–8 are over a dominant pedal of key D minor; bars 139–42 are similarly over a dominant pedal in key B flat minor, while the pedal moves to the dominant of C minor at 143. Then comes a diminished seventh at 147, resolving on to a dominant seventh of the tonic key at 149. The pedal is taken over by the two horns at 153, as it reaches its climax. Then, as the music quietens down, the pedal is given to the two bassoons, so that the last four bars are woodwind alone. The entry of the violins at 105 after four bars without strings and resolving on to the tonic chord after all this suspense, is quite exquisite.

Notice also how this figure begins with four-bar phrases at 104, is shortened to two-bar phrases when the series of pedals starts at 134, and finally gets down to two beats at 153 when the horn pedal starts. The four-bar swing of the phrase when the recapitulation begins is another reason for the sense of fulfilment felt at this point. What a wonderful development section this is! The student should be very interested in seeing how it has all been achieved, and the knowledge should add to his appreciation.

In the recapitulation the first subject is exactly as in the exposition. The transition (184) starts the same but modulates almost immediately, so that it gets to E flat major for the *tutti* section at 191. This section is much extended, with antiphonal contrapuntal treatment between upper and lower strings, alternating between the original figure from 28 and a quaver counter-theme. It passes through F minor (198) and E flat major (205), reaching G minor at 211. Bars 211–26 correspond to bars 28–43, except that they are in the tonic minor instead of the relative major. In other words, bars 191–210 are an interpolation, as compared with the exposition.

The second subject (227) is in the tonic minor, so its chromaticisms sound even more poignant than they did when they were in a major key in the exposition. The extension, at 241, modulates to E flat major, so that it becomes a fifth above the exposition version instead of the expected sixth. A further extension occurs at 247, but 254 corresponds to 66. The rising form of the theme, the second section of the second subject, then occurs as before, and leads to the codetta at 260.

The codetta is very similar to that in the exposition. The cadence extension, starting at 276, begins in the same way, but changes at 281, so that it might be said to merge into a coda at this stage. It breaks off on a discord at 284 and is followed by further references to the first subject figure in the second violin, the first violin, the viola and the woodwind. But bars 293 to the end correspond to the end of the exposition.

The *second movement* is an *andante*, in sonata form, in E flat major. The viola starts a repeated note figure which is imitated by the second violin and then the first violin. Notice the eloquent chromatic movement in the 'cellos in bar 2, and the throbbing, reiterated notes in the horns at bars 4–6. The rhythm of two demi-semiquavers followed by a *sforzando* in the violin in bar 7 is made much use of later. This phrase ends with descending chromatic semitones.

The answering phrase starts at bar 9 in the 'cellos and horns and is imitated as before. But this time the 'cello part from bars 1–4 appears minus its quavers, as a counter-theme in the violins. The relationship between the two is not, perhaps, so very noticeable at this stage but it becomes more obvious in the recapitulation. The demi-semiquaver figure appears in the 'cellos at bar 15; and then, at 16, it is taken up by the first violins and leads to a cadence at 19.

The transition starts in B flat major at 20. Its two notable features are the cross-rhythm in the first bar in the violins and 'cellos and the use of the demi-semiquaver figure that was first heard in bar 7. This figure is tossed about between wind and strings continuously until the entrance of the second subject. There is also a reference to the first bar of the first subject in 29–32.

The transition ends "in the air" on Ic in the dominant major, and the second subject starts in violins and violas only at 37. It sways between tonic and dominant and is repeated an octave lower at 41, this time with woodwind and 'cellos added. The demi-semiquaver figure reappears at 46 as the cadence approaches, and the codetta, which starts at 48, also makes use of it.

The development section is based mainly on the reiterated quavers from bar 1 and the demi-semiquavers from bar 7, which alternate in wind and string parts. It takes on a dark colour at the beginning with the unison C flat, which returns at 56. Then the bass slowly climbs up by semitones, a bar at a time. It reaches G at 64, and swings round this note with chromaticisms above it until 69. Then the reiterated quavers return in the first bassoon, answered by the second bassoon and then by the second violins. The 'cello figure from bar 2 is heard in the oboe and the flute at the same time, and the fluttering demi-semiquavers continue.

All this resolves itself imperceptibly into the recapitulation at 74. The first eight bars of the first subject are as in the exposition. In the answering phrase, starting at 82, the counter-theme in the violins uses the chromatic quavers in the second bar and makes its relationship with the bass of the first bars of the theme more obvious.

The first subject is much shorter than in the exposition, and it merges into the transition at 86. This is a fourth lower than before, is modified and is longer, but it is based on the same material, though it also makes use of the 'cello part from bar 2. Bars 97–107 correspond to 26–36, so that again the additional material occurs at the beginning of the section.

The second subject starts at 108, and it and the codetta are the same as in the exposition except that they are now in the tonic key.

There is nothing particularly dance-like about the *minuet*, and it is a restless, syncopated movement. The first section **A** ends in the dominant minor, and the second section **B** begins with the opening figure in the relative major and passes through G minor (20), E flat major (23) and C minor (24) before reaching the dominant chord of the tonic key and the return to **A** at 28. This contains an imitation of the opening figure in flute and second violin, and ends, as expected, in the tonic key. But the little codetta, starting in the woodwind at 36, is unexpected and is wholly delightful.

The trio, in the tonic major, is much gentler in mood and provides a good contrast to the minuet. The first phrase is in strings alone and the next phrase in woodwind alone, while the strings take up the third cadential phrase with a little support from the oboe. This can all be called **C** and it ends in the dominant key.

The second section **D** continues with the idea of **C**, but returns to the tonic key and contains imitations between 'cello and woodwind. It is very short and ends with an imperfect cadence at 68.

When **C** returns at 69, the two horns add a lovely quality to the texture, both in the string and wind phrases. The wind phrase is modified so as to end in the tonic key; and the third, final phrase is similar to the final phrase of the first section of the trio, though it is rather more fully orchestrated.

The *finale* is again in sonata form. But the first subject is in binary form with repeats and feels rather dance-like. It is quick and gay with a leaping crotchet figure contrasted with a quaver figure running round one note. The second section starts with *forte* and *piano* octave leaps, and then ends in the same way as the first section, so that the plan is **A B** :||: **C B** :||. This is real string writing: it is impossible to imagine this theme on anything but the violin.

The transition, starting at 32, continues with gay, fussy quavers in the violins which are transferred to the lower strings at 49. By 56, upper and lower strings are running after each other in gay abandon, but the violins win, and the lower strings settle down to a dominant pedal of the relative major at 65.

Feeling rather breathless we are glad to slow down into a quieter, more melodious second subject at 71. It is a graceful, long-phrased tune and again makes use of chromaticisms. Its first statement is given entirely to the strings, then it is repeated in a decorated form in the wind, but this time its ending is slower moving, consisting largely of minims moving by semitones.

A sudden *forte* at 101 leads to another gay spate of quavers, and these continue up to the double bar.

The development section starts with a humorous treatment of the first subject, full of unexpected pauses and surprisingly chromatic intervals. Then, at 135, we settle down to imitative entries of the first subject, the violin alternating with the flute, the bassoon and the oboe in turn.

At 146 the entries come closer together (in *stretto*), each string part having a turn. At first, two parts enter at a bar's distance, as at 146 and 158, but by 161 all four string parts are interrupting each other and the woodwind has entered with semibreve chords.

At 175 the woodwind takes up the imitations, alternating with the lower strings, while the violins have an upper pedal on G sharp.

At 191 all the woodwind and strings play *forte*, but the texture is simplified, as each entry appears in three octaves in wind and strings combined. The horns enter in the last few bars, to add to the power.

The recapitulation enters unexpectedly at 207. The first subject is the same as in the exposition except that the sections are not repeated. The transition starts the same, too, but it changes after three bars, so as to lead to the second subject in the tonic. It keeps up the same figures as before, but is shorter.

The second subject enters at 246 in the tonic minor, and contains several modifications. The melody, now being minor, sounds much more plaintive than before. The last eight bars are identical with those at the end of the exposition except that they are now in the tonic key.

Bassoon Concerto, K. 191: Mozart

Mozart wrote this concerto when he was eighteen, so that it is a comparatively simple work that needs little to be said about it. He wrote many concertos for a great variety of instruments, and this one is played quite frequently—though there is always a temptation for the audience (and the performer) to laugh when the soloist has his long runs and large leaps!

It is scored for two oboes, two horns and strings—a slight orchestra. The exposition of the first movement is stated by the orchestra first, as was customary with Mozart, both first and second subjects being in the tonic. The soloist enters with the first subject at 35, and the exposition is then repeated, with a transition at 45 leading to the second subject in the dominant at 59. It is played by the violins as before, while the bassoon embroiders round it.

A *tutti* at 71 leads to the development section, in which the soloist, at 80, develops the transition. Then (at 89) violins and bassoon answer each other antiphonally with a new figure. A short dominant pedal leads to the recapitulation at 98. The transition starts a tone lower at 112. It is longer than in the exposition, but eventually leads to the second subject in the tonic at 138. Now the bassoon and the violins change round, the violins having the counter-theme. The ensuing *tutti* leads to the usual pause on the chord Ic at 160, at which point the soloist is free to improvise his own cadenza, and a *tutti* brings the movement to an end.

The *second movement* is a simple example of modified sonata form. The first subject is stated *tutti* before the soloist enters with it at 7. A two-bar transition (11–12) leads to the second subject in the dominant. A four-bar link (23–6) leads to the recapitulation, in which the soloist enters in the second instead of the seventh bar. Bars 4–9 of the exposition are compressed into 31–2; but the transition, 34–7, is four bars long instead of two, so that the second subject enters in the tonic at 38. Bars 46–52 form a coda.

The *finale* is in minuet style and rhythm, but in a simple kind of sonata-rondo form. The second subject, **B**, is not as contrasted in mood and key as it would be with Beethoven. The plan is as follows: **A**, 1–20, tonic; **B**, 21–44, beginning in tonic and ending in dominant; link, 45–50; **A**, first section only, 51–8; **C**, 59–80, relative minor; **A**, first section only, 81–8; **B**, 89–106, beginning in tonic as before, but changing so as to end with a dominant pedal of the tonic key; pause for *cadenza*; **A**, 107–37, with a long extension; coda, based on **A**, 138–50.

Overture to the Magic Flute: Mozart

"The Magic Flute" was written in 1791, during the last year of Mozart's life. Though rather coldly received at first, it rapidly grew in popularity, and performances of the opera were being given while Mozart lay on his death bed. The libretto is a nonsensical hotch-potch of a story, a mixture of fairy tale and allegory, with references to Freemasonry, in which both Mozart and his father were interested. But it has good dramatic moments, and the music is some of the best that Mozart ever wrote.

The overture starts with an *adagio* introduction. The rhythm of the first three chords is supposed to be linked with Freemasonry and these are used later in the opera, where Tamino appears at the Temple of Wisdom. The chords are very impressive because they are played by three trombones in addition to the usual instruments which Mozart used in a symphony orchestra. Trombones were often used in operas—another effective use of them is in the statue music in "Don Giovanni". After these *ff* chords, the introduction is mainly soft and grave, and contains a good deal of syncopation.

The *allegro* is in sonata form. But the first subject is unusual in that it consists of a complete fugal exposition. The subject enters in the second violin at bar 16, and there is a tonal answer in the first violin at 20. A short (fugal) codetta at 24 leads to the subject in the violas, 'cellos and bassoons at 27. At the same time the first violins have a counter-theme which recurs frequently enough to be designated a countersubject, though it was not used at 20. Notice the descending scale at 28 and the syncopation at 29, as both of these figures are used later. Finally the answer (real, this time) enters in the 'cellos and basses at 33, while the countersubject is heard against it in the second violin.

A series of partial entries starts at 39, acting as a transition to the second subject. They can be followed in the string parts, though they are doubled by the wind. The first halves of the subject and the countersubject occur in upper and lower strings alternately in bars 39–43, then the second halves are used similarly in 43–9. This is followed by the first bar of the subject, which keeps recurring in the strings against a counter-theme in the flute, and leads to the second subject.

The second subject begins at 64, and consists of a dialogue in the dominant key between the oboe and the flute; but the first bar of the first subject is still heard against it, and the syncopation from the fugal counter-subject is also heard from 69 onwards. This section is repeated at 74 with the addition of a long-held note in the horns; and a codetta, starting at 84, brings the exposition to a conclusion on a pause at 96.

The development starts with a repetition of the *adagio* Masonic knocks, but now each chord is played three times. Then the first subject and its countersubject are developed in fugato style, in B flat minor at bar 103, and in C minor at 109. The scalic figure of the countersubject is heard in *stretto* in bassoon, oboe and flute in bars 111–13, while the subject continues in the violins in C minor, E flat major and G minor. A *stretto* of the subject starts in the strings at 117 and is treated in falling sequences. After a bar's pause at 127 a dialogue occurs between the strings playing the first subject and the flute and bassoon, two octaves apart, hinting at the rhythm of the second subject, and this leads to the recapitulation.

The recapitulation starts at 144, but only the first half of the fugal subject is used at first, and the answer appears in the first violin in *stretto* at 146. Two more *stretto* entries appear in the viola in the dominant at 148 and the 'cello in the tonic at 149. While this is happening there are woodwind entries in *stretto* of bar 12 (the countersubject).

The transition starts at 154 and is the same as in the exposition up to 167. Bars 167–74 are an interpolation; but bars 174–85 correspond to 53–64, except that they lead to the second subject in the tonic key instead of the dominant.

The second subject, starting at 185, is considerably modified. The opening melody, though still moving in quavers, is different, and it is played by flute and clarinet in octaves, instead of having the previous antiphonal treatment between the oboe and the flute. Even the syncopated figure which follows is different, though the codetta figure, which starts at 203 is similar.

A short coda starts at 212—notice the diminished third between D flat and B natural, which occurs twice. Bar 219 refers for the last time to the fugal first subject; and brass and percussion are added to make a brilliant final cadence.

10

Haydn and Mozart: Vocal Works

Haydn and Mozart were both very prolific writers and both wrote an immense number of vocal works of all kinds. Haydn wrote many operas for Prince Esterhazy, including several puppet operas. Some are completely lost, while in others the score but not the libretto remains. They are all slight and unimportant and are never performed today. Haydn himself said that they were intended for production in the Esterhaz theatre and would not achieve their effect elsewhere.

Haydn also wrote a large amount of church music, at all periods of his life. Some of his twelve masses are still heard today.

But the one vocal work of his which has stood the test of time and is still regularly performed today is his oratorio "The Creation". "The Seasons" is also sometimes heard, and his "Seven Last Words" gets an occasional performance.

On the other hand, Mozart was very interested in opera, while much of his church music was perfunctory—perhaps because of his unfortunate experiences with the Archbishop of Salzburg. The "Requiem", written on his own death-bed, is much more deeply felt than his earlier church music, and is still frequently performed.

Mozart's first opera was composed at the age of twelve, and nothing gave him greater delight than the chance of composing an opera. Works such as "The Marriage of Figaro" and "The Magic Flute" are among the finest operas ever written.

Although Haydn and Mozart had given up the use of a *continuo* part in orchestral writing they still used it in their church music, which usually had an accompaniment for orchestra and organ. And a harpsichord was still kept in the theatre for accompanying *recitativo secco* in operas. But the idea of a conductor who beat time, instead of directing from the organ or harpsichord, was growing at the turn of the century, and we are told that Haydn conducted performances of "The Creation" round about 1800.

The dramatic quality which is found in the symphonic works of Haydn and Mozart is also found in their choral music. On the whole there is less dignity and less contrapuntal writing than in the writing of Bach. Haydn said he could not help praising God with a merry heart, and at times Haydn's and Mozart's masses seem rather superficial and theatrical. But the sense of drama comes into admirably full play in "The Creation", as in parts of Mozart's "Requiem". And both composers could write a good fugue when they wished to do so, though it might not be as regular as some of those by Bach.

As Mozart died young and as Haydn's most famous choral works were written at the end of his life it happens that the two Mozart works analysed in this chapter were written before the two by Haydn. So they are discussed first. Three of the four are full-length works lasting a whole evening, and there is not room to include an analysis of the whole in a volume containing such a varied assortment as this, so only the first section of each is analysed.

The Marriage of Figaro, Act I: Mozart

"The Marriage of Figaro" is based on the comedy by Beaumarchais (1732–99), the famous French playwright. He wrote a trilogy of plays on "Figaro". "The Barber of Seville", the first of the three, was set as an opera by Paisiello and later by Rossini. The second play "The Marriage of Figaro" is the subject of Mozart's opera, though it has been set by lesser composers, too. And incidental music has been written for both plays, as they were popular in the theatre.

Mozart always enjoyed writing for the stage, but he had not, so far, found a librettist who would give him what he wanted. He first met Da Ponte in 1781 and hoped he might have the chance of a libretto from him. When, finally, Da Ponte adapted the Beaumarchais comedy, reducing the number of characters and toning down the political implications in the plot, Mozart had found what he needed, and he wrote the music in a month.

The Emperor of Austria gave his consent to the work and it was produced in Vienna in 1786. It had a brilliant cast, and so many numbers were encored that the Emperor prohibited encores in succeeding performances.

The work was then transferred to Prague and here it met with even more enthusiasm. Mozart went to hear it there and found everyone talking about the opera and humming its tunes. But, in spite of all this success, the hoped-for regular employment never materialized. Unlike Haydn, Mozart never had a secure post throughout his life, apart from his early uncongenial service with the Archbishop of Salzburg.

A feature of the opera is the amount of concerted music for soloists, as distinct from the arias which normally made up such a large part of the conventional opera of the period. Act I contains three duets and a trio; act II a duet and a trio; act III two duets and a sextet (Mozart's favourite number); the recitatives are frequently in dialogue; and acts II and IV contain finales in which a large number of the soloists take part. Mozart is famous for his elaborate operatic finales.

In the first play of the Beaumarchais trilogy Count Almaviva manages to win the heiress Rosina with the help of Figaro, the cunning Barber of Seville. (This is the story of the Rossini opera.)

When "The Marriage of Figaro" opens the Count has already become tired of his wife and he is now making love to her maid Susanna. But the latter is about to be married to Figaro, who has now become the Count's valet.

When the curtain rises Susanna and Figaro are preparing for

their marriage, each engrossed in what seems to be of importance to them, Figaro measuring the bedroom they have been assigned, Susanna trying on the hat she has made for the wedding. At first, Figaro sings his measurements in short disjointed phrases, taking little notice of Susanna, while she has longer and more florid phrases in which she is admiring herself and asking Figaro to admire her too. Finally, she attracts his attention and he joins in the admiration, switching over to her musical theme. Both their themes are used in the instrumental introduction, and they are effectively contrasted musically as well as dramatically. When Figaro changes to Susanna's theme in the middle of the duet it momentarily appears in the dominant key, but Susanna soon changes back to the tonic, and they sing on the one theme in this key until they reach quite a long coda. This duet is simple and charming, and it sets the mood for the opera.

It is followed by a recitative (*secco*) in which Figaro says how convenient the room is. He describes, in the following duet, how the Countess can ring her bell for Susanna or the Count for him, and they can come at once. But Susanna points out that the Count will also find it convenient for coming to make love to her. She keeps to the same style as Figaro (no contrasts this time) but she starts in the relative minor. Then, when she gets to the point of the Count finding his way to her, she reverts to Figaro's theme, thus ramming home the point that the "convenience" works both ways. While they are discussing the situation in the following recitative, the Countess's bell does actually ring and Susanna goes to answer it, leaving Figaro to sing his Cavatina (no. 3.).

It starts in the style of a minuet, modulating to the dominant in the conventional way in the second stanza. But then the music quickens up over a dominant pedal while Figaro sings *staccato* interjections as he gets more excited. He starts with a seventh, then the interval is compressed to a sixth, a fifth and so on. The pedal resolves into the relative minor and after a pause the return to the tonic is a *presto* in which Figaro resolves on ways to defeat the

Count. It is now in $\frac{2}{4}$ time but the shape of the tune—the phrases rising by steps—is similar to the opening. After this excitement the music returns to the sedate minuet opening, and Figaro leaves the stage to a short final *presto*.

Dr. Bartolo, a lawyer, who had been Rosina's guardian and had hoped to marry her himself, and Marcellina, his elderly housekeeper, now come on to the stage. They sing a recitative in which Marcellina tells Bartolo that Figaro has signed a contract to marry her if he does not pay her some money he owes her, and asks Bartolo for help in preventing his marriage with Susanna.

Bartolo now sings his famous "buffo" aria (no. 4), in which he sees his chance of vengeance on Figaro who cheated him of marrying Rosina. It starts with a fourteen-bar sentence in D major, then moves to the relative minor on its way to the dominant, in which key Bartolo cries out in short disjointed phrases, first high then low, before he settles down to a quaver "patter". At the end of this section an effective *sf* Italian augmented sixth is used three times as a climax. Then he returns to the tonic key comparatively quietly, but soon is off into "patter" again as his rage engulfs him. After a pause he returns to the opening theme, and ends with a grand coda in the Italian style. It is obvious that the marriage broker in Smetana's "Bartered Bride" owes much to Dr Bartolo: the similarity of their arias is very marked.

After Bartolo's exit Susanna re-enters and Marcellina manages to get in a number of spiteful asides in recitative, suitably answered by Susanna, before she attempts to leave the stage.

During the duettino, no. 5, they get in each other's way, and each is elaborately polite in pretending to give preference to the other, getting in more barbed shafts in the process of doing so. Notice how, on the second page, they are almost in canon with each other, as they get to the end of the first section in the dominant key. The orchestral figure which was first heard in the accompaniment in bar 3 starts the second section in the dominant key, and extends it (higher each time it is repeated) until it returns to the tonic key. As exasperation grows triplets appear in the accompaniment. All this second part of the duettino is then repeated, and merges into a long coda, which works up to a climax and ends as Marcellina finally leaves the stage.

Cherubino, the page, then enters and tells Susanna that the Count is angry because he found him alone with Barbarina, his sweetheart, and unless the Countess intercedes for him he will be sent away. Cherubino seems to be in love with everyone, Barbarina, the Countess, "every woman in the castle", and is a young edition of Don Giovanni. In his aria, no. 6, he tells Susanna of the fever of his love. At first it appears as if this is going to be a little aria in ternary form with a middle, very chromatic section, **B**, in the dominant key. But after the repetition of **A** another section **C**, starting in the subdominant key, appears. It returns to the tonic and is followed by yet another section which is entirely in the tonic and which ends in the same way as **C**. But there is no return of the theme **A**. Finally there is a short coda beginning with a few bars of *adagio*.

Now follows an entertaining situation. The Count enters Susanna's room, and Cherubino, who naturally does not wish to be seen there, hides behind the chair. The Count vainly importunes Susanna for favours, but he is interrupted by Basilio who is heard outside. As the Count should not be in the maid's room any more than should Cherubino, he, too, goes to hide behind the chair. Cheribino hurriedly moves away and springs *into* the chair, while Susanna covers him with a dress just as Basilio enters. Basilio is the music master (he also is in the cast of "The Barber of Seville"). He taunts Susanna about the attentions of Cherubino and tells of Cherubino's adoration of the Countess, until the Count can bear no more and comes out of hiding. All this is in very effective recitative.

In the following trio (no. 7) the three are all, at first, engrossed in their own situation, the Count telling Basilio to find the scoundrel Cherubino at once, Basilio full of insincere apologies, and Susanna full of dismay. Then Susanna pretends to faint, so the two men combine in solicitously coming to her rescue. Susanna revives and tells the Count that Basilio's story is untrue; but the Count then tells them how he found Cherubino hiding in Barbarina's room the previous day. As he recounts the story of finding Cherubino under a cloth he demonstrates by removing the dress from Susanna's chair, only to find Cherubino again in hiding. This is a highly dramatic number. Notice the rhythmic contrast of the themes—the angry determination of the Count in disjointed rhythms, the unctious minims of Basilio and the fluttering quavers of Susanna on the first page; also observe how Basilio's unctious theme serves the Count when he is self-righteously telling of his discovery of Cherubino.

The following recitative is concerned with explanations, but it is interrupted by a chorus of peasants who come with Figaro bearing the bridal veil. They sing the same chorus twice in praise of the Count, and in between the choruses there is another recitative. (The Count has just abolished the ancient privilege whereby he had the right to spend the night with every about-to-be-married bride in his employment.)

During the next recitative the Count, who has dismissed Cherubino, gives him a regimental commission, and then Figaro sings the final aria in Act I, in which he tells Cherubino of the life that is in store for him. This is one of the most popular numbers in the opera, and at the first orchestral rehearsal it brought many bravos, both from Mozart for the singer and for Mozart from the orchestra and stage performers. Mozart was on the stage in a crimson coat and a cocked hat, and they cried "Bravo, bravo, Maestro; viva, viva, grande Mozart!"

The aria is a gay rondo, full of dramatic opportunities. The main theme, **A**, is in C major. **B** is in the dominant, followed by **A** in the tonic again. **C** starts in the tonic but modulates several times and ends in the dominant with some delightful skirmishings, both in voice and orchestra. After the final return to **A** there is a grandiloquent vocal coda in the tonic, and a final flourish in the orchestra as the curtain falls.

Requiem Mass: Mozart

Everyone knows of the tragic circumstances in which the "Requiem" was written; and of how Mozart, as he was dying, felt he was writing it for himself and not for the mysterious "man in grey" who had commissioned it. It is now generally thought that most of the vocal parts and the *continuo* are Mozart's own, while the orchestration is largely the work of his pupil Süssmayer. But the "Sanctus", "Benedictus", and "Agnus Dei" may contain more Süssmayer than Mozart, and probably we shall never know. The repetitions which come at the end of the work are a makeshift of Süssmayer's, so as to get the work completed and handed over to the "man in grey".

The student should know something about the words and meaning of the *mass*, which is the central religious rite in the Roman Catholic Church. It is customary to have a "requiem" mass specially sung (or said) for the dead.

The introit "*Requiem aeternam*" is entirely Mozart's work. So notice the orchestration, which consists of basset horns, bassoons, trumpets and drums in addition to strings and *continuo*. The basset horn is a tenor clarinet, pitched in F, and therefore requiring, like the cor anglais, to be transposed a fifth downwards. It became almost obsolete, but has been used recently by a few composers. It has a gloomy tone, well suited to this introit. The organ *continuo* enters with the voice part, and the imitative contrapuntal style is very like that of Bach.

"Requiem aeternam" starts with imitative entries, first in the woodwind and then in the voice parts. Notice the leaping octave accompaniment figure in the violins. The style then becomes more harmonic. A short soprano solo is followed by further imitative entries at "exaudi", accompanied by a quick leaping figure in the strings. Then the octave leaps return, against more continuous semiquavers in the voice parts; but the accompaniment quietens down towards the end. The orchestration of this number is as interesting as the voice parts.

"*Kyrie eleison, Christe eleison*" is Greek, not Latin. It means "Lord have mercy upon us, Christ have mercy upon us". Mozart has written a double fugue to these words, with the instrumental parts doubling the voice parts. The words "Kyrie eleison" are used for one subject, and "Christe eleison" for the other. In the exposition (bars 1–15) all the four-voice parts have both subjects in turn, in the usual tonic and dominant keys. In the middle section there are entries of both subjects in F major (bar 16 soprano, bar 17 bass), G minor (bar 20 tenor, bar 31 soprano), and C minor (bar 23 bass, bar 24 alto). Then follow four entries in B flat major (soprano 27, tenor 28, bass 29, tenor 30), three entries in F minor (alto 32, bass 33, tenor 34), one starting in C minor (alto 35), one starting in B flat major (soprano 36), and one starting in D minor (bass 37). The last five of these entries (all of the second subject) are in *stretto*.

The final section starts at 39 with the first subject in the tonic key in the bass. The second subject appears in the soprano at 40 (and reaches top B flat!). Further entries appear in the alto (43), the bass (44), the soprano (45), the alto (46) and the soprano (47), and they are again in *stretto*. They lead to a diminished seventh in bar 50, followed by a pause; and two *adagio* bars finish the fugue.

The next section (from "Dies Irae" to "Lacrimosa") is, like the introit, a special section that belongs only to a requiem mass.

"*Dies Irae*" has a striding quaver *continuo* part over which the voices sing in solemn minim and crotchet block chords. The first part, which starts in D minor, passes through F major (10) and G major (13), and ends in A minor (the dominant minor) at 19. The second part starts in A minor and passes through C minor (31) and D minor (36). At bar 40 the bass voice starts a quaver figure ("quantus tremor est futurus"), while the other voices answer with "dies irae", as before. But soon all the voices have the quaver figure (51). Then all revert to the quieter block chords and the tonic key.

"*Tuba mirum*" is for S, A, T, B solo voices and a magnificent trombone *obbligato*. Notice the *arpeggi* in both trombone and bass voice parts, and the large leaps in the latter. The tenor voice part is quicker and more syncopated, and so are the alto and soprano when they come in. After all the solo voices have had their turn, they all enter together at 51, *sotto voce*, and gradually build up to a climax.

The dotted scales in the strings are the chief feature of "*Rex tremendae majestatis*". "*Recordare, Jesu pie*" is much longer. It is again for S, A, T, B solo voices, and has a long instrumental introduction, with imitation between the violins, before the voices enter. The bass voice imitates the alto a seventh lower, and then the tenor imitates the soprano in the same way. All the voices imitate one another in the section starting at bar 26, and this section ends in the dominant key, C major. Another imitative instrumental interlude, starting at 34, leads to further imitative entries in the voice parts, and this section ends in D minor at 52. It is followed by a B flat section, 54–68. A chordal section then leads to a return of the opening figures in the tonic key at 93. A short coda starts at 118.

"*Confutatis maledictus*" uses the trombones again, though at first they are in unison with the tenor and bass voices. The strings have a busy figure at the same time. When the soprano and alto voices enter for the first time at 7 they are *sotto voce*, the busy figure and the trombones cease, and a complete contrast results. These two contrasting sections occur again. Then all four voice parts enter *p* at 26 against reiterated semiquavers in the strings. The chorus ends in F major; and a dominant chord leads straight into the next number.

This is the lovely and plaintive "*Lacrimosa dies illa*", which Mozart tried to sing on his death-bed. It is short, but obviously deeply-felt. The rising sixth, falling to the cadence, in the opening bars, and the rising *crescendo* scale in bars 5–8 are both very poignant. After a short middle section, the opening bars return to the words

"Dona eis requiem" at 22, but this time the scale figure falls instead of rises, and leads to a quiet Amen.

"*Domine Jesu Christe*" is a long and "busy" number. The voices start together in harmony, and the first section ends in C minor, the subdominant minor, at 14. The opening figure is then used again in A flat major and B flat minor. A *fugato* starts at 21 on a figure consisting of a series of descending sevenths, and all voices have the figure in turn. At 32 the solo voices enter with the first theme again in the tonic key, but now treat it in *fugato*. The chorus enters again at 44, with yet another *fugato*. It uses three different figures in three bars, and all are developed freely for some time. From bar 67 to the end there is a series of falling sequences.

"*Hostias et preces*" begins in a simple hymn-like style. Then the "quam olim" section of the previous number is repeated.

The "*Sanctus*", the "*Benedictus*", and the "*Agnus Die*" were finished by Mozart's pupil, Süssmayer, and no one really knows how much is the work of Mozart himself. Certainly the work declines at this point. "*Lux aeterna*" begins by repeating the opening bars of the "Requiem", and then repeats the "te decet" from bar 21 of the first number. It ends by repeating the fugue of the "Kyrie eleison" to the words "Cum sanctus tuis". These repeats were written by Süssmayer at the request of Mozart's wife, so that the work could be completed and handed to the "man in grey", and so produce some badly-needed money; but it is very unlikely that Mozart would have ended the work in this way.

The Creation, Part One: Haydn

"The Creation" was the fruit of Haydn's second visit to London, in 1794–5. While there he heard and was impressed by performances of Handel's oratorios, so he looked around for a suitable libretto, which he might use for an oratorio himself. Lidley (or Linley ?) had written a libretto on the story of the creation, compiled from the Bible and from Milton's *Paradise Lost*, and had intended it for

Handel; but it had not been used. Saloman, the impresario for whom Haydn wrote his London symphonies, showed this libretto to Haydn; and Haydn was sufficiently impressed to take it back to Vienna, and have it translated into German, his native language. In the course of translation it was considerably altered; and the version of the words, in the older English editions which are still used today, is a re-translation into English of this translation into German. So it is not surprising that, at times, the words do not make sense, or fit the music very well. Nowadays the work is often sung to a more recent translation, but the older, and better-known one, is referred to here.

Haydn set to work as soon as he returned to Vienna, and he was busy from 1796–8. He was in his middle sixties, an old man in those days, but he worked at it with great vigour. "Never was I so pious," he said. "I knelt down each day and prayed God to give me strength to finish the work."

It was first performed privately at the Schwarzenburg Palace, Vienna, on 29 and 30 April 1798. The first public performance was on 19 March 1799, in the Vienna National Theatre. Various noblemen paid the expenses, and handed over the proceeds (£320) to Haydn, as a birthday present. It was a great success; and performances began to be given everywhere, including many in England. Choral societies were formed especially to produce it.

As Haydn grew older he appeared in public less and less; but his last appearance was at a performance of "The Creation" given by Vienna University in 1808. He was carried there in an arm chair, and received a great ovation. He became so agitated, however, that it was decided to take him home at the end of Part I. As he was carried out, everyone pressed around him in homage, and Beethoven fervently kissed him.

In Parts I and II the archangels Gabriel, Uriel and Raphael tell the story of the Creation. They describe the details in recitative, then enlarge them lyrically in arias; and they are often followed by the chorus singing a song of praise to the Creator. There are a number of trios, in which the archangels sing together. Part II ends with the creation of Adam and Eve; and it is interesting to note that as a tribute to his greatness, the aria "In Native Worth", which occurs in Part II, was sung to Haydn on his death-bed by a French officer during the French occupation of Vienna.

Part III introduces Adam and Eve as characters. Professor Tovey thought that most of this section should be omitted, because the work is complete and long enough without it, and it forms an anti-climax. Audiences of the eighteenth century were used to much longer performances than we are today.

The orchestral accompaniment to this oratorio is more interesting than that of any of Handel's. The intervening fifty years had produced great differences in orchestration, as is realized if we compare a Handel *concerto grosso* with a Haydn symphony. In this work Haydn uses three flutes, two oboes, two clarinets, two bassoons, a double bassoon, two horns, two trumpets, three trombones, drums and strings. This is the standard orchestra of Haydns' later symphonies, with the addition of a third flute, a double bassoon and three trombones. Some of the orchestral effects, particularly in "Chaos" and in the recitatives, must have seemed very surprising when they were written; and even today they can delight us, though they may occasionally bring a smile to our faces, as, for example, when Haydn uses the double bassoon to describe the worm.

"*The Representation of Chaos*" is a most wonderful introduction. It starts with a bare octave C. After a pause, an E flat is added, so one expects the tonic chord of C minor. But no! the next note is A flat—VIb in C minor? How simple and yet how chaotic an effect is obtained just by baulking the listener of an expected tonic chord! The next chord is a diminished seventh, and it is followed after a few notes of melody by another VIb. When finally we reach a dominant ninth it resolves on to Ib, instead of I, thus still evading a strong chord progression. A chromatic supertonic seventh then leads to a chord of E flat, and several hints of the key of E flat major occur in the next few, very chromatic, bars; but the first real cadence that is heard is in the key of D flat! Given the accepted harmonic idioms of Haydn's day, what could give a better representation of chaos than these shifting harmonies?

The miniature second subject, which starts at bar 21 in D flat, settles into E flat, the relative major at 28. A recapitulation begins at 40, with the second subject, more or less in the tonic key, appearing at 45. A coda, starting again on VIb, begins at bar 50; and a chromatic passage appears which, as Tovey says, almost foreshadows "Tristan". But the music eventually comes to rest on a tonic chord of C minor. This introduction can be said to be a simple example of modified sonata form, that is, sonata form without a development section.

Raphael now sings, in *recitativo secco*, "*In the beginning God created the heaven and the earth*", and broods over the words "and darkness was upon the face of the deep". The chorus then enters quietly with "And the spirit of God moved upon the face of the waters", but bursts into a *fortissimo* chord of C major on the word "light". Haydn must have deliberately chosen this chord, the fundamental chord in music, here; just as deliberately as he has avoided it until this moment. And at his last public appearance, when the singers came to the word "light" he said, pointing a hand upwards, "it came from thence".

The light, bright key of A major is chosen for the ensuing aria "*Now vanish before the holy beams*"; but the music reverts to C minor at the words "affrighted fled Hell's spirits, black in throngs"; and there are some wonderful chromatic effects as they "sink into the deep abyss". The chorus has imitative entries to the words "despairing, cursing rage" but eventually settles into the happy key of A major, and a succession of primary triads at "A new created world". These two pictures in words and music alternate to the end of the number. Surely Elgar had this wonderful music in mind when he conceived his choruses of angels and demons in "The Dream of Gerontius"?

Raphael now sings in *recitativo secco* "*And God made the firma-*

ment"; but, after a few bars, Haydn introduces *recitativo stromentato* for the rather naïve but very charming musical descriptions which foreshadow the storms, the winds, lightning, thunder, rain, hail and snow. Gabriel and the chorus follow this with "*The marvellous work behold amazed*", which is in ternary form, with a coda.

After another dry recitative, Raphael sings the aria "*Rolling in foaming billows*". This begins in D minor with a foaming accompaniment. It has a middle section in the relative major with enormous leaps in the vocal part describing the mountains with their tops ascending into the clouds, and with a meandering vocal description of the winding rivers. The final section returns to the tonic key, but is now in the major and the effect is quite different from the foaming billows, because the music now describes the purling brook.

After a short recitative comes the famous aria "*With verdure clad*". This is in ternary form, but with the repeat written out because it is different, particularly at the end. Notice the long extensions of the sentence "Here shoots the healing plant", combined with delightful *coloratura*, and the rather free modulations in the short middle section.

The chorus then sings "*Awake the Harp*". This includes a fugue on the words "For He both heaven and earth has clothed in stately dress". Notice the characteristic interval of the seventh on the words "and earth", which makes the subject easily recognizable every time it enters. The answer is tonal, and there is a redundant entry in the bass before the middle section starts in the relative minor. A few bars later the subject enters in the bass in E minor with the first bar in augmentation. After a short episode the final section begins in the bass, with a prolonged first note in the tonic key. The fugue proper ends on a dominant pedal; and a coda in harmonic style has some *coloratura* runs on "stately".

Uriel now takes up the story, in a recitative which includes contrasting descriptions of the sun and moon. This runs straight in to the most famous chorus in the whole work "*The Heavens are telling*". It is popular because it is so direct and diatonic, with an almost Handelian simplicity. It has short sections for the angelic trio, in contrast to the full chorus; and it contains an amazing amount of the tonic key, C major, a fitting key to end Part I. It might be analysed thus: **A**, bars 1–22; **B**, 22–37; **C** (including a development of **A**), 37–54; **D** (including a development of **A**), 54–95; **C**, running on into a *fugato* section, 95–153; coda, 153–end. The coda begins with an upper tonic pedal, and continues with a dominant pedal in the bass, over which a fine climax is built. Beethoven surely had this coda in mind when he wrote his choral symphony.

The Seasons, Spring: Haydn

Haydn wrote "The Seasons" in the years 1800–1. It is scored for three flutes, two oboes, two clarinets, two bassoons, double bassoon, two horns, two trumpets, three trombones, drums and strings. The orchestration is very similar to that in his symphonies.

Haydn takes the same delight in descriptive writing that he had previously shown in "The Creation", and there are many charming orchestral effects.

As with "The Creation", Haydn took his libretto from England. This time it was a long poem by James Thomson (the author of "Rule Britannia"), describing the four seasons of the year. The work suffers from a double translation, just as does "The Creation", and Thomson's original poem is almost unrecognizable.

"The Seasons" is not the sort of work one normally associates with an oratorio, and Haydn was, at first, unwilling to set it. It is not as popular as "The Creation" today, partly because it is not on a sacred subject, partly because it is very long. But the four sections can be performed separately.

The *overture* "expresses the passage from winter to spring". It is in a very free sonata form, and the first subject is a blustering description of winter. The second subject, which appears in the relative major at bar 55, is much more spring-like. The development section, starting at 76, brings a return to the wintery bluster and modulates freely. The recapitulation starts at 121, but contains no reference to the second subject. It leads straight into the opening recitative.

"*Behold where surly Winter flies*" is *recitativo stromentato*, and reminds one of the description of the weather in "The Creation".

The ensuing chorus "*Come gentle Spring*" is perhaps the best-known number in "The Seasons". It is a gentle *allegretto*. There is a touch of the "cold's returning blast", starting *forte* in C minor, but the charming opening theme soon returns.

A short *secco* recitative leads into the beautiful aria "*With Joy the impatient Husbandman*". The opening theme is played first by the orchestra and then repeated by the voice. Then, at bar 17, the orchestra begins to quote the opening theme of the slow movement of the "Surprise" symphony. But, as this is more of an instrumental than a vocal melody, the voice has a counter theme when it enters at bar 20. The two themes run together until the end of the first section of this *da capo* aria. The middle section, which starts at 48, moves to C minor and then G minor in the orchestra before the voice enters in E flat major at 53. After a *coloratura* climax on "golden" bar 84 returns to the bar 53 theme; but then (at 92) the singer modulates to C minor ready for the return of the opening section in C major at 104. The repeat is written out because it is curtailed a little, and it runs on to a short coda on a tonic pedal.

After another short recitative there is a beautiful trio and chorus "*Be propitious, bounteous Heaven*". At first the style is harmonic, simple and spacious, with the soloists acting as a kind of *concertante* against the *ripieno* chorus. This section is sung twice. The first time is mainly given to the soloists, but the second time, starting at bar 45, uses the chorus most of the time and has a fuller, semiquaver accompaniment.

Then, at 74, the chorus takes over entirely with a fugue. It has an independent, semiquaver, orchestral accompaniment throughout. The exposition is quite regular, with the subject entering in the alto, soprano, bass and tenor voices in tonic and dominant key alternately. The answer is real, and there is no regular counter-subject. The middle section starts in bar 82 with an episode modulating to D minor, and this is followed by middle entries in G minor in the bass (86) and B flat major in the soprano (88). Another, longer episode, starting on the last beat of 90, leads to the final section, starting at 98 with an entry in the bass in the tonic key. A dominant pedal, which starts at 104, ends at 112, and then a short coda, in harmonic style, brings the chorus to an end.

After another short, *secco* recitative Jane and Lucas sing a short duet, "*Spring, her lovely charms unfolding*", describing the delights of the country scene. Jane sings the first stanza and Lucas repeats it. Then they sing the second stanza in harmony together. This modulates to the dominant key, E major, and ends in the tonic key at 63.

But now this runs on into a chorus, with interjections from the trio of soloists. It modulates freely, and does not end in the original key of A major. Jane and Lucas move to A minor at 64, and the chorus enters in C major at 82. At 88 the four chorus parts enter in imitation of each other at the words "Let us wander"—doubtless a touch of word painting on Haydn's part. This section ends in C major at 98.

Then Jane and Lucas make further comments, modulating through D minor (102), E minor (104) and B minor (110). When Jane refers to the lambkins at 113 the orchestra imitates the caper in the following bars. Similarly there are descriptions of the fish (116–20), bees (120–4) and birds (124–8). This may again remind the student of the descriptive recitatives in "The Creation"; but in this case the descriptive orchestral passage always occurs after the verbal comment, not before it.

By now the music has reached G major, and the chorus enters again at 128 with "All is lovely", ending at 144 in D major. Then Simon makes his comment before the chorus enters for the last time at 155. It starts in G major, modulates to E minor (160), and, remarkably near the end, moves to D major at 171 for the final cadence.

Obviously Haydn has treated this number with the key freedom that he normally uses for a recitative. It passes through many keys, without any balanced key-scheme, and it ends in a key quite remote from where it began. It is descriptive music, and therefore, in his mind, not subject to the normal laws of key balance.

The final chorus "*God of Light*" starts with a solemn choral introduction. The *poco adagio* section which follows, starting at 13, begins with the soloists in harmony, but the chorus soon joins in. The introductory theme returns at 30, and (at 34) the soloists each have a short phrase over a dominant pedal, which serves as a preliminary to the final fugue.

This starts at 38 and the voices enter in ascending order, the answer being tonal. There is a countersubject, and the bass has a redundant entry of the subject at 44, so the countersubject is heard above the subject for the first time at this point. The tenor has another redundant entry at 48, with the first note in augmentation.

The episode which starts the middle section has three references to the first few notes of the subject in augmentation, in the soprano and bass at 49 and in the bass at 53. A middle entry in E flat major occurs in the alto at 57, and then there are further references to the first few notes of the subject in augmentation. Bars 64–71 are more harmonic in style. The bass has the melody, while the other three vocal parts are in three-part harmony above it. Then, at 71, all the voice parts become contrapuntal again.

Bar 77 starts the final section, with an entry of the subject in the tonic key in the soprano. The alto and bass enter in *stretto*, in bars 77 and 78. There are two more entries in the bass, in 84 and 89, but by now the style has become more harmonic. Notice the frequent movement from dominant to tonic in minims in one or other of the parts. Bars 91 to the end form a dramatic coda.

11

Beethoven: Piano Sonatas

Beethoven had lessons from Haydn and possibly also from Mozart. He was certainly familiar with their sonatas, so he was able to take their methods of composition as a foundation on which he could build. He was not as much of an innovator as was Haydn, but he developed his predecessor's ideas, and wrote his works on a larger scale. He is often thought of as being one of the first romantic composers, and certainly his works are more impassioned than those of Haydn and Mozart.

By Beethoven's time the piano had practically ousted the harpsichord and clavichord, though the touch of the piano was lighter than it is today, and its range was not as great. So we may find Beethoven modifying a theme when it recurs in the recapitulation because his piano did not go high enough or low enough to allow of an exact repetition in a different key. In such cases performers of today often play what Beethoven would undoubtedly have preferred if his piano had made it possible.

The sustaining pedal was invented by Broadwood in 1783. It enriched the sound of the piano enormously, and made possible new poetic effects of harmonic tone colour. Beethoven realized its potentialities immediately. It is possible to play many movements by Haydn and Mozart with little or no pedal, but the first movements of the "Pathetic" and "Moonlight" sonatas would be unthinkable without it.

Whereas Haydn and Mozart tended to write their sonatas in three movements Beethoven quite often used four, as was more commonly found in symphonies. But he also experimented with the order of the movements. For example, the "Moonlight" sonata starts with a slow movement.

His slow movements tended to be very slow, and were often heavy and even tragic. So the rather sedate minuet did not seem to him to provide sufficient contrast for the next movement, and one of his chief innovations was to write a quick, playful scherzo in its place, though it was usually still in triple time and in minuet and trio form.

Beethoven still used sonata form for the first movement and often for other movements of his sonatas. But it was usually on a larger scale and more highly organized than the movements by Haydn and Mozart. Transitions were less obvious, and Beethoven showed great skill in developing his ideas in the development section. Also his codas were sometimes so long as to be almost like another development section.

He rarely used the old rondo form for the finale, but preferred to use sonata-rondo form, though sonata form is just as frequently found.

Beethoven had a very highly developed sense of tonality. So although he began by writing his second subjects in the usual dominant or relative major keys he was soon experimenting with other possibilities, such as the mediant minor. And he often moved very far from his original key-centre in his development sections and even in his codas. But he could always get safely back again, and there is invariably a satisfying key-balance in the movement as a whole.

Op. 2, no. 2, in A

The *first movement* of the Beethoven sonata, op. 2, no. 2, is in sonata form. The first subject contains four rhythmic figures between bars 1 and 12, all of which are used later. It begins to repeat the first subject at bar 20, though with omissions and modifications, and it leads to a perfect cadence in the tonic at 31–2. Macpherson states that the transition begins at 32. Tovey prefers to avoid the term in this movement, though he uses it elsewhere. Presumably he feels that the figure at 33 is yet another theme belonging to the first subject. But as it is one continuous section up to 58, containing modulation, and ending with the dominant chord of the key of the second subject, perhaps "transition" correctly describes it. Notice that 42–6 continues the descending scale of the previous bars over a dominant pedal, and that 46–58 is still dominant harmony.

The second subject is unusual in that it begins in the dominant *minor* key, but it is in the major by 84, and stays in that key until the end of the exposition. Bars 58–70 consist of a sequential phrase in E minor, G major and B flat major, which must have seemed surprising to contemporary ears. It is followed by another transposing sequence (70–6) through E major and F sharp minor, and ending with a diminished seventh. The first two rhythmic figures of the first subject then, rather surprisingly, reappear, and the subject ends with a repeated cadence in the dominant major key at 92. Bars 92–114 form a codetta. The exposition could have ended at 92, but 92–114 round it off with a reference to the transition. A codetta often refers to previous material in this way. Notice that the two hands overlap at 94, 96 and 98, there being four imitative entries, and that the falling quavers start to rise at 104, over a tonic pedal.

Bars 121–60 develop the opening bars of the first subject. The change, in 114(*b*)–20, from a major to a minor chord on E, plus the rests, make it possible to start in the remote but effective key of C major. At 130 the bass slides up a semitone into A flat major. Then follow a series of six-bar phrases, based on the tonic chord of A flat, the dominant of A flat, and the dominant of F; then four-bar phrases of Ic in F minor, and a diminished seventh; and finally five bars of the dominant of F, all making use of the opening eight bars.

At 161 Beethoven begins to use the figure that started at bar 9, and continues with it until the recapitulation. It passes through F major (161–75), D minor (176–82), F major (183–90), D minor (191–95) and A minor (196 up to the pause that leads to the recapitulation). Notice the three part *stretti* in bars 181–98.

The recapitulation begins, as expected, by repeating the start of the exposition, but, at 244–51, instead of repeating the opening bars Beethoven adds a charming interpolation, repeating the last few bars in D major and then in A major. The transition also starts in the same way, but changes at 254, so that, by 261, it has reached the dominant pedal of the key of A, instead of E. Otherwise it is very similar.

The second subject starts at 277 in the tonic minor, thus corresponding to the dominant minor of the exposition, and it has similarly reached the major by 303, and by the corresponding modulatory steps. Apart from the transposition, this second subject is practically identical with the exposition. It ends quietly and with no coda.

With the *slow movement* we come to more controversial ground. Thiman calls it "episodic", and Macpherson "episodical" form. To them the plan is: **A**, 1–19; **B**, 20–31; **A**, 32–50; Coda, 50–80. Notice that **A** is a small ternary form in itself: 1–8, 9–12, 13–18; and that **B** is binary: 20–3, 24–31. The **B** section (20–31) occurs once only, which makes it an episode: hence the term "episodical" form. The plan is essentially the same as "Minuet and trio" form, but it is not so symmetrical, with repeats and double bar lines, because it has not developed from the dance. In episodical form the sections may merge into each other, as at 31; and there may be transitional passages, though there are none in this movement.

Dr Lovelock thinks of the movement in the same way, but does not like the term "episodic", because he points out it is not the only form to have episodes—rondos have them too. So he calls it "ternary". One drawback to this is that the pupil will be using the word "ternary" for the movement as a whole and also for the **A** section, and this may cause confusion.

Professor Tovey differs from the above authorities in considering that it is not in three part form at all, but is a rondo. He calls 50–67 a second episode, instead of the beginning of a long coda; 68–75 another short return of **A**; and 75–80 the coda.

Now here is a case where the student should consider both the alternatives. He should play the movement through several times, in order to decide whether he feels 50–80 is a long coda, or that 50–67 is another episode followed by another **A** at 68–75. He may think one thing at first, and change his mind later when he knows the music thoroughly well. We have no idea how Beethoven conceived it; and any examiner will have to accept either alternative.

The *third movement* is a scherzo. Beethoven probably felt that a minuet would be too slow after the *largo* second movement. This particular scherzo is certainly playful. The entry at 32 after the bar's rest, and the sudden *pp*s and *ff*s, with the cross rhythm at 43 and 44 are all humorous effects.

As far as the whole movement is concerned, the form is "Minuet and trio". The scherzo itself is as follows: ||:**A**, A major, 1–8: ||:**B**, a development of **A** moving into F sharp minor and G sharp minor, 9–19, followed by a new theme which moves into a series of sevenths ending with the dominant seventh of the tonic key (19–31); **A** (32–40) followed by four bars of coda, A major :||. Most people would call this ternary. The first section ends in the tonic, and is repeated identically at the end. But notice that the beginning of **B** is not new material, though a new theme appears later. When the scherzo is played with repeats, it does not *sound* as if it is in three parts.

The trio produces another difference of opinion. The plan is clearly: ||:**C**, A minor to E minor (1–8) :||:**D**, C major, through D minor and A minor (9–16); merging into **C**, A minor, changed so as to end in the tonic (17–24) :||.

Authorities such as Macpherson and Scholes call this plan ternary, because of the digression and the return to the opening section. Tovey calls it binary, because the first section does not end in the tonic key, and is therefore incomplete; while others would call it binary, because 9–16 is not new material but uses the same idea as 1–8. Thiman uses the term "extended binary" for the plan, which is very common in the minuets and the trios of Haydn and Mozart. This use of conflicting terms to describe the same thing is very unfortunate. The student should weigh the arguments of the protagonists, decide on one method of terminology and keep to it, knowing that any examiner will accept it. Fortunately it is possible to describe the form quite clearly without giving it a title at all, and an understanding of the structure is really all that matters.

The *finale* is in sonata-rondo form. Every time the first subject returns it is in a more decorated form, otherwise no special comment is required. Here is an outline plan of the whole movement set out in tabular form.

Exposition

1–16. First subject, tonic key.

17–26. Transition—semiquaver passage work, leading to dominant key.

27–39. Second subject, dominant key, followed by two bars link, leading to

41–56. First subject tonic, with melody decorated.

Middle Section. An episode, in binary, ternary, or extended binary form (according to the terminology preferred).

57–66. **A** in A minor, modulating to its relative major, C.

67–74. **B**, a development of **A**, but in C major.

75–9. **A**, modified, so as to end in A minor.

80–99. A repetition of **B** and **A**, but written out, because the end is extended, leading into the

Recapitulation

100–15. First subject, tonic key, with further decorations.

116–23. Transition, slightly changed and shorter.

124–35. Second subject, tonic key, with modifications.

135–48. First subject, tonic key, with further decorations.

Coda

148–61. Based on first subject

161–73. Based on episode.

173–87. Based on first subject.

Op. 10, no. 3, in D

The first four notes of the *first movement* are used so much that they almost form a "motto" figure, of the kind that Brahms used later. The phrases beginning at 4^4 and 10^4 grow out of it; it is much used from 66 onwards; it ends the exposition and begins the development section.

Macpherson considers that 16–22 is transition and that 23 starts the second subject in the relative minor, whereas Tovey considers that 23 starts the transition and that the second subject is reached with the establishment of the dominant key at 53. Bar 23 comes after a pause; it is a tuneful theme and quite possible as a second subject. But by 31 it has merged into rather uninteresting passage work; and it reaches a very definite perfect cadence in the dominant at 53, after which comes another tune in the more normal dominant. If one refers to the recapitulation in order to reach a decision, one finds 220 corresponding to 23 now in E minor—i.e. the same relationship to the tonic that the original B minor had to the dominant. There are slight changes towards the end of this section, but it ends with a perfect cadence in the tonic, and 233 corresponds to 53, now in the tonic. Obviously, whatever an examiner may feel personally about this, he is bound to accept 23 (220) and 53 (233) as alternative positions of the start of the second subject.

Another section of the second subject starts at 67, and it broadens out to a climax at 87–93. A final section, starting at 94, is derived from the "motto" in bar 1. Notice that the parts are inverted at 97, and that the phrase is repeated again at 102 with the L.H. an octave lower. R.H. would have been an octave higher throughout if the upward compass of Beethoven's piano had made it possible. Bars 114–24 form a link leading back to the repeat or on to the development section.

The development section is based mainly on the "motto" figure of bar 1. There is an abrupt change of key at 133 (*soh*, key D = *te*, key B flat in 132). The music passes through G minor (149) and

E flat major (157) on its way to a dominant pedal of the tonic key starting at 167.

The first part of the recapitulation has already been discussed. The second subject passes through the same sections as before, but now in the tonic key. The minims starting at 286 merge into a coda, in which there is further development of the "motto" figure, with a tonic pedal from 327. The silent bar at the end is necessary to complete the phrase.

The *second movement* is a hybrid form, a mixture of sonata and episodical form. It has an exposition and recapitulation containing two subjects, as in sonata form, but the middle section is an episode. The first subject ends with a perfect cadence in the tonic at 9, and a subsidiary theme (9–17) acts as a transition leading into the second subject in the dominant minor. A codetta (26–9) rounds off the exposition.

The episode, starting in the relative major, is built on a steady throb of quavers, over which plaintive little figures occur from time to time. A dominant pedal, starting at 37, leads into the recapitulation.

In the recapitulation the first subject ends in G minor at 52; and the subsidiary transitional theme omits its first phrase, while its second phrase is unexpectedly a seventh higher than before, and ends in B flat major at 56. The second subject, now in the tonic, begins at 56; and we see why it was in a minor key before, as it can be in D minor, the same key as the first subject, without having to change its mode. A coda starts at 65, and is built on the first bar. The tension rises throughout 65–72, with a gradual *crescendo* from *pp* to *ff*, the instruction *poco a poco agitato*, chord changes occurring gradually more frequently, quicker notes in the accompaniment and rising pitch. Then it gradually sinks to rest, and a pathetic little figure starts at 76. The whole of this movement is a masterpiece of tragic eloquence.

The *minuet* is in ternary form. **A** ends in the tonic at 16, and it returns at 25, with a trill making an upper dominant pedal. There are two extensions in the second half of **A²**, resulting in eleven bars instead of eight. A coda, based on **A**, starts at 44.

The trio, which is in G major, the subdominant, has an "Alberti" bass, and consists of only one sentence repeated. The repeat changes at the end, so as to finish with a dominant seventh of D major, thus leading back to the minuet.

The *finale* is in old rondo form. A transition starts at 9, and leads into **B** in the dominant at 17. **A** returns at 25, and a *ff* interrupted cadence at 32–3 leads to **C**, starting in B flat major at 35. It passes through G minor and E flat major and leads to a pause (45) after which a link based on **A** leads to the third return of **A** at 55. Notice that Beethoven uses no key signature from 35–55. The music is never in C major or A minor, and one wonders why, if he was going to change from two sharps, he did not use two flats, which would have required fewer accidentals in the course of the passage. **A** returns again at 56, and is followed by a modified form of the transition first heard in bar 9. **D**, which starts at 72, is really a development of **A**, which is rather unusual. There is no settled tonality until **A** returns again at 84. The pauses in the theme are now filled in with little comments in the bass. A coda, which starts at 92, is mainly a development of the first three notes of **A**.

Op. 13, in C Minor (The Pathetic Sonata)

Beethoven's "Grande Sonate Pathétique", op. 13, was probably written in 1798, though the date of composition of most of these earlier works is not known with certainty. Beethoven had written quite a number of small works for clavecin or pianoforte before this date, in addition to ten sonatas, one unfinished sonata and four sonatinas. But he was still in his "first period" and had been in Vienna for only six years. The sonata was dedicated to his friend and patron Prince Carl Lichnowsky, and was doubtless often played by Beethoven himself when he gave concerts. He was thought of as a brilliant pianist at this time.

The *first movement* starts with an introduction, and was the first of Beethoven's sonatas to do so, and the first to be given a title. The passionate introduction was doubtless the reason for the title, which was given to it by the publisher. Nothing so full of dramatic contrasts had been heard before in piano-writing, though Mozart had written works which were quite as full of deep feeling, and the sonata is not "pathetic" throughout.

The rhythm of bar 1 is repeated in bar 2 and then compressed into half-bar units in bar 3, leading up to a climax in bar 4 and a modulation to the relative major.

The rhythm is repeated quietly in E flat in bar 5, and alternates with *ff* interjections in a lower register. Then, starting at the end of bar 7, the last part of the rhythm is worked up to a climax in bar 9, and the introduction ends with a torrential descending chromatic scale in bar 9 over dominant harmony, which leads into the *allegro*.

But even now we have not heard the last of these sudden changes of dynamics. Beethoven was exploiting to the full the new instrument, the *piano-forte*, which could play both soft and loud. The *allegro* starts *p* but rises rapidly, through an *sf* and a *crescendo* to a climax in bar 6, from which it sinks to another *p* in bar 9 and a repetition of bars 1–8. But the first sentence ended with a perfect cadence at bar 9 whereas the second sentence lengthens the diminished seventh chord at bar 16 so as to end with dominant harmony at bar 17. The cadence is elaborated for eight bars and leads to a transition at 25.

This is built on the first subject idea over a *tremolo* bass which rises in semitones until it gets to the dominant seventh of the relative major at 35, ready for the second subject.

The second subject starts at 41, but it is unexpectedly in E flat *minor* instead of E flat major—another touch of the "pathetic". The imitation of the first bar of each phrase at a higher octave has an antiphonal effect. At 53 the music drops into D flat major which has a calming effect, but it returns to E flat minor at 69; and after touching on F minor at 73 it leads to the second section of the second subject in E flat major (the normal key) at 79.

This section, after remaining static for a bar or two, moves outward in the outside parts, reaching a climax at 88, from which it moves inwards again to a repetition at 91.

A third section of the second subject starts at 103, and is little more than cadence chords played twice over.

A codetta starts at 111 and is based on the first subject theme, now in the relative major. It does not end in this key however: bar 121 is a fundamental seventh with D as root, and leads in 122a to a dominant seventh of the tonic key and the repetition of the exposition; while in 122b it is repeated as the dominant seventh of G minor, in which key the development starts at 123.

The development starts with an unexpected return to the introduction. It is very effective, and the student may refer to other examples of this device, such as the first movements of Beethoven's sonata, op. 31, no. 2 and the César Franck symphony. The opening-bar figure is used three times, with an enharmonic change from E flat to D sharp in the third bar resulting in a lovely modulation to E minor.

The *allegro* returns in this key at 127 with a development of the transition, followed by a reference to the introduction at 129, now in quick tempo. These two figures are repeated in G minor; and then at 139 the first two notes of the transition figure are developed in the bass over a *tremolo* in the right hand which falls by step with increasing frequency until it reaches a dominant pedal of the tonic key at 157.

This is a long and exciting dominant pedal, over which chromatic broken chords alternate with references to the first subject. It ends with a tempestuous descending run, leading into the recapitulation.

A dominant pedal is a very common method of leading into a recapitulation but it is none the less effective for that. The student should refer to other examples such as the first movements of the "Waldstein" sonata or Mozart's G minor symphony, or any other works that he may happen to know.

In the recapitulation the first subject begins as in the exposition, but instead of ending with an imperfect cadence, as at 17, it merges into a transition at 197 which is quite different from the original transition. It takes the second half (the minim section) of the first subject and modulates sequentially through D flat major (198), E flat minor (202) and F minor (206), ending with an imperfect cadence in F minor at 209.

The second subject starts in this unusual key, the subdominant minor, but it reaches dominant harmony of the normal tonic key at 223, where it continues with the figure, though its treatment is not quite the same as in the exposition.

The second section starts at 243 in the tonic key, and again it is different in detail while keeping to the original idea. The third section, starting at 267, is the same except for the change of key, and so is the codetta until 283, where it breaks off on a diminished seventh and a pause.

The coda starts with a *p* return to the *grave* introduction. It is broken by effective pauses and leads to a climax in F minor at 287, from where it sadly descends into a final *allegro* in which the first subject is heard for the last time. Notice the bar's rest at the end, which is necessary in order to complete the four-bar rhythm used in the last twelve bars.

The lovely opening melody of the *slow movement*, combined with the fact that it is deceptively easy to play, has made it very popular. It is "deceptively easy" because a pianist requires a very good feeling for rhythmic and melodic shape, combined with a technique which can express this, before a really sensitive performance can be given.

The movement is in rondo form, and is in A flat major, the sub-mediant major. The bass of the first theme is quite as tuneful as the melody, and the theme is repeated an octave higher (9–16) with a thickened accompaniment before going on to the second theme in the relative minor at 17. A five-bar link (24–8) leads to the return of the first theme at 29, which is now heard just once.

The third theme starts at 37 in the tonic minor, A flat minor. (Notice that the music is really in compound time from here to the end of the movement, but Beethoven has not changed the time-signature.) The theme starts with a dialogue between the treble and the bass, and in bar 42 it reaches the key of F flat major, the sub-mediant major of A flat minor, but it is written enharmonically as E major in order to be easier to read. The theme continues for a time in this key, but changes the notation back to flats with the diminished seventh in 48, ready for the return of the first theme at 51 in the tonic key. The accompaniment is now in triplets, otherwise the theme is the same as at its first appearance.

A short coda starts at 67, based on repetitions of dominant and tonic harmony.

Macpherson suggests that this movement might be thought of as being in episodical form, with 17–28 being merely a middle section *within* the first theme. Either analysis will probably be accepted by examiners; but the fact that bar 16 starts with a contrasting idea in a different key and is not heard again when the first theme returns near the end, makes it appear a genuine episode in a rondo scheme. Tovey considers it to be a rondo.

This sonata has only three movements and the *finale* is in sonata-rondo form. It is a typical last movement, with nothing particularly "pathetic" about it.

The first subject consists of an eight-bar theme, with the second phrase repeated and then extended twice so as to make a seventeen-bar sentence.

The transition starts at bar 18 with a modulation to F minor. The four-bar phrase is then repeated sequentially in E flat major and leads into the second subject in the relative major at 25. It changes to E flat minor at 31, and an extended cadence (33–6) leads to a second section at 37. This is based on imitative triplets, and leads to yet another section at 44. Then the second, triplet, section returns at 51 and reaches a climax on the dominant seventh of the tonic key at 58, from where it leads to an exact repetition of the first subject starting at 62.

The middle section, starting at 79, is an episode in A flat major.

Bar 83 begins by repeating 79–80 with the melody syncopated and with some notes at a different octave. At bar 87 a repetition of the previous eight bars begins, with the right hand an octave higher and additional thirds making thicker harmony.

A four-bar link (95–8) leads to yet another repetition with the melody an octave higher again, against a counter-theme in quavers. At 103 the bass of the theme is heard against quavers in the right hand, and this leads to a dominant pedal of the tonic key starting at 107.

In the recapitulation the first subject returns at 120, and the first eight bars are identical with 1–8 in the exposition. Bar 129 appears to be about to repeat the second phrase as before, though now the melody is in the bass, but it moves sequentially into F minor and merges into a transition, quite different from that in the exposition, but leading into the second subject in the tonic major at 135.

The first section of the second subject is similar to its first appearance in the exposition, though it does not change to the minor mode; but the second section (143–53) is longer than before. The third section (154–70) is extended sequentially through C minor (195), E flat major (161), G major (163) and C minor (165), and leads straight into the final return of the first subject at 171.

This states the first eight bars as at the beginning, and is followed by four bars corresponding to 9–12 and built on the same chord scheme, but with the melody so decorated that it is almost unrecognizable.

The coda starts at 182 with a reference to the second section of the second subject, modulating from F minor to C minor. Bar 186 begins a repetition an octave lower, but this time it is extended up to 193.

A new figure starts at 193 and works up to a climax on the dominant seventh of A flat major, in which key a final reference to the first subject appears at 203. The music appears to be dying away, but it is interrupted by a *ff* descending scale over a final perfect cadence in the tonic key.

Op. 27, no. 2, in C Sharp Minor

About this time Beethoven seems to have been experimenting with the order and plan of movements in a sonata. Op. 26 begins with an *andante* and variations, and its scherzo comes before its slow movement. The two op. 27 sonatas were both labelled "sonata quasi una fantasia", presumably because the plan of their movements was so irregular. Op. 27, no. 1 has no movement in sonata form; and op. 27, no. 2 opens with a song-like *adagio*, which made an enterprising publisher give it the title "Moonlight". This movement is much played by itself, because it is deceptively easy.

The first movement uses continuous quiet triplets. After five bars of introduction, the song theme starts at bar 6. It is one long, continuous melody, though three "motives" can be distinguished in it: (*a*) at 6, 23, 43 and in the coda starting at 60; (*b*) at 16 and 52; and (*c*) at 28.

There are only three movements in this sonata, and the *second movement* is in minuet and trio form. The repeat of **A** in the minuet is written out (9–16) because syncopation is added. **A** ends in the tonic, and it returns in a modified form at 25, so the minuet may be considered to be in ternary form. But the trio is in binary form, because the first part does not return.

The *finale* is in sonata form, and though difficult to play, it is quite simple to analyse. The first subject leads to a dominant pedal (9–14) ending with a pause. The transition (15–21) is based on the first subject, but moves to the dominant minor, in which key the second subject enters at 21. A second section, beginning at 43, is quieter, because it is based on quavers instead of semiquavers. A codetta (58–63) is followed by a two-bar link, leading to the repeat or the development.

The development section begins by using the first subject figure and modulating to F sharp minor. At 71 the second subject is introduced in the same key, first in the treble, then in the bass. After passing through G major (79), F sharp (83) and C sharp (85) it reaches a dominant pedal of the tonic key at 87, and this leads into the recapitulation at 102.

The recapitulation is very similar to the exposition, except that there is no transition, and that, as was expected, the second subject is now in the tonic key.

There is a long coda, which is almost like another development section. It starts at 159, using the first subject in F sharp minor; then, after two diminished sevenths in broken chords, the second subject enters in the tonic. It is heard in the bass at 167 and the treble at 171, and quickens to a climax and a series of cadenza-like broken chords. There is a quiet reference to the codetta at 190, and a rapid *crescendo* brings the movement to an exciting finish.

12

Beethoven and Schubert: Chamber Works

Beethoven settled in Vienna when he was twenty-two years old, and it was natural that he should write chamber music, because Vienna was full of music-loving amateurs, as well as professionals, who delighted in playing chamber music whenever they had the opportunity. Beethoven rapidly made friends with members of the musical aristocracy, though unlike Haydn and earlier composers he never took a paid appointment in any of their establishments. But he dedicated many chamber works to them and was sometimes paid for the dedication.

He wrote sixteen string quartets and nine piano trios including the "Archduke" trio which is analysed below. It was natural that he should write so many piano trios, and also violin-and-piano and 'cello-and-piano sonatas, because he was a pianist who could play in such works himself. Most of the general comments at the beginning of the previous chapter apply to Beethoven's chamber music as well as to his piano sonatas.

Schubert was born near Vienna and lived there most of his life, but in more humble circumstances, so that he did not come into contact with the aristocracy as did Beethoven. But he, also, was surrounded by lovers of chamber music, and he played in a family chamber group in his own home when he was a boy. His chamber works include fifteen string quartets, one of which is analysed below, two lovely piano trios, an octet, and the "trout" quintet which is also analysed below.

He was a generation younger than Beethoven and admired his

works from afar, only meeting him on the latter's death-bed. But he unconsciously acquired much from playing and hearing the chamber works of Haydn, Mozart and Beethoven. He did not spend as much time in polishing his works as did Beethoven, and he was often content to repeat the second half of an exposition note-for-note in the recapitulation, apart from the necessary change of key. But he, like Beethoven, had a strong sense of tonality, and at times has some entrancing changes of key. He was particularly fond of changing the mode from major to minor or vice versa on the same tonic, and he also liked an abrupt change to a key a major third below the tonic.

The Archduke Trio, op. 97: Beethoven

The *Archduke* trio was the last full-length piano trio that Beethoven composed, and it was written in 1811 when he was forty, in the same year that he wrote the seventh and eighth symphonies. Emil Ludwig states that it is one of the few works in which no one movement is the most beautiful since every one is perfect and important to the whole. He calls it "the most consummate outpouring of harmony which ever reflected Beethoven's spirit".

It was dedicated to Beethoven's friend and patron, Archduke Rudolph, a brother of the Emperor and a good pianist, who had been a pupil of Beethoven's at the age of fifteen. He became a priest at twenty-three and an archbishop at thirty. This did not prevent him from patronizing the arts and holding a position at court. Beethoven dedicated more works to him than to anyone else, including the "Les Adieux" sonata and the "Missa Solemnis"; and he was one of the royal patrons who guaranteed Beethoven a life pension in 1809.

The *first movement* is in sonata form. Its first subject is a spacious theme of serene nobility, and it is introduced by the piano. When it reaches its cadence at bars 7–8, the 'cello speaks in solo recitative for a few bars and then the violin joins in with a similar comment. Then, at 14, they all settle down to a spacious statement of the theme, with the tune in the violin and a few imitations in the piano.

The first subject ends at 33 with a perfect cadence in the tonic, and this overlaps with the start of the transition. First the 'cello and later the violin make comments upon bar 1, and by bar 39 they have reached the rather remote key of D major. At 43 they enter a kind of "no-man's-land", in which syncopation is a feature, and this leads to the dominant chord of G major at 49 and to the second subject in this key, starting on the last beat of bar 51.

G major is an unusual key for the second subject, and it stays in this key until the end of the exposition, instead of finally establishing the key of F, as would have been more usual.

The first section starts with the piano, and 'cello and violin take up the theme in imitation at bars 56 and 57. The second section starts in the 'cello at 60 and is imitated by the violin at 62. The piano takes the tune in the third section, starting at 68. Then the 'cello reverts to the second section theme at 73 and the violin and piano bring back the third section theme at 77.

The cadence is delayed with imitations at 82 and 83, and then the codetta starts at 84, and is mainly based on a tonic pedal. Bars 94–8(a) form a link modulating back to B flat major for the repeat of the exposition.

The development section starts by modulating to E flat major, and then, at 107, bar 1 of the first subject enters, first in the 'cello, then in the violin and piano in imitation. At 115 the imitations get closer, in *stretto*, and consist of three beats of the figure only. A dominant pedal in key G is reached at 129, and over it the 'cello proceeds to develop bars 3 and 4 of the first subject, starting at 134. A tonic pedal starts at 137, and the violin takes up the theme. The tune and the accompaniment are *pp*, and they come to a standstill at 143.

The piano, left to itself, has a gentle *legato*, *pp*, recitative-like figure over a dominant chord of key C. Its contemplation is interrupted twice by bars 3 and 4 of the first subject, played *pizzicato*, *pp*, first by the 'cello, and then, in imitation between 'cello and violin.

C minor is established at 152. Then, as the music moves to E flat major, bars 3 and 4 are heard in diminution in the strings at 156; and at 158 the piano joins in too. From here until 180, all the instruments have these quaver scales. At first the piano has trills alternating with the scales, but at 170 it drops the trills and has the scales in contrary motion to the strings.

At bar 181 hints of bar 1 are heard in imitation in the strings, and the piano has it in diminution at 187. Two bars of trills lead into the recapitulation.

The recapitulation starts gently at 191, with a decorated version of the first subject in the piano in the treble register. The 'cello and violin recitative-like comments are more elaborate than in the exposition. When the theme returns in full harmony at 204 the 'cello has the theme instead of the violin, and piano and violin have arpeggios round it.

At 210 the music merges into the transition, and there is a large cut, so that 210 is the equivalent of 43. Bars 210–13 move round the dominant of the tonic key, and 214–17 similarly move round the tonic chord of the tonic key. The dominant chord is reached at 219, ready for the second subject in the tonic.

The second subject starts at 222, and, apart from the change of key, it is almost identical with its appearance in the exposition until it reaches the coda at 264.

The coda is based on the first subject. The theme appears *ff* in the piano at 268 and is joined by the strings at 270. The movement ends with a fine, vigorous climax.

The *second movement* is a scherzo, the slow movement being delayed until the third movement. (Perhaps this is because the first movement is not very quick and would have been too much like the *andante* if they had followed on one another.) It is in minuet and trio form. The "minuet" section of this form is normally on the plan ||: **A** :||: **B A** :||, and this plan is followed in this scherzo. But it may not be so obvious to the score reader, because the repetitions are written out and considerably varied.

A is from bars 1–16 and is played by strings alone. It consists of two sentences, the first one modulating to the dominant and the second one starting in the dominant and returning to the tonic.

The repetition of **A** is from bars 17–32. The first sentence is played by the piano alone, and the strings accompany the second sentence, *pizzicato*. Otherwise the two versions of **A** are alike.

B starts at 32, overlapping with the cadence of **A**, and it continues up to 62. The piano has the theme in the first sentence, then the violin takes over at 40, lengthening the theme and modulating to the dominant at 46. The piano takes it up again at 54 and returns to the tonic key. **B** is therefore twice as long as **A**.

When **A** returns at 63 it is played by the strings in octaves, while the piano has a counter-theme in quavers. In the answering sentence, starting at 70, the strings and piano change round. But this time **A** is extended, the two hands of the piano part imitating each other a beat apart at 78.

This **A** does not end in the tonic key, as expected, nor is there the conventional exact repetition of **B A** by means of repeat marks. Instead, **A** modulates to E flat, the subdominant major, in which key the repetition of **B** starts at 86 in the 'cello. The piano takes it up at 90, and develops it in syncopation. The strings repeat this at 107 in the tonic key. The **A** which follows at 107 and continues to 125 is considerably varied.

The trio is much less regular in form than the scherzo. It consists of two themes which can be labelled **C** and **D**, but their repetitions and their key plan are most unusual.

C starts at 126 in B flat minor (the tonic key) and is a four-part *fugato*, starting in the 'cello and continuing in the left hand of the piano part at 133, the violin at 141, and the right hand of the piano part at 151. It is a tortuous, syncopated, chromatic theme, and it is not repeated immediately but goes on to D at 160.

D is a magnificent waltz-like theme in D flat major (the relative major of B flat minor) and it is almost a piano solo. It contains a good deal of development of its third bar in bars 168–79, and it ends in D flat major at 182.

C now returns, but in D flat major. The voices enter in the same order as before, but they are now in *stretto*, so this section is much shorter than the first **C**. Also the theme falls chromatically instead of rising.

Towards the end it modulates unexpectedly and reaches E major at 196, in which key there now follows a complete and exact repetition of **D**.

C returns yet again at 219, with a still closer *stretto*. It starts in E major, but, by means of an enharmonic change, reaches B flat minor by 227. The strings have a tonic pedal in this key at 230, while the piano continues with the syncopated chromatic figure. Then the parts change round at 238, the piano having the dominant pedal and the strings having the figure.

This leads to yet another statement of **D** in yet another key, B flat major, the tonic key at last. It starts at 257 and is the same as before, apart from the key. It is known that this trio was the last piece that Beethoven played in public, and perhaps he liked his "valse brillante" so much that he had to introduce it in three different keys!

The scherzo returns at 287, and 287–302 are identical with 1–16, though they are written out because of the join at 286–7. For the repetition of **A** the reader returns to bar 17, and thereafter the scherzo is repeated exactly up to 125. There is no attempt at shortening it by cutting out repeats—obviously this would not be possible because of the modifications and the repetitions.

For the coda, the reader has to turn on to bar 303. It is based on **C** up to 327, then there is a last reference to **A**, *pp*, ending with an unexpected *ff* in bars 334–5.

The *third movement* is an *andante* in variation form. It is in D major, which, though not a related key, sounds just right after two movements in B flat. The theme is in binary form. The first sentence is played first by the piano alone and then repeated with the strings added; and the second sentence also has the piano alone first, before bringing in the strings for a repetition of the second half of the sentence.

In variation I (bar 29) the piano "shadows" the theme in wide-spread triplets, with occasional support from the strings.

In variation II (bar 57) a variant of the theme appears in the piano in disjointed chords, while 'cello and violin alternate with semi-quavers. For the repetition of the first half (65) all have semiquavers; and at 73 'cello and violin alternate with a rhythmic variant for the second half.

In variation III (85) the piano has semiquaver triplets, which again "shadow" the theme, while strings join in occasionally.

Variation IV is *poco piu allegro*. The theme starts in the violin with a counter-theme in syncopated quavers in the piano, but this soon merges into the main theme. The syncopated quavers are transferred to the strings for the repetition of the first sentence at 121. The strings revert to the original rhythm for the second sentence at 129, but return to the syncopated quavers for its repetition at 136.

Variation V (141) returns to the original theme, but it is now divided between all three instruments. Also it modulates more than before, to F major at 143, D minor at 151, E minor at 153 and E major at 155. The two halves of the theme are not repeated and the music merges into the coda at 160.

Spacious triplet chords lead to a dominant pedal at 166, and this resolves on to the tonic chord at 174. From here to the end all three instruments make brief references to the theme in turn. The movement really ends at 193, and 194 is a link chord leading into the next movement.

In spite of Emil Ludwig's comment, quoted earlier, I feel that the *last movement* of this trio falls far behind the others in musical worth. I felt this very strongly when I first played the trio as a student, and I still feel it now, when I look at it with more mature judgment. The tunes are trite, the development feeble, there are long passages that say nothing of value, and the parts are not well written for the instruments. The piano part is not pianistic, the violin part is unnaturally low and the 'cello part is, at times, unnaturally high—look, for example, at 152 onwards, where the 'cello takes the tune higher than does the violin. Finally the key balance is unsatisfactory. The key-signature is B flat but the movement really begins in E flat, and bar 10 feels like a modulation to the dominant; and the return of the recapitulation at 136 is based on a dominant seventh of E flat and leads to a return in that key of both first and second subjects.

I have been unable to find anything significant about the composition of this movement, but I should not be surprised if it were an adaptation of an earlier work of Beethoven's (perhaps for a different set of instruments or in a different key), put in hurriedly to complete the work, or even if it was based on material supplied by someone else, such as the dedicatee, the Archduke.

(I make this personal comment, in order to stimulate students to think for themselves, and see whether they agree with this assessment or not.)

The movement is in sonata-rondo form. The first subject starts in E flat, and reaches B flat by bar 10. This section then has a decorated repetition. The second sentence starts at 19, in B flat, and it, too, has a decorated repeat.

The transition starts at 35 and is based on bar 1. It reaches the chord of F (the dominant of the key signature, but not of the opening first subject) at 43, and the second subject starts in F major at 51. It has an awkward gait and is mainly for piano. When the strings do come in, as at 59, they appear to be "out of step" with each other. Perhaps Beethoven was just feeling "contrary" at the time, or maybe it shows his sense of humour.

The first subject returns at 73 and is the same up to 104, where it extends itself so as to lead to the episode.

The episode starts in the subdominant major, E flat, at 110. It passes through C minor (120) and G minor (130), and reaches a dominant pedal of E flat at 136 which leads into the recapitulation.

The first subject starts at 152, in E flat, as before. This time it is in the strings, with a chordal accompaniment in the piano. The transition starts at 184 and changes at 189. It is extended and reaches the second subject in E flat major at 206.

The return of the second subject is normally in the tonic key—but what *is* the tonic key of this movement, B flat major, as stated by the key-signature, or E flat major, in which key the first subject starts? Beethoven himself seems to be unsure, and here he, perhaps instinctively, returns to E flat, the key of the beginning of the first subject. To my mind, it *does* feel like the tonic key—but the movement is going to end in B flat! Perhaps this is why he takes such an unconscionably long time in establishing B flat at the end. Listen to the whole movement several times on the gramophone, and see what you feel about the key balance.

The second subject is extended considerably, and hints of the first subject, starting at 246, lead to a pause on a dominant seventh of the unexpected key of A major at 253.

Now follows a *presto* coda in $\frac{6}{8}$ time, based on the first subject, starting in the remote key of A major, and making a lot of fuss about nothing. Perhaps this emphasizing of A major is meant to make the listener forget the earlier confusion about the key centre. But Beethoven returns, after all, to E flat and not to B flat at 293, and it *still* feels like the tonic key!

At about 306 he begins at last to establish B flat, and spends the rest of the time from here to the end (104 bars) in doing so. There is a tonic pedal from 364–96. Do you really think he needs to be such a terribly long time in saying "finis"? Personally I cannot feel that this is Beethoven at his best.

String Quartet in A Minor, op. 29: Schubert

This work was composed in 1824, the same year as the octet and the string quartet in D minor ("Death and the Maiden"). Schubert thought of these works as studies for the grand symphony he intended to write. The year 1822 is the dividing line in Schubert's life, and most of his great works, including the three best quartets (the D minor, the G major and this one) were written after this.

The *first movement* is in sonata form—Schubert never departs from this for an opening movement. The exposition is clearly and simply constructed, with the transition starting at 32, and the second subject at 59, in the relative major. Notice that both first and second subjects start with a tonic pedal in the bass, and that the rhythmic figure which begins the viola and 'cello parts is used almost continuously up to the transition. The first subject is of a melodic nature, as often happens with Schubert; and at bar 23 he brings it back in the tonic major. He is particularly fond of a change from tonic minor to major, and vice versa.

A rather obvious link leads to the development section, which to my mind, is based entirely on the first subject. But readers of the Boosey and Hawkes analysis will note that it says the second subject is also used. Here is another case where students must decide for themselves. After a few bars of imitation, the whole of the first eight bars are re-stated, without development, in D minor. Notice the canon between the 'cello and first violin which follows in bars 118–27, and which uses the rhythm of the first subject. Bar 130 begins a close *stretto* between the three upper instruments, using the rhythm of the first three notes of the first subject. It results in a syncopated second violin part, and possibly the leaping sixth in bar 130 seems to the Boosey and Hawkes analyser to be derived from bar 60 of the second subject. After a dramatic *ff* interrupted cadence in bar 140 the rhythmic accompanying figure to the first subject starts again, *pp*, and a wonderful modulatory sequential passage begins, finally leading in to the recapitulation at bar 168. The first subject has a cut of twelve bars, but the transition is considerably longer. The second subject is very similar to its appearance in the exposition, and a coda, which starts at 267, continues to develop the first subject.

Schubert was so fond of the theme of the *slow movement* that he used it four times, in the "Rosamunde" entracte, the B flat

"Impromptu" for piano, the "Wanderer Fantasia" and this movement. It is perhaps rather surprising that he uses C major for this movement, as, being the relative major, it has been used so much in the first movement.

The form is irregular, and two analyses are possible. It can be considered as modified sonata form, with a long development of the first subject interpolated between the first and second subjects in the recapitulation (74–94); or as sonata form, with the recapitulation of the first subject (53) occurring *before* the development section (74–94). However, the *facts* are not in dispute, and the terminology hardly matters.

The first subject is a complete short piece in binary form, with repeats, and this also is unusual in a sonata from type of movement. Bars 46–52 are a modulatory link joining the exposition and recapitulation, as is customary in modified sonata form; and there is a coda from 110 to the end.

The *third movement* is in minuet and trio form, with an opening figure in the 'cello which is used like a motto. There are many pedals in both minuet and trio. The second section of the minuet is much longer than the first, and contains a good deal of development. Notice the effective enharmonic change at 34–5, followed by an unexpected modulation to C sharp minor.

The *finale*, in the tonic *major*, is exactly the same shape as the second movement. The Boosey and Hawkes analysis says it is a rondo, but this seems to me to be untenable.

The first subject is in two repeated sections, but with both parts ending in the tonic. Notice the five-bar phrases in the first part. The transition, starting in 26b, leads to the second subject in 72. This begins in the unusual key of C sharp minor, but it is in the conventional dominant by 88. Like the first subject, the first part of the second subject consists of two repeated sentences, but the repeats are written out. It is followed by a second section at 104; and a link at 127 leads to the recapitulation at 133. After the repetition of the first subject, Schubert begins to develop it at 172, as in the second movement; and at 183 he adds the triplet figure from the second subject. By 219 he has got to the transition, a third lower than in the exposition, and this leads to the second subject at 254, in F sharp minor and then A major, the corresponding keys to those in the exposition. There is a coda from 293 to the end.

The second and fourth movements both show Schubert experimenting with a new shape; and as it hangs together quite well, it does not matter that theorists have not given it a name.

The Trout Quintet, op. 114: Schubert

This quintet, written in 1819, is named "The Trout" because the theme of the variation movement is the tune of the song called "The Trout" written by Schubert two years earlier. He must have been fond of it because he wrote five versions of it as a song before using the theme for this quintet. There are other instances of his using a tune in more than one work. The song "Death and the Maiden" was used in the "Death and the Maiden" quartet; and the song "The Wanderer" was the foundation of "The Wanderer" fantasia for pianoforte.

Schubert was commissioned to write this quintet by Paumgarten, a wealthy 'cellist who lived in Steyr in Upper Austria. Schubert was on a walking tour in Upper Austria with his friend Vogl, the singer, and a sense of happiness comes through into the music. Paumgarten asked for this rather unusual combination because he had these instrumentalists available; but Schubert intentionally keeps the piano part, to a large extent, in its higher registers, because of the weight of the 'cello and bass in the lower registers of the strings. A double bass is rarely used in chamber music, though it is also found in Schubert's octet. It is also rather unusual to find five movements. The variation movement is the extra one, interpolated between the scherzo and the finale.

The *first movement* is in sonata form. The piano starts with an upward darting triplet arpeggio which is to be heard frequently throughout the movement. The violin has the theme, supported by the 'cello. But no sooner has the key been established than the music moves to F major at bar 11, where the viola has the theme supported by the piano in high, quick octaves. The triplet arpeggio is heard in violin and 'cello in turn, while the bass has a tonic pedal, F, throughout this section, just as it had a tonic, A, in the opening bars. But at 23 the F slips down a semitone to E, over which Ic V in the tonic key leads to a return to the tonic at bar 25.

Although the whole of this opening section is *allegro* it appears as if Schubert is thinking of it as an introduction. The modulation to key F occurs very early for a first subject, whereas when he starts again at bar 25 he settles down into the tonic key for quite a time. Also (and this perhaps is the convincing reason for the supposition) when he returns to the first subject at the beginning of the recapitulation it is bar 25 to which he returns, not bar 1.

However this may be, bar 25 starts a long statement of a slightly altered form of the theme as compared with bar 3, one with a greater sense of rhythmic impetus. It appears in the violin with a quaver accompaniment in the viola and 'cello, *pizzicato* crotchets in the bass, and the occasional triplet arpeggio in the piano. At bar 40 the piano takes over the melody, again in high octaves, while the viola and 'cello change their figure from quavers to triplets, and the violin takes over the triplet arpeggios. By 51 everyone is playing in triplets in turn; and after two abortive attempts at a modulation to C major at 55–6 and 60, the music modulates to the dominant major for the second subject in that key at 64.

The whole of the second subject is really in $\frac{12}{8}$ time, though Schubert does not change the time signature. The first section (64–84) consists of a duet between 'cello and violin with an almost continuous triplet accompaniment in the piano, and a touch of E minor at 75.

A second section, still in E major, starts at 84. The piano has ten bars to itself, then the tune is taken up by the violin, while the piano continues with the triplet accompaniment.

A third section starts at bar 100, with the violin and piano in imitation of each other. Notice the lovely touch of C major at bars 106–9.

A codetta starts at 114. It is unusually long, but nevertheless feels codetta-like, with its scales and assertive dotted figures. The exposition could have ended at 114 or 118 or 122, as dominant and tonic harmony keeps being reiterated. But then Schubert is off on another modulatory excursion, to C sharp minor at 123, and A major at 124. However he soon returns to the dominant key, and by 134 we really feel the end is approaching.

But no! There is a sudden hush and a *pp* entry of yet another new theme, in yet another key, D major this time. However, it is a false alarm, because after four bars we are back at a *ff* cadence in the dominant, ending at 146 with the double bar.

But the development starts in C major, a third below E major, the note E acting as a link between the two keys. Over a *pp* dotted accompaniment in the lower strings the violin takes bars 3 and 4 (the introductory form of the first subject) and develops them, with the last note rising by step at each repetition.

The piano has been silent, but at bar 157 it takes the tune over in high *pp* octaves while the strings continue the dotted rhythm. The 'cello has it at 165, by now in the key of E flat major.

Notice the triplet figure preceded by a tied note which starts in the piano at 167. It is based on the rhythm of bar 1 but is now scalic, and it is used in this form for some time, at first in the piano, and then, at 173, by imitation in violin and 'cello. The music passes through B flat major at 173, G minor at 178, and returns to E flat major at 180.

This time Schubert is long enough in the key to think it would be worth while to change the key signature. The theme is in the violin and viola while the 'cello and bass have the triplet rhythm beginning with the tied note, and the piano has a semiquaver broken chord accompaniment.

A flat major is reached at bar 189, where the piano takes over the triplet figure again. Rising sequences pass through B flat minor (192); C flat major (193); E minor by means of an enharmonic change (196); F minor (199); and F sharp minor (202). Then a dominant pedal of key D (why key D, one wonders?) begins at 203, and crescendos into the tonic chord at 210.

And now we discover the reason for the key of D. Schubert intends to repeat the whole of the exposition note for note, except for the change of key; and if he starts in key D, the subdominant, he will get to the tonic key for the second subject without any need for change! There is an occasional altered note here and there, but that could be accounted for by Schubert transposing from memory and forgetting a few details. It was a lazy man's solution, but the music is so lovely that the listener can make no objection.

So, apart from the change to a key a fifth lower, 210=25; 249=64; and 269=84. The third section of the second subject (100–14) is omitted, perhaps because Schubert felt the movement was getting a bit too long. But the codetta starting at 285 is the same as in the exposition; and it makes such a good ending that there is no need for a single extra chord!

The *second movement* is very easy to follow, if one does not try to make it fit into a standard musical form, or expect it to follow a conventional modulatory scheme. It consists of a succession of four themes which are then repeated with practically no alteration except that of key. Someone might try to fit them into modified sonata form, but the recapitulation of the themes does not start in the tonic but in a very remote key. Nor is the conventional dominant used for the first statement of the second, third or even fourth themes. It is wiser to think of this movement as a string of lovely tunes, making, with their repetition, a satisfying key-scheme of an unconventional but typically Schubertian kind.

The first subject is in F major and starts with the melody in octaves in the piano. At bar 5 the first phrase is repeated in the violin. Bar 9 brings in another phrase, five bars long this time, shared between piano and violin; and bar 14 reverts to the first phrase, though now it is extended to six bars by means of imitation between violin and piano. This first subject ends in the tonic key at bar 19.

Five bars of modulatory link, consisting of a series of arpeggios, lead to the second subject at 24 in the remote key of F sharp minor. Schubert has got there by changing one note of his chord at a time. F A C becomes F sharp A C, then F sharp A C sharp, which then moves to the dominant seventh of F sharp minor and proceeds to establish the new key.

The second subject (24–36) is mainly in thirds and sixths in the violin and viola, and is very reminiscent of the piano part between the verses of Schubert's popular "Serenade".

It modulates at the end to D major, in which key the third subject appears at 36. This key is a major third below F sharp minor—Schubert often drops into a key a major third lower. But D major is still remote from F major. The piano has the lion's share of this subject, and is again mainly in octaves in the treble, but the violin joins in at 44, and the two continue in imitation. The 'cello reaches a pedal on D at 49, and leads to the fourth subject in G major.

This starts *ppp* at 53, and is quite short. It is very like the third subject but is rather more tuneful and makes no use of the triplet figure heard in the third subject. It comes to an end with a pause at 60.

The pause on G makes it possible for Schubert to make a mental change of key, which he expects his listeners to follow. G as *doh* becomes *te* in A flat and at 61 he quietly returns to his first theme in A flat major. Put a dominant seventh of key A flat underneath this G, and you will appreciate the process.

The first subject is exactly as before except for this unexpectedly remote key, which has nevertheless been reached by logical musical means. It is followed at 79 by the same modulatory link, which leads by the same means to the second subject at 84, a semitone higher as it was before, that is, in key A minor. The cycle of keys is now getting nearer home.

The second subject is again exactly the same, with the same key relationships on either side of it. So it leads to the third subject at 96 in the tonic key. However the third subject, when it first appeared in the exposition, modulated at the end into the key a fourth higher. This time it does not do so, because it has now reached the home key. So it changes at 104, moving a fifth higher, with the theme still in the piano instead of being transferred to the violin. This is the only change in the whole of the recapitulation, and by its means 110 corresponds to 49 but with the 'cello pedal now on the dominant of the tonic key.

So the fourth subject, when it reappears at 114, is, like the third, in the tonic key, though otherwise it corresponds to 53, and it is exactly the same to the end.

How simple it all is—but it takes a Schubert to have thought of it!

The *third movement* is a scherzo in A major, the tonic key. **A** reaches a perfect cadence in the dominant key at bar 12, but cadence repetitions, treated antiphonally between strings and piano, extend the section to bar 18. The repetition of **A** is written out because it changes at 27 and modulates to C major. The four-bar phrase at 9–12 becomes nine bars at 28–36. It is followed by the antiphonal cadential extension as before (36–42), but now in the unexpected key of C major.

B, starting at 43, is a development of **A**. It starts with imitative entries, first in F major (43–50), then in G minor (51–8). Then the second half of the theme (first heard at 47–50) is played antiphonally in piano and strings over a series of fundamental sevenths on E (59–62), A (63–6), D (67–70), and G (71–4). Then six bars modulate back to the tonic key.

A returns at 81, but its second half (89–104) modulates to the tonic key, though otherwise it is exactly the same as 28–42. Then **B A** is repeated in the usual way.

The trio is in D major and again has antiphonal treatment between strings and piano. **D**, which is a development of **C**, modulates sequentially through F sharp minor (123), D major (125), B minor

(127), G major (129), and B flat major (139) before reaching Ic V of the tonic key at 149–52, preparatory to a return of **C**. **C** (155–70) is fuller than before and is considerably modified, ending in the tonic key.

The *scherzo* is then repeated.

In the *variation movement* each instrument has the theme in turn, thus making it an excellent example of the tone qualities of the various instruments. The theme is changed very little but it has different adornments in each variation.

The theme is stated by the strings alone, the violin having the tune. It is a clear, little example of binary form. The piano enters with the tune in the first variation, while the strings have darting figures round it. The viola has the tune in variation II, with the violin running above it in happy triplets. In variation III the 'cello and double bass play the tune together, while the piano runs round in demi-semiquavers—four notes as compared with the three of the previous variation.

Now follows a change. Variation IV is in the tonic minor, and the tune has temporarily vanished, though the chord scheme and rhythmic structure are similar. However, the fifth bar modulates to the relative major, and the first section ends in that key instead of the dominant.

Variation V moves to B flat major, a major third below the tonic key, a relationship which Schubert quite frequently used. The 'cello has a variant of the theme, which changes to minor at the beginning of the second half, and then moves as far afield as D flat major before returning, by means of an enharmonic change, to the original key of D major for the last variation.

Here, for the first time, we find the original accompaniment of the song in the piano part. The tune is taken by the violin and the 'cello in turns. This is more like the song than any other variation, and a comparison should be made between the two.

The *finale* is in the tonic key, and although its form is quite clear it is rather unusual.

It starts with a held dominant note, *fp*, in the viola, 'cello and piano, and two bars later the first subject enters over the dominant pedal, four bars in the strings followed by four bars in the piano. Then the strings have a fuller version of the theme for eight bars (11–18) followed by the piano for eight bars, during which modulations occur to B minor (20) and G major (22). Bars 27–36 are a repetition of the first ten bars, and bring the first subject to an end.

The transition starts at 37 with a development of the first subject played *f*, *tutti*, and modulating through A minor (40) into C major (44). There is a varied repetition of 37–44 an octave higher, *p*, played by strings alone. Then 37–44 is repeated exactly at 53–60, and 61 starts a repetition of the second sentence (from 45), but in the piano, not the strings. It breaks off, however, at 66 and is followed by antiphonal treatment of the last two bars in strings and piano alternately, modulating through A minor (70) and F major (74) into D minor (78).

This leads into the second subject at 84 in D major. Here is the first unusual feature. The dominant key is much the most usual key for a second subject. Beethoven quite frequently goes to the mediant, but this is still on the sharp side of the tonic. The subdominant key is unexpected, as modulation to the flat side of the tonic is more usually reserved for the later parts of a movement.

The first section of the second subject consists of a swinging tune which is passed from violins to 'cello, accompanied by a dotted figure in the piano. It is repeated at 92, and bar 100 starts another repetition, but it changes at 103, modulating to F sharp minor.

The second section of the second subject starts at 108 and consists of a quaver figure in the strings acting as an accompaniment to another swinging tune, now in the piano, which includes a hint of the first subject. It begins in F sharp minor with a tonic pedal in the 'cello; then at 116 it slides up to G major. At 125 the bass begins to change more rapidly, sliding up by semitones till it reaches D at 131.

This leads to what feels like a codetta in D major at 135. It is built over a long tonic pedal (135–50) with fragments of the first subject above it. This is just how one would expect the exposition to end, as D major is the main key of the second subject.

Four bars of tonic chord triplets plunge into the chord of B flat at 155, and everything points to this being the beginning of the development section, except for the fact that there is no double bar line and repeat mark in the copy. A listener who is without a copy cannot, however, know this, particularly as the repetition of an exposition is often omitted in performance.

At first the second section of the second subject is developed in B flat major, with the triplets continuing in the piano as before. Then, at 171, the first subject reappears, *pp*, in the piano in D major, and this continues up to 194, with an occasional touch of B minor. Then, at 195, the piano continues with bars 3 and 4 of the first subject in harmonic outline only, the rhythmic figure having vanished. A *ff* interruption in D minor occurs at 231 and modulates to F major, but after a two-bar pause the music reverts to D with what seems like a second codetta, ending with an extended cadence in D major.

And *now* appears the double bar line and repeat mark! The last eighty-one bars, beginning with the abrupt change of key to B flat major, have really consisted of development, though the key centre has tended to revert to D, the key of the second subject, instead of moving further afield, and there was no sign of leading into a recapitulation. Irregular as it may seem, this "development" is all thought of as being an extension of the exposition.

But now follows something even more surprising. The whole of the rest of the movement consists of an exact transposition of the exposition, a fifth higher. There is no development section, as one would expect in sonata form, perhaps because there has been so much development already. But neither is this movement in the conventional modified sonata form, as a recapitulation normally begins by returning to the tonic key as well as to the first subject, and here the first subject returns in E major, the dominant! One wonders whether Schubert planned his second subject in the subdominant key in the exposition so that, by starting the recapitulation in the dominant, he could repeat the exposition note-for-note and end in the tonic key: A major to D major becoming E major to A major. He quite frequently transposes the second subject note-for-note; and we have seen how, in the first movement of this quintet, he returns to the first subject of the recapitulation in the subdominant key so as to be able to transpose the complete exposition, a device which is sometimes found in Mozart. But in the first movement the order of keys was: tonic dominant, balanced by subdominant tonic, which seemed a more natural order. To repeat a complete exposition twice in one work is quite a unique example of labour-saving! Perhaps one ought to remember that, not only was Schubert happy-go-lucky by nature, but he was on a walking tour in the summer, and writing music takes a long time. It is much easier to transpose than to think out afresh, including modifications which may be improvements but which take time.

So, to sum up, we have in the finale a movement in modified sonata form, with the exposition containing the second subject in the subdominant key, followed by a good deal of development, all as part of the exposition; and a recapitulation being an exact repetition a fifth higher, and starting, therefore, most unusually, in the dominant key

13

Beethoven and Schubert: Orchestral Works

Beethoven and Schubert normally used the symphony orchestra as it had been established in the later works of Haydn, consisting of two flutes, two oboes, two clarinets, two bassoons, two horns, two trumpets, two timpani, and strings. But Beethoven used only one flute in his slight fourth symphony, and he required a piccolo in the fifth. sixth and ninth symphonies, and in the Egmont overture, all of which wanted extra brilliance at some stage. The fifth and ninth symphonies also used a double bassoon.

Although two horns was still the standard number he used three in the "Eroica" symphony—probably for the first time in an orchestral work—and four horns in the ninth symphony, a number which was to become general later in the century. The "Egmont" and "Leonora" overtures, which were intended for the theatre, naturally used a larger orchestra, and also had four horns.

But what added even more to the volume of tone was the use of three trombones, which are found in the finale of the fifth symphony, in the scherzo and finale of the ninth symphony, and in the "Leonora" overtures.

Schubert's fifth symphony in B flat, which is analysed below, was written for an incomplete amateur orchestra connected with his family, and used only one flute and no clarinets, trumpets or drums. But his later symphonies not only required the normal woodwind and brass but added three trombones, as did also his theatre music. such as the "Rosamunde" overture.

Perhaps all this does not sound very much fuller scoring than that of the later Haydn symphonies, but most of Beethoven's and

Schubert's works sound much fuller and grander. This is partly because the brass is used more freely, but largely also because of the greater emotional contrasts and variety of intensity. Beethoven could be turbulently angry one minute and full of deep pathos the next, whereas Haydn's and Mozart's emotions were on a more controlled and delicate scale.

Also many of Beethoven's symphonies are much longer. The average length of a Haydn or Mozart symphony is twenty to thirty minutes, but Beethoven's "Eroica" symphony is forty-five and the ninth is seventy minutes long. And Schumann spoke of the "heavenly length" of Schubert's great C major symphony.

Whereas Beethoven made many experiments with the number and order of the movements in his piano sonatas, he accepted the traditional plan for his symphonies. They all had four movements in the usual order, except for the sixth which, owing to its "programme" had five movements, and the ninth in which the slow movement is the third instead of the second movement.

His only change in the over-all plan was to write scherzos instead of minuets for the third movement. The third movement of the first symphony is called a minuet but it is really quite an elaborate scherzo. In later symphonies he used the work "scherzo" except in the eighth, and here the previous slow movement had been unusually quick, so it was followed by quite an old-fashioned slow minuet. But the scherzo was mainly a speeded-up minuet, though often with a humorous or sardonic twist. It was still in triple time, with clearly defined sections and double bars, and it was in minuet and trio form.

The contributions which Beethoven made to sonata form, such as his skilfully welded transitions, his wonderful development sections and his long, powerful codas are magnificently shown in his orchestral works.

Schubert was primarily a lyrical composer, so that we find a greater use of melody in his instrumental works than in those of Beethoven. Compare, for instance, the first subject of the first movement of his "Unfinished" symphony with that of a typical rhythmical, pithy statement of a first subject by Beethoven. His transitions also tended to be shorter, though they were often very poetic.

Mozart established the form and style of the piano concerto, and Beethoven owed much to him, particularly in his early concertos. Mozart usually stated some or all of his themes in a preliminary orchestral exposition before the soloist entered, though he usually kept mainly to the tonic key. Then the soloist entered and decorated the themes in a kind of second exposition which now, however, modulated to the dominant or relative major key for the second subject. A *tutti* then led to the development section, which consisted largely of decorative passage work for the soloist. The recapitulation followed the usual lines of sonata form, but at the end of it another *tutti*, ending on Ic of the tonic key, led to a cadenza for the soloist, which was often improvised by the performer at the concert. The soloist indicated that he was coming to the end by returning to Ic and resolving it on to V, usually with a trill, which was the cue for the conductor to take up his baton and bring in the orchestra for the final *tutti*.

Beethoven modified this plan in several ways. In the first piano concerto the piano enters at bar 16, without waiting for the orchestra to play a complete exposition. In the third piano concerto the orchestra reverts to the plan of starting a complete exposition before the soloist enters, but the second subject is in the relative major and not the tonic key. In the fourth concerto the soloist enters first, and in the fifth the soloist enters with a *bravura* cadenza-like passage after one chord in the orchestra.

But the violin concerto reverts to Mozart's method of having a complete exposition in the orchestra first, with the second subject in the tonic key.

Beethoven wrote no less than three cadenzas to his first piano concerto, and he also wrote his own cadenza in his last piano concerto, instead of leaving it to be "improvised" by the soloist. Later composers have followed this custom.

Concertos normally had three and not four movements, there usually being no minuet or scherzo. Beethoven ran straight on from the second to the third movement in his fourth and fifth piano concertos.

Schubert wrote no concertos.

The works analysed in this chapter are given in chronological order. In addition to one concerto and four symphonies, two by Beethoven and two by Schubert, there are two overtures by Beethoven, one written for a play, "Egmont", and the other for his one opera "Fidelio". Both are highly dramatic, and are on a large scale, quite different from the slight overtures Mozart wrote for his operas.

Piano Concerto in C, op. 15: Beethoven

The orchestral exposition of the first movement follows Mozartian lines except that Beethoven introduces his second subject in E flat major at 47 and reproduces it in sequence in F minor and G minor. However he returns to C major at 72 with imitative entries based on the first subject; and he introduces a second section of the second subject in C major at 86.

When the piano enters at 107 it is with a new theme, of which no use is made later. But the orchestra soon enters with the first subject and it modulates to A minor on the way to the dominant, in which key the second subject enters at 155. Notice the figure starting at 174, which grows from the beginning of the second subject. The second section of the second subject, previously heard in C major in the orchestral *tutti*, begins in the dominant at 182 and the exposition ends with some exciting *bravura* passages for the piano.

A *tutti*, starting at 238, and based on the first subject, leads to the development section, in which the piano enters with a new theme at 266 in E flat. The orchestra soon brings in further references to the first subject, however, while the piano continues with its figuration.

The recapitulation starts at 346. The first subject cuts to the equivalent of bar 24 at 354, then changes; and by 360 it has cut to the equivalent of 145. But the second subject, starting at 370, is practically the same as in the exposition, except for key.

The *tutti* starting at 452 is similar to that separating the exposition and the development section except that it is now in the tonic, and it leads to the customary Ic at 464. But here Beethoven, instead of leaving the performer to improvise his own cadenza, has written no less than three cadenzas. They all begin with a development of bar 72, and the first has been left incomplete. The third was probably composed rather later, and it is a magnificent example of his style of extemporization. After the opening figure, based on 72, and some broken chords, he deals with the first bar of the first subject, in gradually ascending figures, until he reaches the second subject in D flat. But he soon returns to the figure from bar 1, in crashing chords, and a trill on D looks as if the cadenza may be about to end. But Beethoven then goes on to treat the second section of the second subject in the dominant, and he finally ends without a trill, though on the customary dominant chord, and leads into the short final *tutti*.

The *second movement* is in episodical form, and in the key of A flat major, a major third below C major. The piano has the first stanza of the first theme, and the orchestra has the second, at bar 8. The first stanza returns at 15, in the clarinet. A transition, beginning at 19, leads to the episode in the dominant at 30. This begins with a dialogue between the wind and the piano. The return to the first section occurs at 53, with different orchestration and a more ornamented piano part. This time the second and first stanzas are repeated again at 74, thus making the plan **A B A B A**. A long coda starts at 84.

The *finale* is in sonata-rondo form. The first subject is stated first by the piano, then by the orchestra. A transition (41) leads to the second subject in the dominant, 66, which modulates freely. Another transition (128) leads to the return of the first subject (152) first in the piano then in the orchestra, as before. This leads straight into the episode in A minor, in which two ideas (192 and 208) alternate.

The transition starting at 273 leads to the recapitulation: first subject, 311; transition, 351; second subject, now in the tonic key, 382; transition, 436; first subject, 486. The coda starts at 506.

Symphony no. 1, in C, op. 21: Beethoven

This symphony was written in 1799–1800, when Beethoven was uneasily detecting the first signs of deafness. But, on the whole, it was a time of happiness, when he was establishing himself in Vienna, and could look forward confidently to the future. The symphony was played at his first public concert in 1800. It is in the style of Haydn and Mozart, though it is not as great a work as, for example, Haydn's "London" symphony or the three last symphonies of Mozart. It contains to our ears, hints of the greater Beethoven to come, though it could not be expected that this would be realized by his contemporaries.

The introduction to the *first movement* must have seemed deliberately perverse to its first hearers. A composer who started his first symphony, in the key of C, with two chords establishing the key of F, and four bars later, at the first cadence, was in the key of G, gave notice of his revolutionary tendencies. Yet the rest of the introduction is quite ordinary and pedestrian.

The *allegro*, which starts at bar 13, begins with a first subject based on the tonic chord. It is then immediately repeated a tone higher—notice the similarity between this and the later "Waldstein" sonata, in which Beethoven repeats his first subject figure first a tone lower, then a tone higher.

The transition starts at 33, and contains a reference to the first subject at 41. It ends with a well-marked cadence on the dominant chord, so that the ear expects the second subject in the dominant key at 52. A second section starts at 77. It is based on the same idea as the first section, but starts in the dominant minor and modulates through B flat major and back to G minor again before returning to G major. A darker, warmer colour is introduced in this section.

There is quite a long codetta, beginning at 88, based on the first subject. It could have ended at 100, but Beethoven rather purposelessly prolongs it to 106. A link based on the dominant seventh in minims leads back to the beginning and also to the development.

The development begins by treating the first subject quavers sequentially, passing throughout A major, D major, and G major. Then (at 122) imitative treatment of the crotchet part of the first subject begins. Bar 136 introduces imitations based on the transition at bar 45; and bar 144 starts imitations of the first bar of the first subject. The term "working out" certainly applies to this development section, which is full of examples of sequence and imitation based on previous material. It modulates quite freely, too, though there is nothing forced about the changes of key.

The recapitulation begins at 178. The first subject is shortened, and merges into the transition, which starts at 189 by modulating into F major. It grows out of the semibreve chords in the first subject (bars 17–19), and does not use the material of the first transition at all. But the second subject and the codetta are very similar to the corresponding part of the exposition, except for the obvious differences of key.

The coda gives a hint of how Beethoven was going to develop this feature in the future. (Few of Haydn's and Mozart's works have codas of any length.) It begins at 260 with imitative entries of the link figure (bars 106–9), combined with the first subject figure. The last twenty-one bars are entirely on a *ff* tonic chord, over which the first subject makes a triumphant final appearance.

It was quite common, at this period, for trumpets and drums to be silent in the slow movement of a symphony, but both are used very effectively in this *second movement*. Beethoven decides to tune his drums to G and C instead of the usual tonic and dominant of the key, F and C. By so doing he is able to provide an effective dominant pedal, coupled with the trumpets, at the end of the second subject in both dominant and tonic keys (bars 53 and 153), as well as at the end of the development section (81). He was not the first to tune the drums in this way—Mozart did the same thing in the "Linz" symphony—but it was certainly unusual; and perhaps it gives some indication of his interest in the timpani and a foretaste of their effective use in, for example, the violin concerto.

The wind, too, is used rather more fully in this movement than was usual, as indeed it is in the symphony as a whole. In fact it was criticized by some of his contemporaries as being more like "wind-band" music than orchestral music. Notice the woodwind dialogue in the second section of the second subject, starting at 42. There is also the effective use of the oboe and bassoon in bars 97–9 leading in to the recapitulation.

The movement is in a very regular sonata form. It starts with sedate fugal entries in the strings, gradually building up to a climax. The first subject could end at bar 19 but the cadence is repeated four times, from 19 to 26. It ends with the dominant chord which can then lead straight into the second subject in the dominant key without any need for a transition.

There are three sections to this second subject, starting at 27, 42 and 54, the last serving as a codetta to round off the exposition. The first section uses the strings, the second the woodwind, and the third brings in the trumpet and drum rhythmic pedal previously referred to, under a figure of continuous triplets.

The development section takes the first two notes of the first subject and develops them, first in C minor, then (at 71) in D flat major. The dotted rhythm previously heard in the trumpets and drums is used continuously from 71 to 93. It reaches the dominant of the tonic key at 81 and starts a pedal which leads into the recapitulation at 101.

The first subject in the recapitulation is now accompanied by continuous semiquavers but is otherwise the same as in the exposition. The final dominant chord at 126, which in the exposition was used as a pivot to the dominant key, now leads straight into the second subject in the tonic. The second subject is just as before, apart from the change of key.

The coda starts at 163 with a return to the first subject and the second phrase of it is repeated sequentially in G minor (171–4) and B flat major (751–6) before reaching a perfect cadence in the tonic key at 182. Then the dotted rhythm is heard once again as a dominant pedal, with hints of the first subject above it. It gradually dies down to two notes of the tune alternating with one pedal note, until it reaches a *f tutti* perfect cadence at 193–5.

The *third movement* is called a minuet by Beethoven, but it is so quick that it is really a scherzo, the first orchestral one that he wrote.

The minuet starts with a tempestuous rush in the strings, and is obviously in one-in-a-bar rhythm. A series of sequences occur after the first double bar, ending up in the remote key of D flat major at 25. Now a little inner melody (s l t d′) is heard four times over a tonic pedal in D flat.

The next twelve bars (33–45) form a mysterious link back to C major, rising by semitones through B flat minor (35) and C flat major (39) to the tonic at 43. Notice that the first two notes of the first theme are used antiphonally in this passage. The return to the first theme occurs at 45 but it is now extended sequentially, so does not reach its cadence until 58.

Quite a long coda follows, with effective use of a Neapolitan sixth over a tonic pedal at 59, 62 and 64, followed by a perfect cadence repeated six times (67–79).

The trio alternates repeated wind block chords with quick violin passages. Notice that it is in the same key as the minuet. The first part modulates to the dominant and the second part returns immediately to the tonic, being based entirely on the dominant seventh until it returns to the first theme at 43. The music changes at 48 however, and the trio ends in the tonic key. The only unusual qualities in the trio are its speed and its use of the wind instruments as a block of sound.

The *finale* plays a trick at the beginning, as did the first movement. Otherwise it is quite a regular movement, very much in the style of Haydn, and is in sonata form.

It starts with six bars of *adagio*, in which a scale tentatively rises with an extra note at each attempt, until, after a pause, it turns out to be the first phrase of the *allegro vivace*.

The first subject consists of two sentences, bars 7–14 and 15–22, with the second sentence repeated at 23–30, differently orchestrated.

The transition starts at 30. It is typical "passage work" at first, but notice the figure in the lower strings starting at 46 and leading to the dominant chord of the dominant key.

The second subject starts at 56, and the first section consists of a gay tune over a springing bass. The second section, starting at 78, consists of imitations between wind and strings; and the codetta, starting at 86, is based on the opening bars of the first subject.

The development, after a reference to the opening bars of the first subject in the violin, begins to modulate. It reaches the key of B flat major at 108, and a few bars of *tutti* occur that are reminiscent of a *tutti* section in an early classical concerto. They are followed by further references to the opening bars, at first in the 'cello, and then, starting at 123, with imitative entries in all the strings. By 130 this has become a duet between first and second violins.

Another *tutti* section starts at 140, but this time the 'cellos introduce the theme from the transition that was first heard in bar 46. Bar 140 also starts a dominant pedal of the tonic key, which continues until the recapitulation starts at 163.

The first subject is as before up to 182. But then, instead of finishing with a perfect cadence in the tonic, it merges into the transition. This is considerably shorter than before, and is based entirely on the 'cello theme first heard in 46.

The first and second sections of the second subject, starting at 192 and 218, are exactly as before, except that they are now in the tonic key. The codetta, starting at 226, is based on the same idea as before, but the bass now falls instead of rises.

The coda starts after the pause at 236. It is reminiscent of the introduction at first, though it is still *allegro*. But at 243 the first subject gets under way again and is heard in its entirety. At 266 eight bars of cadential chords are heard, with the horns well to the fore, and they are repeated immediately with the addition of the opening scale from the first subject. These two ideas are then continued to the end of the movement.

Sir George Grove, in his book on Beethoven's symphonies, says that this movement is the weakest part of the work, and has an antiquated flavour of formality. In other words, it is too like Haydn for his taste. But that was written over sixty years ago. It is doubtful whether musicians of today would agree—they are not as sure as Grove was that Beethoven is always an improvement on Haydn and Mozart.

Symphony no. 2, in D, op. 36: Beethoven

The second symphony was composed in 1802. Though appearing soon after the first symphony it is a much longer and more ambitious work. Yet it belongs, in style, to Beethoven's first period, though the piano sonatas comprising op. 31, which were written about the same time, bear much more evidence of maturity. It is also coincident in time with the famous letter he wrote to his brothers, which is full of the tragedy of his loss of hearing. Yet the symphony bears no evidence of this, and is predominantly a happy work.

It is scored for the usual classical symphony orchestra: two each of flutes, oboes, clarinets, bassoons, horns, trumpets and drums, and the usual strings. But the woodwind instruments are used more independently than in most works of the period. For example, the clarinets start the theme of the second subiect of the first movement; and they repeat the two halves of the opening theme of the second movement after they have been played by the strings. The oboes open the Trio; and there is an effective use of the bassoon at the end of the exposition of the Finale. Such individualization was still comparatively rare.

Horns, trumpets and drums are used mainly for punctuation in the noisier passages, as was customary at this period, and, as usual, no trumpets or drums are used in the slow movement. But there are occasional imaginative uses of the horn, as, for example, in bar 8 of the introduction to the first movement, in bars 90–3 in the slow movement, and in the opening bars of the scherzo. There was not much that could be done with the restricted brass instruments of this period: they had less interesting parts than they had had in the time of Bach and Handel, when the higher ranges of the harmonic series were used.

The symphony opens with quite a long *introduction*, rather in the style of Haydn. After an opening unison *ff tutti* chord a theme is introduced in the woodwind and then repeated by the strings. Then follows a series of scalic passages in strings and wind alternately over or under slow quaver *arpeggios*. The music modulates freely, but finally gets to a dominant pedal at 24, over which imitative figures, based on triplets, build up a *crescendo*, leading into the *allegro*.

This is a vigorous, almost martial, *first movement*. Its first subject is predominantly rhythmic, and after the first regular eight bars it is extended another six bars by the addition of a counter-theme in the wind and a development of the last bar of the theme in the bass.

The transition starts at 47 with the first subject figure in the bass, and touches on G major (51), G minor (55), and B flat major (59), before reaching the dominant pedal of key A at 61, over which a new figure is heard in the violins.

The second subject starts at 73 in the usual dominant key. The first part of the rather square but vigorous theme is heard *p* in the clarinets and bassoons, and is then answered *ff* by the strings. After a decorated repetition of this (81–8) a second section starts at 88. It bears a rhythmic resemblance to the first bar of the transition figure first heard at 61, but this syncopated first bar is now developed and used in imitation between the strings and the wind. An extended cadence (96) breaks off abruptly at 101, and after a pause a *pp* entry of the first subject in the strings starts the codetta at 102. It ends with an extended and noisy plagal cadence (120–32). A two-bar link leads back to the repeat of the exposition or on to the development.

This starts with a statement of the first subject in D minor, followed by a development of its last two bars (142–6). Then the figure is used in imitation between lower and upper strings against a counter-theme in quavers, and leads to a *ff* statement in C major (158). This contains further development of the semiquavers of the first subject and leads into a quiet statement of the second subject in G major at 182. Again the second half of the theme is developed in imitation. Then (at 198) a dotted rhythm appears in F sharp minor which has some affiliation to the first bar of the second subject. It ends on a *ff* C sharp, which changes to a sudden *p* at 212 (typical of Beethoven), and then crescendos into a dominant chord of the tonic key and diminuendos into the recapitulation at 216.

The first subject is as before, but the first four bars of the transition are different. By 233 the music is the same as 61 except that it is a fifth lower, as it is now on the dominant of key D instead of key A. The second subject, starting at 245, is in the usual tonic key. Its opening bars are played by the oboes instead of the clarinets, and the scoring is, in general, fuller than in the exposition. There is the same discordant *ff* chord at 273 as in the exposition, leading to the *pp* semiquaver figure starting the codetta.

The coda starts at 303, and is based on the first subject. It works up to a climax and has a final reference to the first subject at 350.

The *slow movement* is again in sonata form. The first subject is in two stanzas, each played first by the strings and then repeated by the wind. The transition starts at 32, and consists of a tuneful figure treated in imitation between wind and strings. It leads into the second subject in the dominant key at 48. This consists of four distinct sections starting at 48, 55, 75 and 82, and the last is particularly tuneful. There is no repeat.

The development starts at 100, with the first subject in the tonic minor. The second, third and fourth notes of the theme are then developed by imitation and ornamentation starting *p* at 108, and again *pp* at 118. Bar 128 starts a *ff* treatment of the subject in F major, and leads to a development of the second section of the second subject at 138.

The recapitulation begins at 158. The transition changes at 198 so as to lead to the second subject in the tonic. A coda starts at 264 and is based on the first subject. This leisurely and tuneful movement is easy to follow.

The *scherzo* returns to the tonic key, and is in a quick one-in-a-bar rhythm, with humorous alternations between *p* and *f*, and between strings and wind. The first section ends in the usual dominant key, and the second section modulates to B flat major. A dominant pedal of the tonic key starts at 33 and leads to a return of the opening theme at 39. This is extended by quiet repetitions of the crotchets, getting to F major at 59, where the oboe and bassoon enter with a development of the theme.

The trio starts in oboes and bassoons with the addition of horns at the cadence. The second section is, by contrast, entirely in the strings, and is built solely on the unexpected chord of F sharp major. It leads to a return of the opening of the trio at 109 in the wind as before, but this time it is afterwards repeated in the strings, with several *tutti* cadence extensions.

The abrupt modulations in this movement, sometimes to quite unrelated keys, are a feature which must have shocked Beethoven's contemporaries, but which delight us today.

The *finale* is the third movement of the work to be in sonata form. The first subject is distinctly odd in character and rhythm, and a great deal of use is made later of its first two notes. Notice their use in bars 12 and 14, and in decorated form in 16 and 18, even before the first subject has come to an end.

The transition starts at 26, and is quite as important and tuneful as the two main subjects. The opening bar in the 'cellos is imitated in the second violin and viola. Then the clarinets and bassoons take it up at 32, followed by the flute a few bars later.

The second subject enters in the dominant at 52, with imitations between clarinet and oboe. It is then repeated with different instrumentation in the minor, and now even the bassoon has the tune for a whole phrase. C major is reached by bar 80, and is followed by a *tutti* passage returning to the tonic key. Notice the link bars (98–108) in which the first two notes of the first subject are tossed about in the violins against an effective bassoon arpeggio.

Bar 108, which heralds the return to the first subject, might be thought by some people to be still part of the exposition and to prove the movement to be in sonata-rondo form. But it changes key very soon and the pages which follow are full of development of the first subject instead of being a contrasting episodical theme, so that bar 108 feels more like the beginning of the development section of a movement in sonata form. It is quite common to repeat the beginning of the first subject at the start of a development section.

At bar 116 the theme moves into the minor key; then bar 119 begins to develop the second limb of the first subject theme, while at 126 the last two crotchets start a further development by themselves. At 131 the quaver part of the first subject is developed against minims in the 'cello, and the two rhythms are heard four times in different parts of the orchestra.

Having heard all three figures from the first subject developed separately, we now hear a new variant in the bass starting *f* at 139 in B flat major, and this is heard for some time against *staccato* crotchets derived from its last two notes. But the first two notes are not going to be left out for long, and they interrupt at 165. They finally win the day, and lead to the recapitulation at 185. But notice the pauses and the changes from *ff* to *pp* which make this passage, and indeed the whole movement, so humorous.

In the recapitulation the first subject is as before, and there is the usual change in the transition—at bar 220—so as to lead to the second subject in the tonic at 236. Apart from slight changes of orchestration the music is then nearly the same as in the exposition until it merges into the coda about 290.

The first subject is hinted at twice *pp* and then bursts out *f* at 294. After one complete statement it begins to change key at 303.

Bar 312 starts a series of references to the transition which come to an end on a *ff tutti* pause at 334. Then comes a magical descending bass repeated several times, over which hints of the first two notes of the first subject are thrown out. Notice the four *staccato* crotchets which first appear *pp* in the bassoon at 346, separated by crotchet rests. They are heard as *legato* minims at 358 in the wind, and finally (at 362) in augmentation, in semibreves. All this has the effect of slowing down the music until it almost comes to a standstill with six bars of the chord of G major, *pp*. But then, with Beethoven's love of the abrupt, we have a *ff* discord at 372 followed by eight bars of dominant harmony in the tonic key.

However, we are still many pages from the end, because this is a very long coda. The first two notes are toyed with again; and then, at 403, the complete first two bars are heard, leading to yet another *ff* pause at 414. Then comes the descending bass from 338, interrupted by the first two notes and a pause. This is repeated, and is followed by a *ff* statement of the complete first two bars, which heralds in the final *tutti* climax.

The symphony as a whole is vigorous and tuneful, but the first three movements give little hint of what comes later. The last movement, however, is so original and full of surprises that it must have puzzled Beethoven's contemporaries, and it gives us a foretaste of the giant of the future.

Leonora Overture; no. 3, in C, op. 72(b): Beethoven

Beethoven's thoughts often turned to the writing of opera, but he would consider only great and noble subjects, and he could never find a suitable libretto. So all he actually produced was the one opera, "Fidelio", a story of a noble wife's devotion to her husband. It was produced in Vienna during the Napoleonic invasion in 1805, and was revised in 1814. Beethoven was so self-critical that he wrote no less than four overtures to this opera, in his attempt to find the ideal form. They are now known as "Leonora" nos. 1, 2 and 3, and

"Fidelio". It was this last which became the overture of the opera. "Leonora" no. 3 is the longest and greatest, but it is on such a scale that it is quite unsuited to be merely a prelude to a longer work. It is, however, often performed as a "concert" overture. Students should read Tovey's masterly articles on the overtures in vol. IV of *Essays in Musical Analysis*.

The overture is scored for a large orchestra: two flutes, two oboes, two clarinets, two bassoons, four horns (two in C and two in E), two trumpets, three trombones, drums and strings. The horns are in two keys so that more notes are available—from two harmonic series instead of one. The overture is in C, but the second subject is in E major in the exposition, so the horns in E come in useful here. At the end of the exposition they have a long rest during which, in Beethoven's day, they changed to C crooks, so that all four horns could play in C from the recapitulation to the end. Nowadays, of course, all four parts are played on the valve horn, which can play any note just by pressing down a valve.

Trombones were in common use in a theatre orchestra, as they have dramatic possibilities in an opera. They were not so common in a concert orchestra, though Beethoven began to use them in his later symphonies.

The overture starts with a romantic *introduction*, though it is not as long as that of "Leonora" no 2, because Beethoven did not want it to overshadow the rest of the overture. The theme in clarinets and bassoons at bar 9 is taken from the aria that Florestan sings in prison. Notice that the music has already shifted from C major to A flat major, and by bar 20 it is in B major—these are rapid changes to remote keys. The music returns to A flat major with a gigantic crash at 27. Then dominant harmony of key C from 33 to 36 leads into the *allegro*.

The *allegro* is in a free kind of sonata form with a long coda. The famous theme of the first subject is in violins and 'cellos over a tonic pedal in the double bass. The chords change very slowly—I for eight bars, VIIb for sixteen and V for eight—finally leading into a *ff tutti* repeat of the theme at 69. This merges into a transition, starting about 92, in which bar 3 of the first subject is heard in the violins by inversion. The music begins to move away from the tonic key at 102, and leads into the second subject at 120 in the unexpected key of E major.

This second subject begins with two themes, one in the horns (compare bar 9), and one in the violins doubled by a flute. The second section of the second subject starts at 144 and makes use of syncopation. A codetta starts at 154, when a figure based on the first subject is used in imitation at half-a-bar's distance in the four string parts. Some strong syncopation occurs at 168, but the music quietens down to a cadence in E major, the key of the second subject, based on the descending figure from the first subject. The violins are then left alone, apart from some quiet chords on the bassoon which change quietly and romantically to E minor at 188. Then (at 192) a sudden *ff tutti* chord marks the beginning of the development.

The development section is full of rapid alternations of *ff* and *p*. The *piano* sections are based on the first subject, and they lead eventually to *f* imitative entries of the first subject at 252, starting in C minor. The music works up to a climax; and 264–7 seem to be about to lead to the recapitulation, but a rush of scales leads to the unexpected and highly dramatic trumpet call in the remote key of B flat major. It is the trumpet call heard from the watch tower in the opera, which heralds the coming of relief for Florestan. At a concert performance it is often played "behind the scenes" to heighten the dramatic effect. The theme which follows is the melody which Florestan and Leonora sing in thanksgiving. The trumpet call is heard again, a little louder, and the song of thanksgiving is then heard in the remote key of G flat major.

Eventually the music leads to the dominant key, and the first subiect returns in this key at 330. The Boosey and Hawkes analysis suggests that the recapitulation starts here. But it is also possible to consider that it starts with the *ff* return of this theme in the tonic at 378. After repeated hearings the student should decide which he feels to be most like the recapitulation. It depends a good deal upon whether he considers the return to the theme or the return to the tonic key is the more important. Personally I feel that Beethoven has not said the last word about development at 330, and that the *crescendo* from 364 onwards is intended to lead to a grand recapitulation in the tonic. Certainly 378 corresponds to 69 rather than to the opening bars of the *allegro*, but a *ff* return is dramatically right here.

Bars 378 to 389 correspond to 69 to 81; then a change occurs, which can be considered as a transition leading to the second subject in the tonic at 404. The next part is very similar to the exposition except for the key, and it leads to a coda starting at 460. Florestan's aria (i.e. the second subject) occurs again at 468, and a long dominant pedal starts at 481, with an effective part for the timpani, which keeps up the suspense. Suddenly a *presto* whirlwind of scales starts in the violins at 514, which leads into a *ff tutti* of the first subject at 534. The horns and woodwind play the second subject theme at 554; and the syncopation which starts *p* at 570 moves rapidly to an exciting and prolonged climax, ending with a triumphant re-statement of the first subject at 614.

Egmont Overture, op. 84: Beethoven

Students will probably know something about Germany's greatest poet, Goethe. They will know of his famous drama based on the old legend of "Faust", which has been used as a basis for a choral work by Berlioz, a symphony by Liszt, an opera by Gounod, an overture by Wagner, and for various works by many other composers. They probably realize that the poem of Schubert's song "The Erl King" was written by Goethe, and may know of other poems of his set by Schubert, Schumann, Mendelssohn, Liszt or Brahms. Those students who know German will probably be familiar with some of his work, but all should realize his greatness.

In addition to the incidental music to Goethe's play "Egmont", Beethoven set two of his poems for chorus and orchestra, and nine as songs for solo voice and piano. The two men met in 1812, two years after the production of the "Egmont" music, when Goethe realized how much Beethoven's growing deafness was affecting him socially, as well as musically. Although each realized the greatness of the other, it is doubtful if they had much in common.

A series of performances of "Egmont" was planned for the Vienna Court Theatre in 1810 and Beethoven wrote nine incidental numbers for it in addition to the overture, though his music was not ready until a month after the opening performance in May. Beethoven enjoyed the theatre and writing for it. He was envious of Mozart's success in the theatre, but his deafness prevented his being any use at rehearsals. His one opera, "Fidelio", was not very successful.

The "Egmont" overture is practically a symphonic poem. It concentrates upon the historical significance of the tragedy, rather than its human relationships. There is a heroic, dramatic contrast of themes, and the work expresses oppression, conflict and victory. At the same time, it falls into the customary sonata form.

The scoring is for the standard classical orchestra of the period, except that in order to have more notes available, there are *two* pairs of horns, crooked in different keys, and the second flute player changes over to the piccolo in the coda. It was unusual to include the piccolo at this period, and its shrill voice adds most effectively to the climax.

The introduction contains two contrasted themes. The opening chords in the strings can be considered as expressing the oppression of the Spanish tyranny, and the contrasting theme (starting with imitations in the woodwind in bar 5) the sorrow of the downtrodden Netherlanders. Alternatively, the string theme can be taken to represent the hero, Egmont, and the woodwind theme the heroine, and her love for Egmont. Both interpretations are in print, but, as far as is known neither is an authentic expression of Beethoven's intentions. There is, however, no doubt that Beethoven was expressing the elemental contrasts that are inherent in the story.

Notice the violin quaver figure that first appears in bar 15. After a number of repetitions combined with the chords of bars 2–5, it appears in diminution in bar 24, and then gathers speed, becoming the accompanying figure which starts the *allegro* in bar 25.

The first subject of the exposition appears in the 'cellos at bar 29. Notice that it begins with the same curve as the previous quavers, and therefore has a link with bar 15 of the introduction. There is certainly a feeling of discontent and revolt in this section. A second section to the first subject starts at 43, and its rhythm adds to the intensity. It leads to a *tutti* repetition of the first section theme at 59.

The transition starts at 66 and is built on the rhythm of the second section theme. It gradually moves to the relative major, in which key the second subject enters at 82. This is based on the introduction (bars 2–5) but it has a different answering phrase. The contrast between strings and woodwind is still present, however. Notice the enharmonic change at 91–2, and the resulting modulation to the brighter key of A major. But the music is back in A flat major again by 98, where the second section of the second subject appears. A codetta starts at 105 over a tonic pedal; and it leads into the development section at 116.

At the beginning of the development section (116–46) the first two bars of the first subject are thrown from one instrument to another. At bar 146 the complete phrase appears in C major, combined with the quaver figure of the second section of the first subject. The continuous quavers that led into the exposition now lead into the recapitulation, which starts at 163.

The recapitulation is very similar to the exposition for some time, though the orchestration is rather fuller. At bar 200 an extra six bars appear, as compared with the exposition, and they lead into the transition, which starts at 207. This begins in D flat major instead of F minor, and it might be expected to lead to the second subject in F, (the tonic key) thus rising a third, as happened in the exposition. But it does not work out like that, for the second subject appears, at 225, in D flat major, the subdominant key. So also does the second section, starting at 241. Even the codetta (247) is still in D flat though, apart from the change of key, bars 225–59 are the same as in the exposition. However, there is still some distance to go before the end of the overture, so Beethoven has plenty of time to re-establish the tonic key.

Bar 259 corresponds to the end of the exposition at 116. It is possible to consider that the coda starts at this moment; or alternatively one may feel that 259–86 is an extension of the recapitulation, and that the coda starts at 287. Bars 259–86 consist of the second subject theme followed by the codetta theme, first in D flat major, then in B flat minor, finally reaching F minor at 275. Four *ppp* chords in the woodwind lead to the *allegro con brio* in F major, which works up to a tremendous climax. The tyrant Duke of Alba ordered the trumpets to drown the farewell speech of Egmont; and Beethoven here quotes his "symphony of Victory", used in the closing scene of the play.

Symphony No. 5 in B Flat: Schubert

Schubert wrote two symphonies in B flat: no. 2 when he was seventeen and no. 5 in 1816, when he was nineteen. All the first six symphonies are cast in the mould of Haydn and Mozart, and the scoring is typical of most of their works. Schubert wrote no. 5 for an amateur orchestra, which did not possess clarinets, and it was quite customary to use only one flute. He also used no trumpets or drums. Schubert took longer to develop as a composer in his symphonies than he did in his songs, though there are unmistakable Schubertian touches in these early symphonies. But they cannot compare with his last two mature symphonies, the "Unfinished", and the "Great" C major, which were written for a large professional orchestra.

The opening bars of the *first movement* are unusual, starting as they do, in the wind, in semibreves, with a perky quaver interruption in the violins. The first subject proper starts at bar 5, with imitations between violin and 'cello based on a simple chord scheme of primary triads. At bar 19 the figure is inverted and the imitations are between flute and violin, while at 26 the flute begins to use the quaver run first heard in bar 10. The first subject is unusually long, and ends, with Ic V I, in bars 40–1.

The transition, which starts at 41 over a tonic pedal, is a *f tutti* that reminds one of the *tuttis* used to separate the *concertante* sections in a *concerto grosso*, or of a *tutti* between the solo sections of a Mozart concerto. It is based on the first subject; and at bar 51 it begins to change key, passing through G minor (53), C major (55) and B flat major (57), before reaching the reiterated Cs in bars 63–4, which prepare for the second subject in the dominant.

The second subject (65) is a graceful charming tune with a haunting lilt. The strings have it first, then the wind, with perky interruptions in the strings. An interrupted cadence at bar 80 transfers the cadence figure from wind to strings and from F to D flat major, and the idea is extended to bar 92. From 92–107 is a long codetta. Notice the alternate ascending and descending minims in bars 92–108. Bars 108–17 reiterate the dominant and tonic chords.

The development begins by making use of the five introductory bars, combined with a diminution of the first subject figure from bar 5. The chords are repeated sequentially in D flat major (118–21), B flat minor (122–5), G flat major (126–9) and E flat minor (130–3). Notice how far Schubert has travelled from his tonic key. Modulatory freedom was a feature of all his works.

At bars 134 the diminuted first subject figure is left to itself, and modulates to F minor (140 and 144), and D flat major (141 and 146). Then it gradually quietens down, loses its quavers, and gets to a B flat pedal at 157. This, with its subsidiary chord on C flat, turns out to be a dominant of key E flat, in which key the recapitulation starts at 171.

Schubert quite frequently starts his recapitulation in the subdominant key. It is then possible to repeat the exposition note for note and end in the tonic key, though sometimes he does make changes. In this movement, for example, the inversion of 19–22 is omitted at 185; and bars 215–28 omit the imitations of 53–61. But the second subject is the same up to 276, when an extra *tutti* passage is inserted. Bars 292–end correspond to 110–18, the end of the exposition.

A tabulated analysis of the rest of this symphony follows. Students may find it helpful to see how to lay out the essential facts in this way.

Second movement

This is in a clearly defined form, but one which has not been given a name.

I. Ternary form.

A. 1–8. Main theme in E flat major. 1–4, strings alone, repeated *tutti*. Tonic.

B. 9–17. A development of the main theme, modulating into F minor (10), followed by a sequence, returning to tonic key; cadential two bars repeated.

A. 18–24. A varied repetition, tonic key, as before. Cadence bar repeated twice.

four-bar link (24–7) leading to II

II

C. 27–41. Dialogue between wind and strings. Beginning in C flat major, an unexpected and romantic change. Note the enharmonic change at 34, from C flat major to B minor. Is in G major by 39.

D. 41–66. 41–52 G minor; 52 begins a repeat a fourth higher in C minor, but with bass transferred to treble in first few bars. Gets to dominant pedal of tonic key at 59.

I.

A. 67–71. Strings only, exactly as before. 71–4, *tutti* as before, but now decorated in melody.

B. 75–83. Exactly as before.

A. 84–9. Now in tonic minor.

four-bar link (90–3), a fourth lower than before

II. Almost identical with first II, a fourth lower.

C. 93–106. As before, but in G flat major, changing to F minor.

D. 107–17. First two bars are repeated so as to get to dominant of tonic key immediately. The section is therefore shortened.

I. Now consists of **A** only.

A. 118–21. Strings only, tonic key, as before. 122–8, repetition contains imitation between wind and strings.

Coda

128–end. Two phrases, each repeated.

Third movement

Minuet and trio form.

Minuet

A. 1–26. Tonic key, modulating to relative major. It consists of an eight-bar sentence followed by an extended eighteen-bar answer. Compare bar 11 with bar 3, and notice how the second sentence is extended first by a pedal (15–18) and then by a chromatic scale (19–23).

B. 27–56. A development of **A**, starting in relative major. Notice how the phrase in the violin (27–31) is imitated in the 'cello, then violin, then 'cello again, passing through G major and C minor. A dominant pedal of the tonic key is reached at 51.

A. 57–88. Notice the extension at 63, and the six-bar phrase with the tune in the bass, falling in thirds, in 69–74. It is repeated. Then, at 81 the music becomes similar to 19, but now in the tonic key.

(Some authorities would call this minuet ternary, because **A** returns; others would call it binary, because it is in two repeated sections, with the first **A** ending in the relative major, and therefore being incomplete. If possible, avoid the use of either term.)

Trio

C. 89–104. Tonic major. Tune very similar to that of the minuet.

D. 105–20. A six-bar phrase in D minor followed by a similar one, a tone lower in C major, but now extended to ten bars.

C. 121–8. A repetition of the second phrase of **C**.

(This would be called ternary by most people, because the first section ends with a perfect cadence in the tonic key, and is therefore complete in itself.)

Notice the prevalence of pedals in the trio.

Finale

Sonata, or first movement form. Very regular.

Exposition

First subject. 1–47. A simple, tuneful theme in binary form, with the second half repeated.

Transition. 47–78. Passage work, leading to dominant key.

Second subject. 79–152. Dominant key. First section 79; second section 111; third section 125.

Development

153–67. A development of the first two bars of the first subject, in imitation between lower strings and wind.

167–75. A similar passage, but with imitations between 'cello and violins.

175–83. One bar imitations between 'cellos and wind.

183–209. Chromatic quaver movement combines with syncopated crotchets.

209–36. Dominant pedal of tonic key, over which the chromatic quaver movement continues.

Recapitulation

First subject. 237–83. Exactly the same as in exposition.

Transition. 283–320. Modified so as to lead to second subject in the tonic. The striding minim figure is the same, but the semiquaver scales are missing.

Second subject. 321–end. Almost identical with the second subject in the exposition, except for the change of key.

No coda.

Symphony in B Minor (The Unfinished): Schubert

It is surprising how many people think that this symphony was unfinished simply because Schubert died in the middle of writing it. Actually, these first two movements were written when he was only twenty-two, six years before his death. But then, as with the "quartetsatz", he lost all interest in the work, and did not return to it, except for making a few sketches for a scherzo and scoring the first nine bars of it. He was seriously ill soon afterwards, so perhaps he unconsciously associated the work with an unhappy period of his life, and was loath to return to it. He did not write another symphony until 1828, the year of his death, when he produced what many people consider the finest of all his works, the "great" C major.

However, Professor Tovey considers the "Unfinished" to be the finest of Schubert's larger works, perhaps because it is unusually terse and well constructed as compared with the rather repetitive meandering of the "great" C major symphony. But both are full of haunting tunes, and both are highly dramatic. They both use trombones, which were still comparatively rare in symphonies, and this adds to their splendour.

The "Unfinished" symphony was intended for a musical Society in Graz, but was never performed there—probably they were waiting for the complete symphony. It was never performed anywhere in the composer's lifetime, though the manuscript was sent to Hüttenbrennen, a friend of Schubert's, and a director of the Graz Society, who did all he could to get his friend's music better known. As he lay dying, in 1865, he passed the manuscript on to the conductor of a Viennese music society, and it received its belated first performance in Vienna that year.

The mysterious opening of the first movement in the 'cellos and basses is one of the great moments of music, which repeated hearings does not stale. It appears, at this stage, to be merely introductory, and the theme which follows at bar 13 teels like the first subject. But the introductory theme is made much more use of later than is the theme starting at 13, so perhaps it is better to consider them both as sections of the first subject.

The theme which starts at bar 13 is unusually melodic for a first subject, and perhaps that is why it is not made use of in the development section. It is also unusual in that it is played by oboes and clarinets in unison. Modern orchestrators consider that one tends to kill the other and that any discrepancies between the intonation of the different instruments will be shown up. But perhaps Schubert was not quite sure that good players on the new instrument, the clarinet, would be available. Schumann doubled instruments in the same way in his symphonies, later; but it is generally felt that, in his case, it was because he was not a very good conductor, and he was playing for safety, in case an instrument failed to come in.

A repetition of this oboe–clarinet theme starts at 22, but this time it is extended, with full orchestration, and reaches its climax and ending with a perfect cadence in the tonic key at 37–8.

We now expect a transition. Sometimes Haydn plunged straight into the second subject in the new key without a transition at all. Usually Mozart had some rather obvious kind of passage work which made the listener aware that the second subject was due. Beethoven made his transitions more significant, more an integral part of the whole. But Schubert rarely wrote such highly organized transitions. Here the transition is short and direct, but how poetic and satisfying it is! Tovey calls it a *coup de théâtre*.

Schubert intends to get to the key of G for his second subject. This, in itself, is unusual. The usual key would be the relative major, D major; and G major is on the flat side of the tonic, which is rather difficult to manage so early in a movement. But see how he does it: a single long, *fp* note, in horns and bassoons, which lasts long enough to make us forget that it is the mediant of B minor, and then melts into three chords which establish it as the dominant of G major. There are other instances where Schubert does the same sort of thing, and the effect is always magical. Elgar must surely have had Schubert in mind when he wrote the held tonic, G, at the end of the eighth Enigma variation, which becomes the mediant of E flat major and leads with such calm beauty into "Nimrod".

The second subject has a lilting, tuneful melody, first in the 'cellos, then in the violins. The submediant major key sounds reposeful after the restless B minor section, and the lilting effect is largely caused by the syncopated accompaniment.

It sounds, at 61, as if Schubert is about to repeat the melody for a third time, but he breaks off abruptly, and after a bar's pause, has a *ffz tutti* interruption which is highly dramatic.

However it ceases equally abruptly at 71 and the syncopated accompaniment returns, followed by a development of the third bar of the second subject, starting *p* in D minor and making a *crescendo* through C major (76), A minor (78), G major (80) and D minor (85), with upper and lower strings having the figure in imitation. This is, in effect, development, before the actual development section is reached.

A series of strong, syncopated chords lead to a perfect cadence in G major at 92–3, and the codetta which follows is based on imitative entries of the first two bars of the second subject. This has been quite a long second subject, but it has been based entirely on one theme.

A *ff* chord, reminiscent of the beginning of the transition, starts a short link of *pizzicato* chords which lead back to the repeat of the exposition or on to the development section.

And now we see why Schubert has developed his second subject in his exposition. It is because he does not intend to use this melody at all in the development section, though he does make frequent use of its accompaniment figure. Nor does he use the oboe–clarinet theme that we have probably previously thought of as being the main first subject. Instead he devotes the development section almost entirely to the introductory theme in the 'cellos and basses, which now assumes a much greater importance than we had expected.

The development starts in 'cellos and basses in E minor (114), but sinks at 118, instead of rising as before, and drops by slow dotted minims to C, the lowest note on the 'cello. This is another wonderful moment in the symphony. Now the violins take it up, followed by the violas in imitation, while the 'cellos and basses play their low notes *tremolo*, gradually rising to F sharp. Over this F sharp, now treated as a dominant pedal, the violins have the first three notes of the theme by inversion against the 'cellos in its original form, both playing strenuously in a high register. Schubert makes full use of the extremes of register available to him in this section. The music reaches a climax on an unexpected G sharp at 146, and then sinks down the chord of C sharp minor.

At 150 we hear the syncopated accompaniment figure from the second subject played pathetically all by itself for four bars, but then the storm breaks out again for another four bars. These two ideas alternate most dramatically until the whole orchestra breaks out with the first theme *ff* in unison in E minor at 170. It continues in the trombones and lower strings at 176 while the upper strings rush around furiously in semiquavers.

A dotted figure in brass and drums is added, at 184, to the bass theme, which now appears in imitation between upper and lower instruments of the orchestra. The music reaches a *ffz tutti* climax at 194 with an inversion of bars 1–2, which is then repeated *pp*. After another contrast in intensity we at last hear a reference to the oboe–clarinet first subject theme, at 208. But it consists of the rhythm rather than the melody, and its purpose is to lead into the tonic key and the recapitulation.

The recapitulation starts at 218 with a repetition of bars 9–20. Bars 1–8 are not used, obviously because they have been used so very much in the development section, and the oboe–clarinet theme breathes an air of solace after so much strenuous conflict.

But, perhaps to make up for the fact that he has not used this theme in the development section, he now proceeds to extend and develop it for some time. It passes through E minor at 231, and after hinting at, but not establishing, a number of other keys, reaches F sharp minor at 252.

The transition starts at 252, exactly as before, but now it leads to the second subject in the key of D major. The tune is very definitely a major one, and D major is the relative major of B minor. All the same it is more usual to have the same tonic at this stage, and Schubert will have to allow time later to re-establish B minor as tonic.

Bars 256–75 correspond exactly to 42–61, except for the change of key, But, instead of having a pause, as at 62, Schubert continues the last two-bar phrase in descending sequence, so that he does not reach the pause bar till 280, and the crash that follows is in E minor, which bears the same relationship to the tonic B that C major at 63 did to G major, the main key of the second subject in the exposition.

From now on all is plain sailing. Bars 281–322 correspond to 63–104, but now centred round the tonic key, and with the codetta in B major.

The next six bars (322–8) are the same as the link which occurred at the end of the exposition, but this time they lead to the coda.

The *coda* begins with the introductory theme, as at 1–8. Then it is used in imitation between upper and lower strings, and blazes up to another climax at 352. It occurs three times more: *pp* in the woodwind (352); upper strings (356) and lower strings (360); and the movement ends with four sharp chords.

The opening of the *slow movement* in the unexpected key of E major gives a wonderful sense of peace after the unhappiness of the first movement. It illustrates Schubert's fine sense of key contrast.

The movement is in modified sonata form but, in spite of having no actual development section, it contains a good deal of development.

The first three bars form a most poetic opening, full of warm tone colour. The horns and bassoons play three simple chords in the middle register while the double basses play *pp pizzicato* quavers against them, Then, lightly poised over the top, comes a slow, ethereal tune in the violins. The first six bars are repeated, but this time they modulate to C sharp minor at the end. A discord at 14 is followed by a curving semiquaver figure which is much used later, and which leads back to E major.

The *pizzicato* quavers start yet again at 16, but this time they lead into G major. The curving semiquaver figure from 15 is used in imitation between wind and strings at the end of this, and it returns again to E major.

Now follows (at 33) a loud *tutti* section with a tune in wind and brass accompanied by *staccato* quavers in the strings. But, in spite of sounding so different, it bears a resemblance to the first theme, with a *staccato* quaver bass and a tune with similar rhythm above it. One might have though it was the beginning of the transition, particularly as it begins to modulate (through B major at 40 to C sharp minor at 44). But the first theme returns in the tonic key in an abbreviated torm at 45. So the theme at 33 must be considered a second section of the first subject; and the first subject as a whole could be said to be in ternary form, with the second section a development of the first.

When the first section returns, bars 45–52 correspond to 9–16, and 52–6 correspond to 28–32 with wind and string parts changed round. So it is obviously considerably curtailed. Then bars 1–3 are stated twice in the tonic key at 56–60, to bring the first subject to an end.

The transition, like the transition in the first movement, is very brief, but equally poetic. A long quiet G sharp is held in the violins. It is the mediant of E major but becomes the dominant of C sharp minor. It quietly rises an octave and then gently falls to the mediant and the tonic and into the second subject which is in C sharp minor, the relative minor.

This has a syncopated accompaniment, similar to that of the second subject of the first movement. The tune starts quietly in the clarinet and modulates through D major (73), F major (74) and

D minor (76) before coming to rest in C sharp major at 82. An enharmonic change then occurs and the oboe takes up the tune in D flat major. Oboe and flute alternate in repeating the last two bars, getting softer each time, until a *ff tutti* entrance of the second section of the second subject occurs in C sharp minor at 96.

This is really a development of the first section, but it is so completely different, both in intensity and orchestration, that it sounds almost like a new theme. The original tune is now *ff* in the bass, and the accompaniment is *ff* syncopated quavers instead of *pp* syncopated semiquavers. When it is repeated at 103 demi-semiquavers are added in oboe, violins and violas.

This breaks off suddenly in D major at 111, and a third section of the second subject starts. This, too, is a development of the first section. It reverts to the syncopated quaver accompaniment of the first section, but the first two bars of the theme are the beginning of an eight-bar melody which occurs in imitation between lower strings and violin. It is heard twice, ending in G major at 121 and in C major at 129.

In spite of the fact that we are now in C major, while the second subject started in C sharp minor, it appears as if this is the end of the exposition. It has contained as much development as any development section. The first subject contained two sections, the second being a development of the first; and the second subject contained three sections with the last two being a development of the first.

Now follows a short link leading to the recapitulation, and dying down to *ppp*. It is based on bars 114–15, the second and third bars of the third variant of the second subject, and is heard imitatively in flute and oboe (130–1), and bassoon and horn (131–2). This is repeated and is then followed by the same figure minus the semiquavers, alternating between various woodwind instruments and the horn. During this time there has been a syncopated pedal on C, and it quietly slides up to C sharp at 140, ready for the return to E major. The horn is most effective in these few bars.

In the recapitulation the first section of the first subject (142–73) is exactly as before. The second section starts in the same way, but moves to A major at 181 instead of to B major, and then to F sharp minor at 183, so that the first section returns at 186 in A major instead of the tonic. Otherwise it is the same.

The transition is the same, except that it is in A instead of C sharp; and so is the first section of the second subject, now in A minor. In the second section, starting at 237 and still in A minor, the melody and bass have changed round and the orchestration is different. Otherwise it is nearly the same until 252, when it reaches F major. Then bars 250–3 are repeated over V VI in E major, and the recapitulation ends in the same way as the end of the first subject in the exposition, bars 257–68 being an enlargement of 50–6 and in the same key, the tonic.

The coda starts at 268 with the *pizzicato* bass of the opening, but the first three chords in horns and bassoons now form the beginning of a lovely new melody in flutes and oboes. This is repeated in the horns at 274–80.

Now the violin plays the transition figure *ppp*. It takes us into another world, particularly when a C natural is added and leads to four bars of the first subject *ppp* in A flat major. It is rounded off with the semiquavers first heard in bar 15. Bars 280–90 are then repeated, ending in E major. From here the music moves quietly to the end of the movement, with a series of cadential repetitions followed by the *pizzicato* quavers of the opening bars.

This is a very wonderful coda, and the whole work is so full of romantic beauty that it is tragic to think, not only that Schubert never heard it, but that the world was unaware of it until 1865, by which time romanticism had spread its mantle over music, and Schumann, Chopin and Mendelssohn were dead. The symphony was before its time, and perhaps if it had been heard in 1822 it might have considerably affected the development of music in the intervening years.

14

German Lieder

Students who wish to study certain songs, perhaps for examination purposes, should first get to know them by singing them, and should become so familiar with them that they can quote from them, or recognize quotations given by an examiner. They should realize that the approach to a song is rather different from that to a sonata or a symphony. Detailed structural analysis is less likely to be required, but the student should know something about the poet (if he is of any importance) and of the methods which the composer used to achieve the mood and atmosphere required by the words.

The songs discussed in this chapter were all written by German composers in the nineteenth century. It is interesting to compare the outlook of the composers who wrote them: Beethoven, half classic, half romantic, who was not at his best in vocal writing, and who did not realize the possibilities inherent in the accompaniment; Schubert, also half classic, half romantic, who had a much greater feeling for the poetry of the words, who realized to what an extent the piano "accompaniment" could be a partner to the voice, and who really established the German Art song; Schumann, more romantic than classic, to whom poetry meant so much, and who set to music some of the finest romantic poetry; and Brahms, a disciple of Schumann, who knew the songs of his greatest forerunners, and who was able to add his own incomparable tone colour to the art of Lieder writing.

Beethoven wrote over seventy songs, but they are rarely heard today. His earliest songs, such as "Adelaide" and "Ah Perfido" are classical in style, and might easily be arias from an opera. By the turn of the century he had begun to realize that the dramatic possibilities of the poem could take precedence over the formal construction; and a song such as the well-known "Creation's Hymn" is an early example of the "Art" song. But he still usually set each verse to the same tune (strophic), as in the song cycle discussed below; and the accompaniments, though varied, are rarely used to enhance the dramatic situation.

Schubert came at a moment of time when the rise of romantic lyric poetry and the development of the piano made possible the combination of the two in the "Art" song. He realized the potentialities more than did Beethoven, and songs such as "Gretchen am Spinnrade" and "Erlkönig", which he wrote when he was only a youth, sound a depth of poetic-musical feeling that was wholly new. Poetry inspired him, whether it was the great poetry of Goethe, Schiller or Shakespeare, or inferior verses written by his friends, and Schubert instinctively let the words decide the form of the music. Some poems of a simple style were set strophically, with the same music for every verse; other, more elaborate poems were composed as a continuous whole, *durchcomponirt*; while others used a mixture of the two styles.

He instinctively developed musical figures, rather in the same way that Beethoven developed his themes in sonata form, and he used similar key schemes, though he had a particular fondness for a sudden change from minor to major mode, and vice versa, when the colour of the words asked for such a change.

Schubert wrote over six hundred songs, and obviously only a representative few can be discussed here. Most of his songs were written as separate items, but he wrote three long song-cycles: "Die Schöne Müllerin", setting twenty poems by Wilhelm Müller in 1823; "Die Winterreise", twenty-four poems by the same poet in 1827; and "Schwanen Gesang", consisting of seven poems by Rollstab, six by Heine and one by Seidl, in 1828, the year he died.

The story of the Wandering Miller, told in Müller's poems,

originated in a family charade. In the first cycle the miller gets employment at a mill, where he falls in love with the miller's daughter. But another suitor, a hunter, comes upon the scene. The miller confides his sorrows to the brook, and then once more goes on his way. Most of this cycle of songs are happy, though when he wrote them Schubert was seriously ill. In the second cycle the lovesick miller continues his wanderings, and most of the songs are now full of melancholy, sixteen of the twenty-four being in the minor key.

In addition to six songs from "Die Schöne Müllerin" and the twenty-four songs of "Die Winterreise" discussed below a few of his other songs are described. He wrote four versions of "Erlkönig" and five of "Die Forelle", while the tune of "Der Wanderer" haunted him sufficiently for him to use it in a piano solo, "The Wanderer Fantasia". "Die Forelle" was used in the "Trout" quintet, and "Der Tod und das Mädchen" gave its name to the quartet which used its tune in its slow movement.

Three of the songs discussed below are set to words by Goethe: "Erlkönig", "Gretchen am Spinnrade" and "Heiden Röslein", while "Ave Maria" is taken from Scott's "Lady of the Lake". But any poem seemed to have the knack of starting off a flow of melody, with an accompaniment which heightened the effect of the words in some wonderful way.

Schumann was almost as interested in literature as he was in music, and his approach to both was essentially romantic. He was a disciple of the writer "Jean Paul" in youth. He set many poems by Goethe, Heine and Burns, and a few by Byron, Shelley, Shakespeare, Thomas Moore, Schiller and Hans Anderson, as well as many by lesser poets. His accompaniments have the same kind of warm, rich harmonies that one meets in his piano music. But some of them have "dated" rather more than have Schubert's, and at times one feels they are too sentimental.

He wrote several song cycles. "Dichterliebe" is one of the most famous, and several of the songs from this cycle are discussed below.

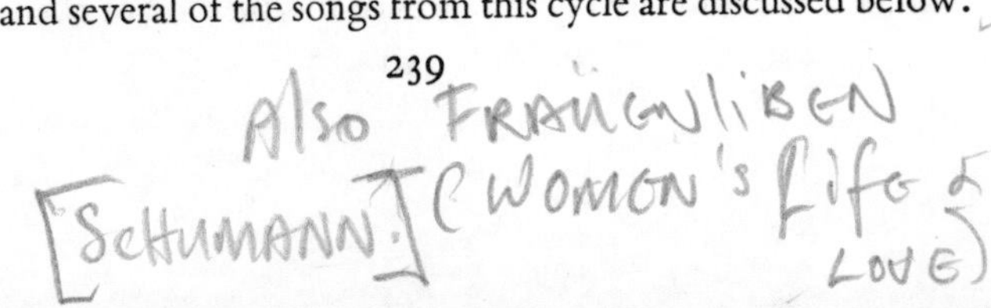

Brahms' songs reach a high level rather more consistently than do Schumann's, though his style was certainly influenced by both Schubert and Schumann. His finest songs show an originality, a power of development, and a warm, though sometimes sombre colouring which are typically Brahmsian. He had a strong sense of melody, and his rhythmical freedom and breadth of design show up particularly well in his songs. But poetry meant rather less to him than it did to Schumann, and his approach to the words of a song was musical rather than literary.

Brahms also wrote a number of songs in simple folk-song style, as well as arranging a large number of German folk-songs, including those written for the Schumann children.

A miscellaneous collection of his songs are discussed below, including the two songs for contralto, viola and piano, op. 91.

German Lieder are published in several English editions with different translations. Also they can frequently be obtained in different keys, for high and low voice. So, in order to avoid confusion the original German titles are given in the comments which follow, and key relationships to the tonic are stated instead of particular keys being named.

An die ferne Geliebte: Beethoven

This song cycle was written in 1816, when Beethoven was forty-six, and had been in Vienna for many years. Jeitteles, who wrote the poems, is a little-known German poet, and these are the only poems of his that Beethoven set. The similarity to Müller's "Die Schöne Müllerin", which Schubert set, is very marked. There are touches in the music, too, which make one wonder if Schubert knew this song cycle, and unconsciously adapted some of the ideas. Look, for example, at the link between songs 1 and 2, in which one note is played seven times, being *me* in the tonic key at first, and, in the course of the reiteration, becoming *doh* in the mediant major. Schubert has some lovely instances of this method of changing key.

Then notice the change from major to tonic minor in the third and ensuing verses of song 3, again a common device with Schubert. This change fits the colour of the words. But surely Schubert would not have set song 5 strophically, keeping the same cheerful major tune at the reference to "tears" near the end of verse 3. One feels that Schubert has taken a number of hints from the Beethoven songs, and improved upon them.

The first song consists of five short verses, set strophically, but with variations in the accompaniment. In song 2, the vocal melody goes into the piano part in verse 2, while the voice sings on one note, thus making a dominant pedal. It gives an impression of quietness which fits the words, and again, perhaps, one thinks of Schubert's "Der Tod und das Mädchen", where Death sings so expressively on one note. Song 3 has two verses in the major key and three in the tonic minor, while song 4 has three simple strophic verses with an accompaniment in triplets throughout.

The verses are rather longer in song 5 and contain modulations to the relative minor and subdominant major, but the accompaniment is almost identical in all the verses. The sixth and last song returns to the key of song 1. It breaks off in the middle of the second verse, and leads into a coda which is based on the first song.

The whole cycle is very slight, with modulatory links between each song, thus giving a continuity more like that of Schumann's "Dichterliebe" than that of the Schubert song cycles.

Die schöne Müllerin, nos. 1–6: Schubert

"*Das Wandern*", *no.* 1, is a simple strophic song, with a continuous murmuring of the brook in the accompaniment, during which the miller expresses his desire to wander. After four bars of introduction the voice enters with a three-bar phrase, which is extended to four bars by the accompaniment. This is repeated, and is then followed by an eight-bar phrase consisting of a two-bar section repeated in sequence, and a two-bar refrain which is repeated *pp*.

In "*Wohin*", *no.* 2, the miller sets off on his journey, and asks the brook for guidance. The song is *durchcomponirt*, and the form is very free, but it is consistently constructed and the phrases are all four bars long, except for a two-bar interpolation at bars 40–1 and an extended eight-bar phrase at the end. The brook murmurs in triplets throughout the accompaniment, and there is a tonic pedal in bars 1–10, which returns whenever the opening theme is repeated, and adds to the deliberate monotony of the ever-flowing brook.

When phrases are repeated they are often varied or developed in some way. In the tabulated analysis which follows, a development of **A** will be labelled thus: $\mathbf{A}^{d}$.

First section

1–2 Piano introduction in tonic key, on tonic pedal.

3–6. **A**.

7–10. **A** repeated. Pedal ends.

11–14. **B**. Modulates to supertonic minor.

15–18. $\mathbf{A}^{d}$.

19–22. Repetition of the last four bars, i.e. $\mathbf{A}^{d}$, therefore ending the first section with a perfect cadence in the tonic.

Middle section

23–6. **C**. Modulates through relative minor to dominant major.

27–30. **D**.

31–4. $\mathbf{D}^{d}$.

36–9. **E**. Modulates through supertonic minor towards relative minor.

40–1. A two-bar interpolation to the words "Wohin? sprich wohin?".

42–5. $\mathbf{C}^{d}$. Establishes relative minor.

46–9. **D**. Now in relative minor, instead of dominant major as before.

Link

50–3. Four bars returning to the first section and the tonic key.

First section

54–7. **A** in tonic.

58–61. **A** repeated, as before.

62–5. **C**, modulating through relative minor to dominant major, as before.

66–9. **D**^{d}. On the same chord scheme as the first **D**, but now in tonic, in which key the music remains to the end.

70–3. A further development of **D**^{d}.

Coda

74–81. An extended form of **A**^{d}.

"*Halt*", *no.* 3, is again *durchcomponirt*, and tells the story of the Miller's arrival at the house where he is later to get work and meet "die schöne Müllerin". It is on the plan **A B C D**, but many short phrases are repeated and the style and the accompaniment are the same throughout, so the song has unity.

Introduction

1–11. Rather a long, bustling introduction. The figure in the first half-bar is used throughout the song.

12–22. **A.** Modulates to subdominant key at the end of the first phrase, which is surprisingly early for a modulation to the flat side of the tonic. But the music returns to the tonic in the second phrase, and the last two bars of it are then repeated.

23–31. **B.** Dominant major. Four-bar phrase repeated. Ends with a sudden change from major to minor in the accompaniment.

32–34. **C.** Returns to tonic key and stays there to the end of the song. The construction of this section is rather more elaborate: two bars voice; one-bar accompaniment; a developed repetition of the first two bars in voice; one-bar accompaniment; four-bars voice; same four bars repeated.

46–end. **D.** Four bars repeated with a different ending, followed by a cadential phrase repeated. There is a tonic pedal in the last eight bars.

"*Danksagung an der Bach*", *no.* 4, introduces "Die schöne Müllerin". The miller asks for employment, and realizes that here is work for both his hand and his heart. The acccompaniment is quiet and contemplative after the bustle of the previous song, but it again keeps to one figure throughout. The phrasing is more irregular than in the first three songs.

1–4. Introduction. Sets the quiet accompaniment figure going.
4–10. **A.** A six-bar sentence in the tonic key.
11–18. **B.** Eight bars, ending the same as **A.**
18–21. Link. Same as introduction.
22–6. **A**^{d}. A five-bar sentence starting in the tonic minor, and modulating to the flattened mediant major—an unrelated key.
28–31. **B**^{d}. Returns to the tonic key, but with internal subsidiary modulations.
33–8. **A.**
38–41. Coda. Same as introduction.

"*Am Feierabend*", *no.* 5, is an exciting song in ternary form. The accompaniment is full of fire and impatience, and the introductory seven bars use firstly the brusque quaver chords that are the basis of the middle section, and then, at bar 5, the semiquaver figure which is used throughout the first section.

The first section (8–24) gives a feeling of enormous vitality, yet with quite simple means. It consists of four phrases, the last of which is beautifully extended to five bars at the thought of "Die schöne Müllerin" in 21. Notice also the syncopation in this bar. The section ends in the tonic major.

Bar 25 changes back to the tonic minor, clouding over as the miller impatiently thinks of his weakness, and wishes he could prove his strength to the girl. The middle section starts at 26 with the brusque chords used in bar 1. Notice that the underlying rhythm still consists of two quavers and a quaver rest, as did the rhythm of the bass of the first section; but now it starts on the first part of the beat, instead of being anacrusic. It effectively gives a feeling of frustration. The music modulates at 29 to the relative major, and vacillates between this key and the tonic key for the next few bars.

A quieter recitative-like passage follows (38–59), modulating rather freely. This is a picture of the family circle round the fire. Notice the unusual discord at 54 which is repeated *sf* at 56.

Bar 59 returns to the boisterous flowing rhythm of the first section. Although it begins the same as the first section it is modified at 69, and 69–73 is repeated at 74–8.

A coda starts at 79, and returns to the contemplative recitative-like style, with a little burst of energy in the piano between the two vocal phrases. At 86 the piano quietly descends the scale to the tonic, and two loud chords bring the song to a finish.

"*Die Neugierige*", *no.* 6, is a thoughtful, delicate song, during which the miller enquires of the brook if the maiden really loves him. It consists of four stanzas on the plan **A B C B**. The first part, **A**, has a quiet simple accompaniment and modulates to the dominant. **B** is a *molto lento* section, in which the sound of the brook is heard again. It starts in the tonic key, but notice the change to tonic minor in 25 at "*Wir bist du Heut so stumm*". It returns to the major at 27, and the cadence (29–30) is repeated in 31–2, with an extra pathetic *appoggiatura* on the first beat.

C starts at 33 in a recitative-like style. There is a sudden change of key on the word "Nein", in 35. The voice rises a semitone, and the key rises a semitone, too, on its way to a cadence in the major key an augmented fifth above the original tonic, about as remote as a key can be. The last phrase is then again repeated with two *appoggiaturas* added. The modulations in this section are wonderfully effective.

An enharmonic change at 42 leads back to the tonic key and to a repetition of **B** which is modified at the end. The piano brings the song to a quiet conclusion.

Die Winterreise: Schubert

There are twenty-four songs in this winter journey. Brief comments on them all are given here. In the first song "*Gute Nacht*" the miller says farewell as he leaves the mill. The first four verses are strophic and in the minor key; but, in the last verse, Schubert moves to the tonic major as the miller thinks tenderly of the girl and say he will not wake her but will leave a farewell message on her door.

In the second song he compares her inconstancy with the fickle weathercock above the house. The two verses begin alike, but the first verse ends in the subdominant minor while the second, after several modulations, ends in the tonic major, though the final bars of the accompaniment return to the minor theme with which the song started.

"*Gefror'ne Thranen*", *no.* 3, a short, sad song, is followed by a longer, *durchcomponirt* song, "*Erstarrung*". This is in the nature of a duet between a 'cello-like tune in the left hand of the piano part and the voice. It is in ternary form, and in the last part of the first and last verses the left-hand tune soars up into the right hand as it reaches the climax. But it sinks again at the end, as the piano part sadly dies away.

"*Der Lindenbaum*", *no.* 5, rings the changes from tonic major to tonic minor, according to the mood of the words. Number 6 is a simple strophic song; but no. 7 is again *durchcomponirt*, and changes from minor to major as the miller communes with the river. In "*Rückblick*", *no. 8* he presses on in the wintry weather. There is an anguished start in the minor key but a change to the major as he thinks of his first meeting with the maiden. Numbers 9 and 10 are two short songs in the minor key, and continue the story of anguish.

"*Frühlingstraum*", *no.* 11, begins happily in a major key but reverts to the minor, as the miller wakens to reality and hears the raven's cries. And in *no. 12*, "*Einsamkeit*", he asks why the world should be so bright and cheerful while he is in such a wretched plight. The anguish in the accompaniment grows throughout this song.

"*Die Post*", *no.* 13, starts in more matter-of-fact mood, with the trotting sound of the horses bringing the post-chaise. But again it changes from major to minor as he realizes there is no letter for him. There are two verses, with the change of mood occurring in each verse. Number 14 is short and recitative-like, and is followed by "*Die Krähe*", a gruesome song, in which he imagines the raven is hovering around, waiting for him to die.

And so the lover proceeds, comparing himself with a broken leaf, no. 16; envying the peaceful villagers, no. 17; identifying himself with the stormy morning, no. 18; following an illusory light, no. 19; shunning the highway and following a by-road over the mountains, no. 20; being rejected at a wayside inn, no. 21; momentarily regaining his courage, no. 22; seeing three suns in a hallucination, no. 23; and finally, in the last song of the cycle, watching an old organ-grinder standing in the cold, ignored by everyone. This last song is stark and bare, with a double pedal and a monotonous little figure in the piano coming between recitative-like phrases in the voice part which sound equally mechanical and comfortless. Schubert has painted a wonderfully convincing picture here, with the minimum of material.

Brief Notes on Miscellaneous Songs: Schubert

"Erlkönig", "Gretchen am Spinnrade" and "Heiden-Röslein", all poems by Goethe, were set by Schubert in 1814 and 1815, when he was seventeen. It seems almost unbelievable that he could write so dramatically in the first song and so pathetically in the second, when he was little more than a boy.

The accompaniment of "*Erlkönig*" keeps up the movement of the rider throughout, while the boy, the father and the erlking sing in turn. Notice how the boy's voice rises higher in anguish each time he appeals to his father, with a very discordant clash at "Mein Vater", and how dramatic is the cessation of the piano triplets as the voice sings the last line in unaccompanied recitative.

"*Gretchen am Spinnradc*" has a continuous figure in the accompaniment, too, this time representing the movement of the spinning wheel; and it too breaks off when Gretchen stops the wheel at the thought of her lover's kiss. The repetition of the beginning at the end, as a kind of refrain, is also most effective.

By contrast, "*Heiden Roslein*" is a simple strophic song, which tells the story in an unsophisticated folk-song style. Notice the six-bar phrase in the middle of the verse, followed by a slow climb up the scale, leading to a pause, and then an *a tempo* ending.

"*Der Wanderer*" is more like a *scena* than a song, with frequent changes of mood. Notice the pedals in the first section, and observe how Schubert gets the changes of mood by means of different styles of accompaniment and changes of rhythm. The opening *lento* triplets recur near the end, as does the phrase "Ich wande still", imitated by the piano. But the song begins in a minor key and ends in a different major key. It is rare for any piece of music to begin in one key and end in another. It is even more surprising that the ending in the major key (the bright key of E major in the original) is very little brighter than the gloomy opening. Perhaps it is meant to express resignation, or perhaps ending in a "foreign" key is meant to express rootlessness.

"*Frühlingsglaube*" is a happy little song with two identical verses and a lilting accompaniment. It has an apt little touch of the minor at "Nun, armes Herz" in each verse.

"*Die Forelle*" is strophic, but with a most effective change of key and accompaniment when the fisherman makes the water muddy. The darting fish is charmingly portrayed, yet the song is essentially simple. The student should hear the variation movement of the "Trout" quintet, and compare it with the song.

"*Ave Maria*" is also strophic, yet very different in style. The student should read Scott's poem, "The Lady of the Lake".

Dichterliebe, Nos. 1–7: Schumann

Schumann set Heine's "Dichterliebe" in 1840, the year that he was married. He was so happy that he wrote over a hundred songs that year, most of them love songs. This set is a duet between voice and piano, with the piano often carrying on after the voice has finished. The songs are short and often incomplete, obviously being intended to be sung as a continuous song cycle. There are sixteen songs, and the first seven are discussed here.

"*Im wunderschönen Monat Mai*" (I) has a maytime grace and charm in the accompaniment, and consists of two short stanzas. The key is deliberately vague. The introduction is in a minor key and is based on the chords IVb V. But when the voice enters in bar 5 it moves away from this key and has its first cadence in the relative major at bar 6. The first verse ends (at 12) with a perfect cadence in the submediant major. The second verse is a repetition of the first, and then the piano ends with the IVb V of the minor key in which it began. It is just as unusual to start a piece of music with IVb as it is to end it with V, and nowhere is there a perfect cadence in the tonic key.

"*Aus meinen Tranen spriessen*" (II) moves to the relative major of the first song. It has an accompaniment which is little more than a support for the voice. The vocal part is in a *parlando* style, and its range is only that of a minor sixth. The phrases are on the plan (*a*) (*a*)(*b*) (a^d).

"*Die Rose, die Lilie*" (III) is nearly as simple as the previous song though the style is more vivacious. The key is the subdominant major of the previous song, and the vocal phrase-plan is (*a*) (*a*)(*b*) (*c*). But the last vocal phrase is extended to five bars, and there is an instrumental coda based on (*a*).

"*Wenn Ich in deine Augen seh*" (IV) begins quietly, with a calm produced by the almost static accompaniment, and the few chord changes. But it soon rises to an emotional climax in bar 8, where the first half ends. It is now in the subdominant major, which is unusual for the halfway cadence—the dominant, or some other key on the sharp side of the tonic, is much more common. But this song does not modulate to any key on the sharp side of the tonic. The second half moves to the relative minor at bar 10 and the supertonic minor at 14, before returning to the tonic at 16. When the voice ends at bar 16 the piano carries on the accompaniment figure for another six bars, and the song ends as quietly as it began, though with a sadder tinge.

Apart from the repetition of bars 9 and 10 in 11 and 12, no two phrases are alike, and the vocal style is almost that of recitative. Schumann has done his utmost to make Heine's words come through clearly and significantly.

"*Ich will meine Seile tauchen*" (V) is another short song, and the voice part is entirely developed from the first two bars. Bar 5 starts the figure a third higher, bar 9 repeats it at the original pitch, and bar 13 reverts to bar 5. The first half ends with an imperfect cadence at bar 8, while the second half is modified so as to end with a perfect cadence at bar 16.

But notice that there is a counter melody in the piano throughout. It consists of continuous quavers with broken chords underneath it. When the voice ends the piano carries on in the same style and rhythm as before, though the melody is different. The last three bars consist of repetitions of a plagal cadence.

"*Im Rhein, im heiligen Strome*" (VI) is longer than any of the previous songs, and as well as being a love song it contains an impression of Cologne and of the grandeur of its cathedral. Schumann was very attached to this city—Cologne was also the subject of his "Rhenish" symphony.

The accompaniment uses a dotted crotchet–quaver figure throughout, and flows with a slow dignified rhythm. The music starts in a minor key and modulates through the subdominant minor to the relative major, in which key the first section ends at 27.

Four bars of accompaniment lead to the second section, which again touches on the subdominant minor key before reaching the dominant chord of the tonic key by means of an augmented sixth chord at 41–2. The voice is left in the air at this point, and the piano rounds off the return to the tonic key. It then continues with a coda based on the opening bars, but now without the voice part.

"*Ich grolle nicht*" (VII) is perhaps the most famous of all the songs in this cycle. It is a cry of passionate despair, all the more effective for its simplicity. Quaver pulsating chords continue throughout. Two features of the song are the steady descending minim bass in the first half of each verse, and the passionate climax in the voice towards the end of the second verse. After this climax the voice sinks in grief to the end of the song. The reiteration caused by the many sequences in the song adds to the despair, as do also the poignant discords.

Two Songs for Contralto, Viola and Piano, op. 91: Brahms

In "*Gestillte Sehnsucht*" the voice and the viola have equally important melodic parts. The piano provides the harmonic basis, and it uses so many kinds of figuration that it conveys a feeling of restlessness in itself. The viola part has a certain amount of chordal accompaniment too, particularly in the middle section (bars 42–64). But at the beginning of the song it has the main theme, while the voice is silent. In bar 14 the voice enters with a counter-theme against the viola theme; and in bar 28 it goes on to the viola theme, while the viola part changes over to the accompaniment figures.

The middle section, starting at 42, is mainly in the tonic minor key. It returns to the major and to the viola theme at 55, but is back in the minor again by 59.

The first section returns at 68, though it is now without the introductory viola solo. However the viola has the coda (the last twelve bars) to itself.

This song could be said to be in ternary form. But the middle section has little real contrast of key or mood; and it contains the main viola theme of the opening section.

"*Geistliches Wiegenlied*" is based on an old carol tune which most students will know. The viola opens with the tune. The words are written underneath for recognition purposes, but are not meant to be sung. The voice never uses the tune at all, though the viola frequently refers to it.

The form of this second song is very similar to that of the first. The viola begins and ends it; and the plan is ternary, with a short middle section (74–89) in the tonic minor. But in this case the middle section changes its rhythm from duple to triple time, and it does not refer to the first section. Notice the cross-rhythms in the viola and piano parts in this middle section. The first section of the song is on the plan: **A** (1–22); **B** (23–33); link (33–9); **C** (40–57); **B** (58–68); link (68–74). Notice that **C** is very chromatic.

Brief Notes on Miscellaneous Songs: Brahms

"*Standchen*" has a zither-like accompaniment, and is in ternary form. The middle verse modulates freely—notice the enharmonic change in the middle.

"*Feldensamkeit*" conveys a wonderful sense of stillness, caused partly by the long vocal phrases, and partly by the throbbing bass and slowly changing chords. It is a very difficult song to sing, requiring great breath control.

"*Von Ewige Liebe*" is *durchcomponirt*. It consists of three parts. The first is descriptive, with two verses that are practically alike. They begin and end in a minor key, with modulations to the mediant minor, the dominant minor and the subdominant minor. The accompaniment has a rich, dark colour, typical of Brahms. Then follows a section which uses a theme from a wedding cantata which Brahms composed ten years earlier. The lover speaks, and an urgency comes into the piano part, which carries on for eleven bars after his voice has finished. The triplets work up, *stringendo*, to a climax as he finishes speaking, and then quieten down into the tonic major section when the girl replies.

She is quietly confident; and although triplets continue, they are low and calm, and the effect of contrast is heightened by the major key. An almost static effect is obtained by the rarity of the chord changes: tonic for seven bars; subdominant for three; supertonic for two; and dominant for eight bars. Her second stanza is similar to the first, but ends in the tonic instead of the dominant key, and works up to a climax and to a cross-rhythm of $\frac{3}{4}$ against $\frac{6}{8}$ in the accompaniment, which continues to the end.

"*Treue Liebe*" is a love song with a warm, rich, broken chord accompaniment. The first two verses are alike, but the third changes and becomes highly dramatic as the waters sweep over the girl, though it ends quietly.

"*An ein Veilchen*" is another love song with a warm accompaniment, though its style is different. It has three verses, and the second and third verses grow out of the first, with the second verse modulating freely and the third returning to the tonic key.

"*Wir wandelten*" again has three verses, with the second and third growing out of the first in a similar way. Notice the delicate canonic writing in this song.

"*Der Schmied*" is a simple, strophic song, in which the accompaniment magnificently gives the feeling of the blows of the hammer; and the large intervals in the voice part, swinging along in slow crotchet rhythm complete the picture.

"*Wiegenlied*" is another simple, strophic song, with a lilting, cross-rhythm accompaniment. It is syncopated, and yet it contrives to give a most soothing feeling.

"*Sandmännchen*" is one of the fourteen nursery songs written for the Schumann children. It is really an arrangement of a folk song.

15

Chopin, Schumann and Brahms: Piano Works

Chopin, Schumann and Brahms are frequently called romantic composers. Yet the term is a loose one and applies to them in varying degrees.

A romantic poet or musician is one who is more concerned with the message of his work than with its formal design. The message is usually an emotional one, and, in the case of music, it is often concerned with feelings or events outside the terms of music itself.

Although all works of art have some element of romance in them the romantic element came to the fore around 1800. Beethoven has been called the first romantic in music, and his music is certainly more emotional than that of his forerunners, Haydn and Mozart. But he was also very concerned with formal design, and the emotion was primarily musical rather than inspired by poetry or any other non-musical medium.

Of the three composers who are the subject of this chapter Schumann was certainly the most romantic. He was a great reader, particularly of romantic poetry and novels, he set romantic poetry in his songs, and his piano works were frequently inspired by non-musical subjects, as for example in both "Papillons" and "Carnaval" analysed below.

Perhaps Chopin is called a romantic with less truth. The springs of his inspiration were purely musical; and although he was at his best in writing short pieces, often in rather irregular forms, he did not give his pieces fanciful titles. But the poetic tone-colour of his music appeals to the romantic element in the listener.

Brahms was even less of a romantic. He was much influenced by Schumann, and something of the romantic texture of Schumann's piano pieces creeps into those by Brahms. But although he, too, wrote short piano pieces, their inspiration was purely musical, and they usually had vague titles, such as intermezzo and rhapsody. Brahms was very much concerned with form and design, and unlike Schumann and Chopin, was a master of the larger forms such as are to be found in chamber music and the symphony.

In the chapter on Beethoven's piano sonatas there were comments on the development of the piano. But although Beethoven made good use of the sustaining pedal, and of the increased range available, he did not fully realize the possibilities of an essentially pianistic style, any more than he realized its value in his songs. He was so much of a classicist that he was more concerned with the essential musical message than with experimenting in new mediums.

So he left the development of the piano as a sensitive accompaniment to the voice to Schubert and Schumann, and the development of pianistic idioms in piano solos to Chopin and Schumann.

Chopin experimented with all kinds of pianistic figuration: spreading arpeggios, delicate arabesques, melodic and harmonic effects that were quite new and belonged exclusively to the piano. He was a pianist himself, and all his finest music was written for the instrument he loved.

He was at his best when writing short works such as studies and preludes. It was natural that he should write Polish dances, mazurkas and polonaises, the dances of his native land. He wrote no less than fifty-one mazurkas in his short life, and three of them are analysed below.

But he was half Polish and half French, and he spent most of his adult life in France. He loved the social life of the French salons, and he was much sought after to play his waltzes to the company assembled there. Four of his waltzes are analysed below.

When Chopin attempted larger, more formal works, such as sonatas and concertos, he was less able to cope with the large-scale design. But his four ballades are very popular, and one of them is analysed below, together with his third and last piano sonata.

Schumann admired Chopin's piano music and wrote very warmly about it in his music journal. Nevertheless he developed a pianistic style of his own. It is well known that he wanted to a be pianist but met with opposition at home. When, at last, his mother gave permission for a musical career, Schumann conceived the foolish idea of tying back the unruly fourth finger, which damaged his hand so much that his career as a concert pianist was doomed. So he turned to composition instead, which was a greater gain for posterity.

Schumann wrote practically nothing but piano music until 1840. He composed seated at the piano, and his works are truly pianistic in style, though the method was entirely new. He developed a kind of orchestral polyphony in his piano writing, by clever use of the sustaining pedal, and by using chords in unusual positions, thus getting new pianistic effects. But he did not use the *bravura* style that one associates with Weber and Liszt, nor did he fully exploit the newly-extended range of the piano. He was fond of syncopation and cross-rhythms, and his harmonies were remarkably rich for the period. He began by composing small pieces, such as "Papillons", and he never attained a complete command over larger forms.

Although Schumann is perhaps better known today for his piano music than for anything else, his interests were much wider than Chopin's, and he wrote in many other mediums. But Brahms' interests were wider still. He wrote every kind of music except opera. He, too, was a pianist. He wrote three massive, but not particularly pianistic piano sonatas in his youth; and two fine sets of variations (one on a theme by Handel and the other on a theme by Paganini) belong to his middle years. But as he grew older his pianistic style became more subtle and intimate, and he wrote many short piano pieces of great beauty, three of which are analysed below. He is fond of widespreading harmonies, often rich and thick in the lower registers, and his magnificent powers of thematic development show in his piano music no less than in his other works.

Mazurkas: Chopin

The mazurka, a Polish country-dance, originated in that part of Poland near Warsaw where the Mazurs live. It was less strenuous and heroic than the polonaise, and was danced by peasants rather than courtiers. There are several types of mazurkas and the rhythm can be very varied, but all are in triple time, though the accents frequently cut across the triple rhythm, occurring on different beats of the bar in a deliberately wayward fashion. Mazurkas are based on folk songs, and are often split up into two or four short sections, each section being repeated. The sections are quite frequently six bars long. Often there is a drone bass, meant to be played by the dudy, the Polish bagpipe, and sometimes the music is modal, or even oriental. The mazurka is usually danced by four, eight or twelve couples, and the steps are often improvised by the dancers. The dance was quite well known in Europe before Chopin wrote his mazurkas. Some of his later mazurkas are quite elaborate, but the three analysed below come in the first three sets he wrote, and are comparatively simple.

Op. 6, no. 2, in C Sharp Minor

This mazurka opens with a drone bass on the tonic and dominant, as it would be played on the dudy. The accent is clearly on the second beat in the opening bars. But a study of the rhythms used throughout the piece shows an extraordinary variety, and the accent quite often comes on the third beat. The sections are eight bars long throughout. The mazurka consists of a number of separate tunes strung together as follows: **A**, 1–8; **B**, 9–16; **C**, 25–32; **D**, 33–40 in A major, repeated in C sharp minor in 40–8; **A**, 49–56; **B**, 57–64 repeated with slight variation in 64–72. Except for the **D** section it is in C sharp minor throughout. But notice the use of *fe* in the first bar of the **D** section, both in A major in 33 and C sharp major in 41. This is quite common in Polish music. The return of **A** and **B** at the end gives the piece as a whole a feeling of being in ternary form.

Op. 7, no. 1, in B Flat

This is one of the most popular mazurkas, perhaps because it is harmonically and structurally so simple. There is not a chord in the whole piece which is not a primary triad, and the form is obviously rondo. But the phrase structure of **A** is interesting. It starts with a four-bar phrase, then the rhythm of the last bar is repeated twice, thus extending the phrase to six bars. The next phrase is also six bars but broken up as 2+1+1+2, with the two odd bars in the middle using the same rhythm as the extension of the first phrase. The whole of this twelve bars is then repeated, thus making twenty-four bars. **B** starts in F major at 25. It consists of two four-bar phrases and has a tonic pedal throughout. **A** then returns, and is followed by a repetition of the whole of **B** and **A**.

C, starting at 45, consists of a single strand of melody in F minor over a double pedal on G flat and D flat. It could therefore be said that this section uses no chords at all. It is, again, eight bars long. Then **A** returns and the whole of **C** and **A** is repeated. These repetitions mean that, though on paper the form is **A B A C A**, in actual sound it is **A A B A B A C A C A**.

Op. 17, no. 4, in A Minor

Superficially this mazurka may seem a little like the last one, as it is also in rondo form. But there the resemblance ends. It is considerably more elaborate, harmonically and melodically, and has many points of interest.

Notice the inner melody, B, C, D, B, C, in the four bars of introduction, as its shape recurs elsewhere. **A** starts at bar 5 and is not harmonized in a conventional way. It is more like a wayward tune with a varied, descending drone underneath it. Notice the descending bass, A, G, F sharp, F natural, E. In bars 9–11 the bass and treble are in octaves and the music is very chromatic, with almost an oriental effect. The eight bars of **A** are stated four times, with the melody becoming more wayward and decorative each time. The arabesques are typical of Chopin.

B starts at 37 and is still in A minor. It is based on a dominant pedal, but notice the G sharp, A, G sharp, F sharp, G sharp, A which, though the changes only occur once a bar, are reminiscent of the inner melody in the introduction. Notice also the chromatic descending melody in the right hand, E, D sharp, D natural, C, which is used again, in augmentation, in the coda.

A returns at 45, and is stated twice, with further melodic variations.

C, starting at 61, is in A major, and is built on a double tonic and dominant pedal. Again there is an inner melody, this time in the right hand, C sharp, D, C sharp, which is similar to the previous inner melodies. Like **A**, **C** is stated four times. The first and third times are alike, but the second and fourth have varied melodic endings.

A returns at 93, and again comes twice, with yet more melodic variants.

Bar 109 starts the coda. It is based on **B**, but the chromatic tune E, D sharp, D natural, C, is now in augmentation, with the notes changing every two bars instead of every beat, and the pedal is on the tonic, not the dominant. The last eight bars form an extended cadence, with the introductory figure returning again at the end.

Waltzes: Chopin

The waltz originated in Vienna and derived from the old German peasant dance, the ländler. The waltz, however, moved to the drawing room and the palace, and has been associated with Vienna ever since the days of Mozart. Mozart himself wrote waltzes for the balls of Vienna, and Beethoven and Schubert wrote both ländler and waltzes, though they were slight and consisted of little more than a string of short sections.

The waltz, in its early days, was considered rather shocking. It was quicker than the stately minuet, and also less decorous, as the gentleman held the lady by the waist. But it rapidly swept over Europe, and has been popular as a dance ever since. It is associated with the famous Strauss family, and with other Viennese composers.

Chopin's waltzes, though written for the drawing room, were not, however, intended for dancing. He was so much admired as a pianist that the ladies and gentlemen in the salons listened attentively as he played.

Op. 18, in E Flat

This waltz begins on the plan **A B A B**; **C D C**, and it looks as if it is going to be in minuet and trio form, which is so common for dances. But, instead of a return to the first section, the music then goes on **E F E**; **G**. It is obviously better to think of this as a series of short waltzes, each in binary or ternary form, of the kind which Schubert used to write, though these are more elaborate. At the point where the **G** section ends Chopin apparently felt that a recapitulation would hold the piece together better. So, after a short link, **A B A** returns. It is followed by a coda, in which hints of **B**, **F** and **A** occur.

Op. 34, no. 1, in A Flat

This waltz starts with an introduction and then goes on to **A B**; **C D**. After a short link we retrace our tracks with **D C**; **A B**; **C**. The two-page coda starts with brilliant passage work, and continues with snatches from **C**. **C**, with its decorated repetition, is really the most important theme in this waltz.

Op. 34, no. 2, in A Minor

This waltz is quieter. The pedal effects in the first section and the minor key give it an unusually plaintive feeling for such a gay dance as a waltz. Its plan is: **A B C**; **D**; **B C**; **D**; **A**; coda ending with **A**. Again the first theme is not as prominent as later themes; and again it is no use trying to give a name to the form as a whole.

Op. 69, no. 1, in F Minor

This waltz is in rondo form. It is in a very simple style and phrases are frequently repeated. The following is a tabulated analysis:

A. 1–32. F minor. An eight-bar sentence repeated four times. The second time (9–16) is more decorative than the first; the third (17–24) is almost identical with the first; and the fourth (25–32) is like the second time except for bar 27, which is more decorative.

B. 33–48. E flat major. An eight-bar sentence, repeated at 41 with slight variants, notably the change of rhythm in bars 42 and 43.

A. 49–64. F minor again. Consists of the third and fourth variants of the first section.

C. 65–112. A flat major. Consists of two ideas. The first one is heard twice (65–72 and 73–80). The second one modulates to E flat but returns to A flat. It, too, is heard twice (81–8 and 96–105). In between the repetitions the first sentence is heard again (89–95). Finally, the first sentence is heard for the fourth time at 106–12.

A. 113–end. Two more repetitions of the first sentence in F minor. 113–20 is the same as 17–24; and 121–end is like 25–32 except for bar 123, which is even more ornate than before.

Ballade in A Flat: Chopin

"Ballade" is the French and German form of the English word "Ballad". The word is Italian in origin and signified a song sung while dancing. But in England we associate the word with long narrative poems and with the tunes to which they were sung.

Schubert and Brahms wrote songs which were ballads in the sense of telling a story, but, as in England, the connection with the dance had been lost. Brahms wrote four ballades for piano, and certainly one of these is connected with a story, as it is based on the Scottish ballad called "Edward". But the others have a romantic element too, and they seem to tell a story in music, though we are given no clue to it in words.

Chopin wrote four ballades for piano, and they too are romantic. They have plenty of musical meaning, but Chopin does not put it into words. They are all four in compound time, and perhaps he felt that this had a lilting story-telling element about it, similar to the feeling we have about our simple ballad metre rhythm in English.

They were written at different times between 1831 and 1842 and are longer than most of his pieces. They each took some time to compose, and as he finished one he started the next. The one in A flat, op. 47, is the third, and was composed during 1840 and 1841.

It may surprise students who are used to sonatas and symphonies that a movement as long as this should not be in a regular form that can be given a label. But Chopin often wrote in very free forms on a plan of his own. He was not very good at developing his ideas, and at making a piece hang together as a whole; so, where Beethoven or Brahms would start a development section Chopin would start a new theme. It is easy enough to hear what is happening at any moment in this piece, and if each theme is labelled **A**, **B**, etc. as it appears, an over-all plan emerges, even though it may be very unusual.

The opening theme, **A**, starts very simply, as if saying "Once upon a time". It is a short theme, with the tune in the bass in the second half, and it ends with a perfect cadence at bar 8. **B**, which follows, is still in the tonic key, but is much longer and more assertive. Notice the syncopation in the right hand—there is a great deal of syncopation in this ballade. Bar 17 starts an extension of the theme; and by bar 25 the style has become very brilliant, though this particular example of *bravura* passage work does not occur again. It modulates to C major, and leads to a return of **A** at 37, though this time it is a little extended. The section ends quietly with a perfect cadence in the tonic at 52, thus making a complete little example of ternary form for the opening section of the ballade.

The next section, from 52 to 115, also contains two themes. **C** starts in F major at 54. This is rather a surprising key. F minor is the relative minor, but F major has no close relationship to A flat major. However, by 65, when the theme **D** first appears, the music has reached F minor, and this key can be said to be the main key of the **C–D** section.

Notice the syncopated tune at the top in theme **C**–*me ray doh* in F major at 54–5, followed by *me ray doh* in C major in 56–7. This is repeated (58–62), and the cadence chord is extended for two bars. **D**, which starts at 65, grows out of **C**, and the tune is a little like an inversion of **A**. **C** returns at 73 in E flat major; then **D** returns at 82 with fuller harmonies than before, and ends with a perfect cadence in the tonic key at 88.

The extension which follows is rather like a codetta, and we think we are coming to the end of this section, but unexpectedly **C** returns at 105, and it is exactly as before. So this second section consists of **C D C D C**, with a long connecting link between the last **D** and **C**.

So far we have had what we might consider to be two main subject groups, and now follows a middle section, which lasts from 116 to 143, and might be thought of as a kind of development section, because the rhythm of the accompaniment of the opening bars has a resemblance to **B**, and 136 onwards is developed from **D**. In between, at 124–36, there is a passage of continuous light decorative semiquavers, typical of Chopin. But the prevailing key of this section is the tonic, which is certainly not usual for a middle section.

We might now expect a return to **A**, but what follows is a repetition of the *second* section, rather more decorative than before, and with the subdominant, D flat, as the prevailing key. **C** starts at 145 in D flat major, then **D** turns into the minor at 156, as it did before. But Chopin apparently feels that D flat minor is too difficult notationally, so he makes an enharmonic change to C sharp minor. From here there are continuous semiquavers for the rest of this section. When **C** returns in C sharp minor at 164 the theme has moved to the bass, and there is an ornate semiquaver pedal above it. **D** returns *ff* at 172—notice the tune at the top. Bars 178–82 are an extension in which *lah te doh'* appears in the tune in sequence in eight keys. By 182 we are in B major, a very remote key from A flat major. This section has been **C D C D** this time, without a final return to **C**.

What next? We might have expected a return to the first section to follow now. But Chopin is very far from home, as far as keys are concerned, and what follows is practically another development section, during the course of which he gets back to his tonic key. **C** appears at 184 over a dominant pedal of key E, and there is a hint of **A** at 188, still over the same pedal. Then the whole of 184–91 is repeated a semitone higher in F major at 192–9. The rising process continues: 200–3 is in G minor, and 240 reaches A flat major, the tonic, at last. The decorative pedals and the alternation of **C** and **A** continue throughout these bars. The crescendo from 208–212 over the dominant pedal leads at last to a full return of **A** in the tonic.

This tonic recapitulation starts at 212 and is a grandiose *ff*. It is extended at 218 and surprisingly reaches E major again at 225. However it is rapidly brought back to the tonic. The recapitulation of this first section is quite short and there is no reference to **B**.

A short coda starts at 230, and is based on the middle section figure from 116.

The plan of the ballade as a whole can therefore be summarized as I, II, development, II, development, I, coda. Perhaps this might be said to have grown out of sonata form, but it stretches the term very much to include an example of this sort in it. However we have had the essentials of good form: contrast of themes and keys (though the keys relationships are unusual), some development, and a return to the first theme and the tonic key at the end. If the piece hangs together well, and the listener feels satisfied, what do labels matter?

Sonata in B Minor, op. 58: Chopin

This sonata was dedicated to the Countess de Perthuis, and was written in 1844, five years before Chopin died. It is one of his latest and most mature works, with many original and beautiful passages.

The *first movement* is in sonata form, though the development section merges into the recapitulation and the first subject does not return in the tonic key.

The first subject consists of a number of themes, so it seems wise to follow Professor Tovey's system of calling them all "first subject group" rather than saying there is a definite transition section. The first theme ends on the dominant chord at bar 8 and is then repeated in the subdominant key. Bars 12–16 develop the opening semiquaver figure and then the second theme starts at 17 with an abrupt modulation to B flat minor. It moves towards G minor in 18, but then heads off with a diminished seventh in 19, and after a few rhapsodic bars leads to the third theme at 23, which oscillates between D major and D minor. The fourth theme starts at 31 in D minor and reaches a dominant pedal of key D, the relative major at 33, which eventually leads to the second subject at 41.

The second subject also consists of a group of themes. The first theme starts in the conventional relative major at 41 and consists of a long melody with spreading arpeggios underneath, typical of Chopin. The second theme is another long-breathed melody in rhapsodic style, and starts in F sharp minor at 56, though it soon returns to D major. The third theme starts at 66 and is more broken up. It leads to a perfect cadence in the relative major at 75–6 and is followed by a codetta. Bars 88–91(a) form a link leading back to the beginning of the exposition.

The development section starts with a continuation of the link theme for some bars and then leads to a development of the first theme of the first subject at 96–7, starting in the tonic key and moving to F sharp minor. By 108 it has reached C minor and then passes sequentially through F sharp minor at 110, A flat major at 112 and C major at 114.

At 117 there is a reference to the second theme of the second subject in D flat major. Its third bar (58) appears in the left hand at 121 and then the theme is repeated in the right hand at 123 in E flat major. The bar 58 figure returns in the left hand at 129–30, and the music modulates freely in the next few bars.

Then, at 133, there is a return to the second theme of the first subject. In spite of the fact that it is in G sharp minor and not the tonic key and that there is no return of the first theme of the first subject, the music appears to be recapitulatory from this moment. Bar 138 corresponds to 31, the fourth theme of the first subject, so that the third theme as well as the first, is omitted. But at this point the music returns to the tonic key. So the return to both first subject and tonic key has been very gradual. The dominant pedal of the tonic key is reached at 140, corresponding to 33; and by 148, when the second subject appears, the recapitulation has returned to normality.

The first theme of the second subject starts at 148 in the tonic major and is almost identical except for key. The same applies to the second theme (163) the third theme (173) and the codetta (183). Bars 195 to the end form a short coda over a tonic pedal, in which the opening semiquaver figure is built up to a climax.

The *second movement* is in minuet and trio form, and is in E flat major, as remote from B minor as it could well be.

The minuet section is based on one idea only and is cast in a continuous whole without repeats. The theme starts in E flat major and is repeated in G minor at 17 and in F major at 25 before returning to E flat major at 34. The only contrast is therefore that of key, though the key scheme gives a feeling of ternary form.

The trio section is more normal in form, though it starts in B major, which is very unrelated to E flat major, the main key of the movement. It does this by means of an enharmonic change, E flat, the tonic in 60 becoming D sharp, the mediant of the new key, at 61.

The first part of the trio is based on a series of pedals: B (61–8); C sharp (69–73); F sharp (73–6); B (77–88). The middle part, starting at 189, is more varied, though pedals still occur. There is a cadence in F sharp minor at 98–9, then the music slips down to F minor at 103 over a tonic pedal. The pedal slips down again to

E at 109, and the A flat upper pedal changes enharmonically to G sharp, the key being changed to A major. The dominant pedal lasts for sixteen bars, and then slips up again to F sharp at 125. This marks the return to the beginning of the trio, though in the first four bars the pedal is on F sharp, not B. Bars 125–52 correspond to 61–88, so that the form of the trio is ternary, too.

Bars 152–6, which are identical to 89–92, form a link leading to the return of the minuet section, which is an exact repetition.

The *third movement* is in episodical form, and it opens in the original key but now in the major mode. After four bars of introduction the main section starts a long, slow melody, which comes to an end with a perfect cadence at 26–7. It consists of four four-bar phrases on the plan (*a*) (*a*)(*b*) (*a*), followed by a codetta from 20 to 27. Bars 27–8 are a link modulating to the episode in E major.

The episode is built of eight-bar phrases on the plan (*c*) (*d*)(*c*) (*d*), followed at 61 by a development of (*c*) and at 69 by a development of (*d*) lasting for ten bars (79–90). Notice the inner melodies in cross-rhythm in (*c*), and also the movement in consecutive fifths in the outside parts in 31–2. The first (*d*) (37–44), modulates from E major to G sharp minor, its mediant minor; but when (*d*) returns at 69–78 it modulates from G sharp major to E sharp minor, its relative minor, enharmonically written as F minor, at 71. Another enharmonic change at 77 leads to the return of (*c*) in E major at 79.

The episode is joined to the return of the main section at 90–8 by means of the codetta to the main theme, first heard at 21. Bar 99 starts the return of the main section, but the accompaniment is more flowing than it was before and the equivalent of 11–18 is omitted, so that 105 corresponds to 19. A short coda starts at 113.

The *fourth movement* is based on two subjects on the plan **A B A B A**, but the key scheme is unusual.

After eight bars of introductory chords the first subject enters in B minor. It swings along with an easy gait, reaching a climax at 24 and then falling by semitones until (at 28) it starts a repetition two octaves higher. The semitone falls are again reached at 44 and are repeated at 48 an octave lower with a cross-rhythm, reaching a perfect cadence in the tonic major at 52.

The second subject starts at 52 in the tonic major, It is unusual for the second subject to have the same key as the first, but it soon begins to modulate. It has reached D sharp minor by 57 and D sharp major on the first beat of 60. It returns to D sharp minor at 68 and reaches F sharp major, the dominant key, at 76. Semiquaver "passage work" in the right hand over broken chords in the left then follows, but it soon moves away from the dominant key and reaches B major at 84. It settles on dominant harmony on B from 90 to 99, and this leads into a return of the first subject in E minor, the subdominant minor.

This is a complete return of the first subject, based on an unusual key—one would have expected the tonic key for the return of the first subject. There are other small differences—the accompaniment is in quadruplets throughout and the repetition is one octave, not two octaves higher.

At 142 *te*, D sharp, enharmonically becomes *doh*, E flat in 143, and the second subject is now repeated starting in E flat major, another very unexpected key. It reaches G major on the first beat of 151, which is the same relationship to E flat major as D sharp major was to B major at the first appearance of the second subject. But by 159 it has reached C minor, not G minor as would have corresponded to the first statement. The passage work starts at 167 as before, but in E flat major, the tonic not the dominant of this section. It reaches A flat major at 175 and E flat minor at 182.

A link starts at 183. It is based on bar 60, but at first it runs round A flat, not D sharp. It continues round a dominant seventh of D major, 187, and B minor, 191; and dominant harmony continues to 207, when there is a final return of the first subject, now in the tonic key.

The accompaniment is now in semiquavers and the repetition is two octaves higher, as in the first appearance. A four-bar extension starts at 250 and the subject ends with a major chord at 251, as it did the first time.

But this time it is the beginning of a brilliant coda in the major key. So the sonata ends in B major, though it began in B minor. It is fairly common, however, for works in a minor key to end in the tonic major, and it feels just as satisfying, because the tonic is the same.

Papillons, op. 2: Schumann

"Papillons" were partly composed in 1829 when Schumann was in Heidelberg and partly in 1831 when he was in Leipzig. He was therefore between nineteen and twenty-one years old. Bach and Jean Paul (Richter) were Schumann's idols in early life. Jean Paul's novel *Die Flegeljahre* (the Clownish Years), written in 1805 inspired "Papillons". (Jean Paul, 1763–1825, was a Bavarian, and a very romantic writer.) The penultimate chapter of this novel describes a carnival, and "Papillons" consists of a series of sketches for a carnival. The title "Papillons" is perhaps a trifle misleading, as it has nothing to do with butterflies, except in the metaphorical sense that the pieces are of a light, fanciful, inconsequential nature. Schumann later returned to the same idea in his larger work "Carnaval", op. 9, written in 1834–5, and in "Faschingsschwank aus Wien", op. 26, written in 1839.

"Papillons" is an ideal work to study, when first starting to deal with musical analysis, quite apart from any examination requirements. All the twelve pieces are short and the form is quite clear. They are meant to be played straight through, after one another, but there is great key freedom from one number to the next, although the first one and the last two are in D major. All but no. 2 are in triple time, which is a natural dance rhythm. Yet it is surprising what rhythmic variety Schumann obtains in spite of this limitation.

After a short introduction no. 1 is a dainty waltz in the hybrid form **A** :||: **B A** :||. The theme is used again in the finale and also comes at the beginning and end of "Carnaval". The chords generally change once a bar, as is usual with a waltz, but notice the syncopation at the beginning of the second half, and also the change of phrasing in bars 11 and 12 as compared with 9 and 10.

No. 2 starts in E flat major, which is quite unrelated to D major. It is very short and butterfly-like, consisting of four bars of introduction in E flat, followed by four bars in A flat major, repeated. It consists of continuous semiquavers, divided between the two hands.

Number 3 is in another unrelated key, F sharp minor, and is in ternary form, with the middle section in the relative major. It is entirely in octaves in both hands, but at the return of **A** the two hands are in canon. At the end there is an upper tonic pedal, while the bass finishes the phrase.

Number 4 sounds more like $\frac{6}{8}$ than $\frac{3}{8}$ time. It is still in F sharp minor and is in ternary form with the first **A** repeated before going on to **B**. When **A** returns after this, there is an effective *appoggiatura* in the third bar of the phrase, otherwise it is the same as before.

Number 5 is a polonaise in B flat major in ternary form. Notice the cadence at bar 8 which ends on a weak beat, a feature of polonaise rhythm. **B** modulates freely, and **A** returns with the tune in octaves, being modified near the end.

Number 6 is a miniature rondo, in D minor. **B** is in A major; **A** has its cadence extended by a pedal; and **C** is in F major.

Number 7 again has a short introduction, followed by sixteen bars in binary form, using the same rhythm in every bar.

Schumann pretended to a friend that no. 8 was a waltz by Schubert. Its introduction is in C sharp minor and the main piece is in C sharp major, written as D flat major with an enharmonic change. Again a one-bar rhythm is repeated throughout. The plan is the hybrid form **A** :|| :**B** **A** :||, with the first **A** modulating to the dominant and the second **A** changing so as to end in the tonic key. Some people call this form binary, others call it ternary.

Number 9 consists of an introduction on a tonic pedal in B flat minor followed by a piece in binary form beginning in D flat major and ending in B flat minor, and using continuous quavers throughout.

Three longer pieces finish the set. Number 10 has two introductions, the second of which is a repetition of **B** in no. 6, now in key G instead of key A. The waltz which follows has the same rhythm in every bar and is in binary form with a short link between the two sections. After this there is a short interruption based on the rhythm of no. 8. This is followed by a pause and then the original waltz rhythm returns for the last bars, as a coda.

Number 11 is another polonaise and it re-establishes the key of D major, the original key of the set. It has a rather unusual form, that of minuet and trio with **A** omitted at the return of the "minuet". After three bars of introduction **A** starts at bar 4 and ends at 11 in F sharp minor with the usual weak-beat cadence. **B** is from bars 12 to 23 and **A** returns at 24, changing at 29 so as to end in the tonic key. The "trio" section is in G major and is *piu lento*. **C** starts at 32 and has broken octaves in the right hand and syncopation in the left. **D** starts at 40 and **C** returns in decorated form at 44. Then the "minuet" returns at 48, using **B**, not **A**; and a final exact repetition of **A** starts at 60.

The *finale*, in D major, begins with an old German folk-tune "the Grandfather's dance". Schumann later used the same tune to represent the Philistines (the old-fashioned pedants) in "Carnaval". It breaks off abruptly at bar 18, and after two bars' rest in the right hand the theme of no. 1 appears. At 27 it is combined with the Grandfather's dance in the left hand. Bar 43 starts a long tonic pedal, over which the two tunes continue, though the waltz tune gradually dies away, the syncopation helping to create a feeling of distance. At 58 the church clock starts to strike six, and at 65 the grandfather's dance ceases too, as "the noise of the carnaval night dies away". There is a bar's pause followed by upper pedals, first on the tonic then on the mediant, then on the dominant, with quiet syncopated chords underneath them. Finally, at 85, Schumann writes the dominant seventh in arpeggio and directs the pianist to take the notes off, one by one, leaving the top note to be heard against the final tonic chord. He used the same device in op. 1, and it is certainly an interesting experiment in the use of the pedal.

Carnaval, op. 9: Schumann

In "Carnaval" Schumann returned to the idea of his earlier work "Papillons". But this time the figures which flit across the scene are more clearly portrayed than they were in "Papillons" and they are often given titles.

Schumann was a complex personality, and several evidences of this are shown in "Carnaval". In 1831 he began working on a novel *Die Davidsbündler*. He never completed it, but he began to identify two characters in it, Florestan and Eusebius, with himself: Florestan when he was in a fiery mood and Eusebius when he was in a poetic one. Later, when he founded a musical periodical, he wrote articles under these two pen-names. The two characters appear as portraits in "Carnaval" as do musical personalities such as Clara Wieck, Chopin and Paganini, in addition to the usual carnival figures, such as Harlequin and Columbine.

The "Davidsbündler" in the projected novel were a collection of "Davidites" who were pledged to fight against the old-fashioned pedants, the Philistines. These groups, too, are shown in "Carnaval". The Davidsbund first appear in the *animato*, *vivo* and *presto* sections of Préambule. Then they come in "Pause", the penultimate number, preparatory to appearing in the fight against the Philistines in the finale, in which, of course, they win. The Philistines are shown by the Grandfather's dance which appeared in "Papillons".

A further instance of Schumann's complex nature is shown in his love of symbols. His op. 1, the "Abegg" variations, was composed as a result of meeting a girl, the letters of whose name "Abegg" could be turned into a musical theme. Later he had a more serious love affair with Ernestine von Fricken, who is "Estrella" of "Carnaval". But when he realized she came from a place called "Asch", that these four letters also occurred in his name, and that they could be turned into musical notes in several ways, he could not refrain from playing about with them, hence the sub-title of "Carnaval", "Scènes Mignonnes sur quatre notes".

In German E flat is called Es, A flat is called As, and B is called H. The four notes which are referred to in the title are E flat, C, B, A, which in German are therefore Es (which sounds like S), C, H, A. They can also be turned into A flat, C, B (AS, C, H) and A, E flat, C, B (A, ES, C, H). These three combinations of letters appear in "Sphinxes", which are not meant to be played. But they also appear as themes very frequently in the various pieces.

"*Préambule*" is one of the longest pieces in the work, but it is little more than a number of short sections strung together without any kind of recapitulation. It begins *maestoso*, and then each section speeds up, until *presto* is reached at the end. The *maestoso* is in mazurka rhythm, and the *piu moto* is in waltz rhythm. Notice the syncopation at the end of this section, a device of which Schumann was very fond. The *animato* section represents the Davidites and recurs at bars 83 and 179 of the finale. Notice the theme in the alto in dotted notes. The *vivo* section occurs again in "Pause", where, perhaps, the Davidites are assembling for their march against the Philistines, and also in the finale: at 99, in the thick of the fray, and at 195 when they have finally routed the Philistines. The *presto* section uses the theme in dotted notes in the alto from the *animato* section, but now it is augmented and syncopated, and it is based on a tonic pedal, thus making it into a kind of coda. The *animato*, *vivo* and *presto* sections are very modern for the period in which they were written (the Philistines would not have approved of the chromaticisms in the *vivo* section), and the piece ends in a whirl of youthful excitement.

The next two pieces are pictures of two conventional figures in a carnival, "*Pierrot*" and "*Arlequin*". Both of them make use of the "quatre notes": "Pierrot" in the tenor, notes 2 to 5 being A, ES, C, H, (C flat = B by enharmonic change); "Arlequin" in the soprano, A, ES, C, H being the first four notes. The form of these pieces is very simple, as is that of most of the others, and requires no special comment. But notice that "Arlequin" is based on two figures: (*a*) the first two bars; and (*b*) the cadence figure at 7–8. The first two notes take flying leaps throughout the piece, quite frequently making the interval of a tenth, and the cadence figure occurs at every cadence. One can almost see the leaping figure of Harlequin making passes at Columbine in every phrase.

The carnival continues with "*Valse Noble*", and the four notes again start the tune, in the form of A, ES, H, C. Then we come to the poetic "*Eusebius*" who wanders absent-mindedly along in septuplets and quintuplets. "*Florestan*" follows, starting with A, ES, C, H, and hinting at himself as the composer of "Papillons" in bars 8–10 and 18–22. This runs, by means of an *accelerando*, straight into "*Coquette*", who dances to the same rhythmic figure nearly throughout. But she, too, brings in the four notes in bar 3 as A, ES, C, H. "*Replique*" is really a continuation of "Coquette", starting with the tenor part from the first two bars of "Coquette", and then continuing with the main "Coquette" rhythm.

After "*Sphinxes*" comes "*Papillons*", which again starts with the four notes A, ES, C, H, but has no reference to Schumann's op. 2, in spite of the title. Then comes "*A S C H. S C H A. Lettres Dansantes*". The first notes of this piece make AS, C, H, but the second set of letters does not appear in this piece, which is strange.

"*Chiarina*" is Clara Wieck, who was fifteen when this piece was written. At the time Schumann was engaged to Ernestine von Fricken, but he began to see more of Clara soon after this, and eventually he jilted Ernestine in favour of Clara, though several years were to elapse before he was allowed to marry her. The notes AS, C, H start the piece and then expand outwards.

"*Chopin*" follows, a short piece which might almost be a nocturne by Chopin. Then comes his fiancée, Ernestine, here called "*Estrella*".

As she lived at Asch it is natural that her piece should start AS, C, H. It is marked *con affetto*, and the second half is full of syncopation, *molto espressivo*.

"*Reconnaissance*" is presumably a meeting between two lovers. It again starts with AS, C, H, and one wonders how many more rhythmic and tonal guises of the *lettres dansantes* can appear. The middle section starts with an enharmonic change, and consists of a duet between right and left hand—presumably the lovers have now met.

Next we revert to the conventional figures of a carnival, "*Pantalon et Columbine*". The first part, Pantalon, is playful and *staccato*, and makes use of the letters; the middle section, Columbine, is sentimental and *legato*.

"*Valse Allemande*" starts with yet another rhythmic variant of the letters, and is followed by "*Paganini*", a picture of the great violinist. Schumann greatly admired him, and had already arranged some caprices of his for the piano. The cross-rhythm broken chords give the effect of double stopping on the violin, with difficult octave leaps, just the kind of feat that Paganini delighted to perform. There is a return to "Valse Allemande" at the end of the piece.

"*Aveu*" is a very short exchange of vows between the lovers, starting with the ever-present AS, C, H. Then the waltz rhythm is resumed in "*Promenade*", with a duet between two tunes, one in large print, the other in small, perhaps meant to represent the male and female. The procession dies away at the end, over a tonic pedal.

"*Pause*" consists of the *piu vivo* section from "Préambule"; and finally comes "*Marche des Davidsbündler contre les Philistines*". In spite of being called a march it is in triple time throughout, but it starts with a majestic *fortissimo*. The grandfather's dance, representing the Philistines, appears in the bass in bar 50, but hints of it occur before that, at 25 onwards over a dominant pedal. Then the Davidites enter at 83 with the theme which first appeared in the *animato* section of "Préambule". The *vivo* section from "Préambule" follows. The grandfather's dance reappears at 121–78, a fourth higher than before, but this is the last we hear of the Philistines, so presumably they are now vanquished. The *animato* and *vivo* sections of "Préambule" have won the day, and they now reappear, a fourth higher than before, followed by the *presto* section of "Préambule", which is extended to make a *ff* coda.

Rhapsody in G Minor, op. 79, no. 2: Brahms

One of the *Oxford Dictionary's* definitions of a rhapsody is "an emotional, irregular piece of music". This piece is certainly emotional, and it has several features of irregularity; but its form is quite regular: it is a clear example of sonata form.

Perhaps its most irregular feature is the tonality of the opening. There is no doubt that G minor is the tonal key-centre of the piece, but it is not usual to start with V VIb, and then to modulate immediately to another key (F major). The first cadence (bars 3–4) is in G major, and it is followed by a sequence a third higher, starting in B minor, passing through A major, and ending in B major. Bars 8–9 produce the first V I in root position, but they are in E minor! After passing through G major and G minor the music begins to modulate towards the dominant, ready for the second subject in that key. The marvel is that it does feel like the dominant, thus proving that Brahms has managed to establish G as the tonal centre, in spite of the many and surprising changes of key. What a wonderful first page this is—striking in its modernity!

The second subject starts in D minor at bar 13, and the first section of it lasts for seven bars (another unusual feature). A second section starts at 21, still in D minor. After four bars it is repeated an octave higher, but this time extends itself to eight bars before coming to a perfect cadence in the dominant and to the repeat of the exposition.

The development section begins at 33, by using the first subject theme. It reaches B flat major at 36, and is followed by four bars of tonic pedal. The bass then slides up a semitone and leads to a sequential repetition of 33–40 an *augmented fifth* higher, landing therefore in F sharp major at 44. The pedal which follows is extended to nine bars, and finally becomes the dominant of B minor, in which key the second subject appears at 54. A short link, starting in G major at 61, leads to a further reference of the first subject, beginning in G minor at 65. The consecutive octaves between the melody and the bass in the next nine bars add to the *misterioso* effect. The key is indeterminate for some time, but finally the section ends with a *pp* perfect cadence in the tonic (82–5), which is an unusual way to lead to a recapitulation.

The first subject of the recapitulation is as before, except for the last three chords, which lead to the second subject in the tonic at 99. This is almost identical, except for key, and leads to a short coda on a tonic pedal at 116.

Intermezzo in A, op. 118, no. 2: Brahms

The "Intermezzo" is in ternary form. The first section begins and ends in A major; the middle section is an episode in F sharp minor and F sharp major; and the recapitulatory section is the same as the first section, except for a little decoration in the first few bars. The texture is rich and warm, with short pedals, sometimes syncopated, as a feature of the first section; and a cross-rhythm of three against two is frequently used in the episode. The contrast of this restless rhythm with the quiet crotchets of the F sharp major section has a breathless beauty.

Ballade in G Minor, op. 118, no. 3: Brahms

The Ballade is in episodical form, and is rather rhapsodic in style. The terms ballade and rhapsody are almost interchangeable with Brahms, and neither has any exact meaning.

The first section is in ternary form. Notice the phrase lengths: 5 + 5; 7 + 7, with bars 17 and 23 as overlapping bars, providing the ending of one phrase and the beginning of the next. A codetta, starting at 32, ends the first section over a tonic pedal, and is followed by a three-bar link (38–40) which anticipates the rhythm of both tune and accompaniment of the episode.

The episode changes to the unrelated key of B major, and feels beautifully placid after the stormy first section. It contains four eight-bar phrases, the first and third of which are alike. The second phrase unexpectedly refers to the first section of the piece, but the last phrase continues in the same style as the rest of the episode. Then a four-bar link (73–6), leads to an exact repetition of the first section. A coda starts at 108, and contains a final brief reference to the episode.

16

Overtures

This chapter is concerned with orchestral music written between 1826 and 1891, and it may seem strange that it should be headed "Overtures". During this period many composers wrote large orchestral works such as symphonies and concertos, notably Mendelssohn, Schumann, Brahms, Dvořák and Tschaikowsky. Also the symphonic poem came to birth at this time.

But this book is concerned with the analysis of the relatively short and simple type of classic that is likely to be analysed by students in the earlier stages of their studies. An Examining Board for the G.C.E. will prescribe a Brandenburg concerto or a Mozart symphony for O Level, but not a Brahms symphony or concerto. The greater length and complexity of design and orchestration make the latter more suitable for A Level candidates, who are not only more advanced musically, but who can devote more time to the study of a large work.

Overtures, however, being shorter, are frequently prescribed at O Level and other similar examinations, and their analysis is more likely to be useful to the reader of this book, whether he is preparing for an examination or not.

An overture, as it name implies, was originally meant to be an "opening" or prelude to a larger work, such as an opera, an oratorio or a play. The first operas and oratorios often had little more than a trumpet fanfare as an introduction. But gradually composers began to feel that something more elaborate was wanted, and two types of overture emerged. These were the Italian overture, consisting of three short movements (quick, slow, quick) which was associated with A. Scarlatti; and the French overture, consisting of an opening *adagio* and a quick fugal movement, often followed by one or more dances, which was popularized by Lully. Bach's suite in B minor, discussed in chapter 5, is really an overture of this type, though it is not the prelude to a larger work. So, also, is the overture to Handel's "Messiah", analysed in chapter 6. Gradually, however, the French type of overture died out, and the Italian type merged into the new form of the symphony, and ceased to be used specifically as an overture.

By Mozart's time the overture in several movements had died out, and a new type, the result of the development of the symphony, had taken its place. This was a single movement in sonata form or modified sonata form. An instance of this is Mozart's overture to "The Magic Flute", analysed in chapter 9. It was Mozart, too, who began occasionally to allude to some theme or themes in the opera which was to follow, as for example, the masonic knocks in "The Magic Flute". Beethoven uses several themes from the opera in his third overture to "Leonora", analysed in chapter 13. And the habit grew to such an extent with later composers that sometimes their overtures became little more than a string of themes from the opera. This was particularly true of writers of comic opera, such as Sullivan.

Three operatic overtures are analysed in this chapter, and all make use, to a greater or lesser degree, of themes from their operas. They are Glinka's "Russlan and Ludmilla"; Smetana's "The Bartered Bride"; and Wagner's "The Mastersingers".

Haydn's overture to "The Creation", called "The Representation of Chaos", described in chapter 10, deserves special, mention because it neither quotes from the oratorio nor acts as a formal introduction to it. It is an integral part of the story, which starts with the first note of the overture. Wagner did the same kind of thing later, in his preludes to "The Rhinegold" and "The Valkyrie", where the atmosphere is created and the story started, so to speak, before the curtain rises.

Beethoven's "Egmont" overture, analysed in chapter 13, is an example of an overture to a play.

But in the period covered by this chapter, 1806–91, a new kind of overture came into being, the "concert" overture, and Mendelssohn is generally credited with its creation. It is a work which is complete in itself, but is based on some non-musical idea such as a story or a visual scene, and which can be played as an independent work at a concert. Mendelssohn's "Hebrides" overture and his "Calm Sea and Prosperous Voyage", analysed below, are concert overtures of this type. His overture to "A Midsummer Night's Dream", also analysed in this chapter, was written when he was only seventeen, and is, of course, an overture to a play, though when he wrote it, it is hardly likely that he actually envisaged it being performed at a stage production of the play. But seventeen years later, when he was famous, he was commissioned to write incidental music for the whole of the play, and then the overture became, like Beethoven's "Egmont", an overture for a play production.

These three overtures are all in sonata form, though they are "programme" music, too. Brahms' "Academic Festival Overture" and Dvořák's "Carnival Overture", analysed below, are also concert overtures and are in sonata form, though the form is more free than in the Mendelssohn overtures.

Two other works are analysed in this chapter which do not quite come into any of the above categories. Berlioz's "Carnival Romaine" is based on themes taken from an earlier unsuccessful opera, but is quite an independent work and is therefore a concert overture. And Wagner's "Siegfried Idyll" is largely based on tunes taken from his cycle of music dramas "The Ring", though it, too, is quite independent, and was written for a special occasion. It is, in effect, if not in name, a concert overture.

The works analysed in this chapter are taken in chronological order, and it will be seen that the scoring becomes heavier and more complex as the century progresses. Mendelssohn uses more or less the same orchestration as Beethoven, though he experiments with the ophicleide and the serpent. But thereafter extra woodwind instruments creep in, the brass gets heavier and more percussion is used. An exception is "the Siegfried Idyll", which, being written for performance in a home, uses only a chamber orchestra.

A student who is unused to reading a large score should start by looking down the names of the instruments on the first page, and making sure that he knows the English equivalents, if they are given in a foreign language. He should not confuse *corni* with cornets, *trombe* with trumpets or *tamburo* with tambourine. The foreign names of many of the percussion instruments are particularly confusing, and they should be looked up in a textbook or a dictionary. Then he should be sure he understands the reasons for the transposition of all the transposing instruments, and knows exactly how much higher or lower they are playing.

When he follows the score for the first time while the music is being played on a record or a tape it may be advisable for him to follow the first violin part throughout. Even that can be quite confusing with a larger score, particularly if the number of staves or sets of staves varies from page to page. At later hearings he can try to follow the main tune as it passes from one instrument to another. If he has plenty of time he may even follow one particular instrument or group of instruments throughout one hearing. There is a good deal to be said for getting thoroughly familiar with the sound of the work and its main tunes, while looking at the score, before starting on its analysis.

Overture to "A Midsummer Night's Dream": Mendelssohn

Mendelssohn, who was well educated and had wide cultural interests, had a warm appreciation of Shakespeare as a youth. He read "A Midsummer Night's Dream" with his sister Fanny when he was seventeen, and it inspired him to write this overture. It was mostly written in the summer of 1826, in the lovely garden of their

Berlin home, near the Deer Park. The family was very wealthy, and their Berlin home later became the German Houses of Parliament. The work received its first performance in their garden house (which was really a concert hall) and had an enthusiastic audience of the family's friends.

The overture is full of lightness and youthful grace, is very well constructed and orchestrated, and is a most remarkable work for a youth of seventeen.

Seventeen years later Mendelssohn was commissioned by the King of Prussia to write incidental music for the whole of the play. The song "You Spotted Snakes", the nocturne, the scherzo, and the popular wedding march are four of the best known of the thirteen numbers he wrote for the purpose. Some students may be surprised to learn that the wedding march they associate with the organ in their local church was really written for a full orchestra for the wedding of Theseus and Hippolyta in the play.

The first performance of the play with the overture and all the incidental music was given in 1843 in Potsdam. Shakespeare was not then well known to Berliners, and some were shocked at so coarse a piece, while others thought it a poor play!

The overture is scored for the normal orchestra of the period: two flutes, two oboes, two clarinets, two bassoons, two trumpets, drums and strings. In addition Mendelssohn used an ophicleide. This was a bass horn, a descendant of the older serpent. It had a coarse distinctive sound that did not blend well with other instruments, though it was quite suitable for the ass's bray, and is so used in the scene with Titania (Act III, Scene I). It was soon superseded by the tuba on which the ophicleide part is now always played. The ophicleide was never a very satisfactory instrument, but at the time composers felt the lack of a bass brass instrument, and this was the best that had then been invented.

The overture is in sonata form, marvellously adapted to fit the story. The evocative fairy horn call in the first few bars starts with two flutes and builds up gradually. (It is also used at the beginning of the finale of the incidental music, and again at the end, while Puck speaks the last four lines of the play.)

The violins enter at bar 6, and their light, high, divisi quavers give almost a shimmering effect, which is further enhanced when the *pizzicato* violas enter at bar 24. This is truly fairy music. There is a momentary pause on a discord at 39, and again at 56; otherwise, the upper strings continue in the same way until bar 62. (They are used again in Act IV, Scene I, in the scene with Oberon and Titania, and also at the beginning of the finale—"Through the house give glimmering light".)

The fairy-like effect is rudely shattered at bar 62 with the entry of the first court theme in full orchestra. The bellow of the ophicleide adds to the *fortissimo*. A second court theme, at bar 70, consists of a hunting call. (This is also used to accompany the hunting party of Theseus and Hippolyta in Act IV, Scene I.) A third court theme, starting with descending thirds, in minims, enters in the wind at bar 78, and this is made use of later in the overture.

The whole of this court theme section, starting at bar 62, may be thought of as a second section of the first subject or as the beginning of the transition. There is an obvious perfect cadence in the tonic at 61–2, which could be said to mark the end of the first subject. On the other hand, the whole of the court section remains in the tonic key, and modualtion does not occur until 97–8 with a *forte* return of the fairy music. So, if preferred, it could be said that the first subject merges into the transition at 97–8. One often turns to the recapitulation to clarify such an issue, but it is no help here, because the court theme does not return at this juncture at all.

Certainly by 98 the transition has been reached. The ophicleide is again heard at 104 onwards, as the clamour grows. But it is suddenly hushed at 122, and a few quieter bars prepare the way for the second subject.

The first section of the second subject enters at 130 in the clarinets, and represents the lovers. It is in the usual dominant major key. The theme continues for some time, being passed over to the strings at

138. There is a hint of fairy horns at 166, in a theme which is used later in the development section. The lovers' theme grows in intensity, until it ends with a descending scale at 192–4.

Now the second section of the second subject enters, again in the dominant key. This illustrates Bottom and his companions, "the rude mechanicals". It is clumsy and heavy, starting with an accompaniment of horns, ophicleide and drums. The ophicleide contributes greatly to the coarse humour of this section. When the tune enters, notice the clumsy leaps of ninths and tenths. (This theme is used as the basis of the Bergomasque dance in Act V, Scene I.)

This section comes to an end at bar 222 with a perfect cadence in the dominant key. A short codetta follows, based on the hunting call from the court music.

So by the end of the exposition all the main groups of characters in the play have appeared, very diversified, as they are in the play. Yet they fit naturally into the conventional sonata-form scheme.

There is some wonderful orchestration in the development section, which starts at bar 250. It is based almost entirely on the fairies' theme. First the violins enter in the dominant minor key, with soft woodwind interjections in a disjointed rhythm. Gradually the lower strings are added, and the wind interjections change to soft arpeggios, starting at 270. The original rhythm of the interjections returns at 278; and then, at 284, the rhythm changes to the fairy horn call first heard at 166 in the middle of the lovers' theme.

Notice the sudden *ff* single note in the horns at 294, and again at 302 and 310. Each time it rapidly dies away as a *pp* roll enters on the drums. Perhaps all this is meant to represent the eerie sounds heard in the fairies' wood at night. The material continues for some time, until almost every instrument of the orchestra is playing, though usually *pianissimo*. The one instrument which does not appear in the development section is the ophicleide. Most of the time the strings are playing their fluttering *pp* quavers. But at bar 324 only the 'cellos and basses are left. The violins enter again at

334, while a scale of descending *pizzicato* crotchets is dropped into the fluttering texture.

Then, at 376, the flutterings cease, and there is a reference to the end of the lovers' theme. Gradually the music quietens down and comes to rest on a reiterated chord of C sharp minor, which marks the end of the development section.

The recapitulation starts at 394 with the opening fairy horn call followed by the shimmering violin quavers as before. But now occasional long notes are added to the texture by means of interjections in various instruments including the ophicleide. Notice the low descending fourth in the ophicleide at 416–20, the effective soft drum roll at 419–27 and the ophicleide note lasting for nine bars at 428–36.

There is no reference to the court themes at this stage. Instead bars 442–50 correspond to 112–30 in the exposition at the end of the transition. But now they are based on the dominant seventh of the tonic key instead of the dominant key. The transition is therefore much shorter.

This leads to the lovers' theme, i.e the first section of the second subject, in the tonic key at 450, and it is almost identical with its first appearance except for key. The second section, the Bergomasque dance, starting at 512, is also as before.

Now follows a belated appearance of the third part of the court theme, starting at 542, and corresponding to 78. This is modified and lasts for some considerable time. Then, at 586, there is a short reference to the first section of the court theme. Its second section, the hunting call, which first occurred at 70 and was also used for the codettta at 238, follows at 594, acting solely now as a codetta. Perhaps Mendelssohn put the court section so much later in the recapitulation in order that it could round it off.

However, as in the play, the fairies have the last word. A coda starts at 620, in which the strings have their fluttering quavers and the wind have the arpeggio interjections heard in the development section.

A pause is reached at 643, on the chord which first interrupted the quavers at 39, but this time it resolves into a series of descending semibreve chords, which get gradually softer. The clarinets and bassoons are the only instruments left with them at 658, and over them there is a soft attenuated reference to the first court theme, getting gradually slower by means of augmentation. Mendelssohn was probably thinking of the court at night, at the end of the play, when the fairies hold sway and all is hushed. The fairy horn call finishes the overture, which thus ends as it began.

The Hebrides Overture: Mendelssohn

"The Hebrides" was written in 1830 when Mendelssohn was twenty-one, and was the result of a visit to Scotland the previous summer, as was also the "Scotch" symphony. He wrote home on 7 August 1829 "on one of the Hebrides", quoting the first ten bars of the overture. It was finished in Rome on 16 December 1830, but a year later he was discontented with it, saying, "the middle section is very stupid, the working-out smelling more of counterpoint than of train oil, seagulls and saltfish". It was heard in London in 1832, and, profiting by this hearing, he made more alterations before sending it to be published. At various times he called it "The Hebrides", "The Lonely Island", "The Isle of Fingal", and "Fingal's Cave".

It is written for the standard classical orchestra and is in sonata form. The little one-bar figure with which it opens is heard six times, on chords of B minor, D major and F sharp minor in violas, 'cellos and bassoons before it swells into a two-bar phrase in E major. It is then repeated in the violins, with a new figure starting at bar 13 which is much used later. The opening figure recurs at 26, but this time it is accompanied by a new theme in the wind, which can be said to begin the transition. The figure heard in the third bar of the new theme, (bar 29) is passed from one instrument to another, and eventually leads to the second subject in the relative major at 47.

This second subject is played by the 'cellos and bassoons, with support from the clarinet, and is accompanied by quiet broken chords in the strings. At bar 57 the tune is transferred to the violins. Bar 70 starts an unusually long codetta based on the first subject. Notice how the rhythm is changed at 77. It is combined with a simplified version in the brass which makes a kind of horn call, and this continues until it is left by itself at 93 and brings the exposition to an end.

The development starts at 96 and uses the first bar of the first subject combined with the horn call, now heard in the woodwind. A new figure, which has a resemblance to the opening figure, starts at 112, and this leads to a reference to the second subject at 123. Other variants of the first subject appear, notably at 149, where strings and woodwind imitate each other, and they lead to a dominant pedal at 169, which, in its turn, leads to the recapitulation.

The recapitulation starts at 180, but the dominant pedal continues for another six bars. Two extra bars are interpolated at 182 before the change to the D major chord; and a similar two bars occurs again at 186. The ensuing passage is considerably shorter than in the exposition, and runs into the second subject in the tonic key at 202. This time the clarinet has the tune to itself, and it, too, is shorter.

The coda starts at 217, with the same pedal effect that was heard at the beginning of the recapitulation. Under it a new figure is heard in imitation in oboe, violas and violins. But soon it is swamped by a rapid *crescendo* which leads to the first subject at 226 in the lower strings. This rises in intensity until it is taken up by the brass at 234. After a climax at 237 the strings are left to themselves for a few bars, but they play *con fuoco* and are joined by the woodwind at 244 and the brass at 249, so that the music builds up to a most exciting climax. Yet, after all the fury, it ends quietly with three references to the first subject in the clarinet.

Calm Sea and Prosperous Voyage Overture: Mendelssohn

This concert overture is based on two sea-poems by Goethe, which are quoted at the beginning of the "Eulenberg" score. Elgar quotes a theme from it in no. XIII of the "Enigma Variations", thus wishing a prosperous voyage to his friend who was on the high seas.

It is scored for a larger orchestra than the "Hebrides", though it was composed at about the same time, and was finished in 1832. The additional instruments are a piccolo, a serpent and a third trumpet, though the Eulenberg score looks much more complex than the "Hebrides" because so many of the pairs of instruments are written on two separate staves.

The serpent, which looked like its name, was a woodwind instrument with a metal mouthpiece like that of a trombone. It was used in churches and in military bands; and Mendelssohn experimented with it in an attempt to give bass support to the wind instruments, just as he used the ophicleide in the overture to "A Midsummer Night's Dream". Nowadays both instruments are obsolete. The part for the serpent is played on a double bassoon, and the ophicleide part is taken by the tuba.

The introduction depicts the calm sea, which, in the days of sailing ships, did *not* mean a prosperous voyage, as the ship could not move until the wind rose. The opening rhythm in the strings is much used throughout the movement. It is passed to the clarinet at bar 10, and the music becomes quieter and quieter until, at bar 45, we are left with a solitary flute. Will the wind never rise?

But at 49 it begins to stir, and Mendelssohn here changes the title to "prosperous voyage", and the speed to *allegro*. The movement is quiet at first, but builds up a *crescendo* while a dominant pedal appears at 71. After six crashing chords the first subject appears *pp* at 99, with the boat now happily under way. A second theme of the first subject appears *f* at 107. It uses the rhythm of the introduction, but the tune is now the one that Elgar uses in the "Enigma". It is combined with the *arpeggio* that appeared at 72. The first theme of the first subject reappears *ff* at 129, and the second theme also appears at 137. The music then begins to move away from the tonic key, and leads to the second subject in the dominant at 149, played alternately by upper and lower strings.

Then the music gradually dies down, as if the sea is becoming becalmed again, and the second theme of the first subject is heard softly in the 'cellos at 185 and in the violins at 209, making a kind of codetta.

By 223 we are back in the tonic key, and there is a very free, shortened repetition of the exposition—an unusual feature. The wind rises, rather in the way it did from 72 to 99, with the brass coming to the fore with the dotted rhythm at 243; but it begins to die down again at 259, and the second subject, in the dominant as before, enters quietly at 271.

The development starts at 286, and is built for some time on a series of ninths and sevenths, with no key established. Then it settles in G major at 345, with a reference to the second subject *pp* in the 'cellos. A dominant pedal, starting at 347, leads one to expect the recapitulation, but it unexpectedly resolves on D sharp instead of D at 355. However another dominant pedal starts at 379, and this time it does lead into the recapitulation which starts at 401.

The first subject enters quietly in the violins, and is much shortened. The second subject enters in the tonic at 424, but this time it is not becalmed. It merges triumphantly into a coda about 442. A tonic pedal starts at 457, and leads to a *ff maestoso* section at 482, in which the trumpets blare out the "Elgar" theme at 500, and are followed by the whole orchestra doing likewise.

Overture to "Russlan and Ludmilla": Glinka

Glinka (1804–57) is considered to be the father of Russian music. He wrote the first Russian opera "A Life for the Czar" in 1836, and it had an immediate success in Russia. "Russlan and Ludmilla", first performed in 1842 at the Bolshoi theatre, was not so popular, though it is generally considered a better opera musically. It is based on a poem by Pushkin, Russia's great poet, but Glinka used five different librettists, which weakened the story. Ludmilla, the daughter of the Great Duke of Kiev, is abducted by a dwarf; and Russlan, a knight, after many fairy-tale adventures, rescues her and wins her as his bride.

The overture is an exciting work, and makes use of a heavy brass section, consisting of four horns, two trumpets, and three trombones. It is in sonata form.

After a noisy *tutti* introduction the first subject appears at 21. The transition starts at 59, and is based on imitative entries in the woodwind of the first subject. It leads into the second subject at 81, played by violas, cellos and bassoon, in the unrelated key of F major. This theme is taken from Russlan's aria in Act II. It is repeated by the violins at 105, and leads to A flat major at 119. A codetta then starts in this key. It is based on the introduction, and consists of dialogue between woodwind and strings in descending sequences.

This merges into the development, which starts at 133, with imitative entries of bars 97–100 from the second subject. After a few bars based on the introduction and a *pp* pedal on the horns, they are resumed at 153 and lead to a development of the first subject at 165. The changes are rung on these three themes and the horn pedal for some time. Then the horns start a tonic pedal at 205, followed by a dominant pedal at 221, over which scales from the introduction lead in a rapid *crescendo* to the recapitulation at 237.

The first subject is exactly as before, and the transition starts the same but changes at 287, leading to the second subject in the dominant at 297. This time the 'cellos have the theme alone, but there are no other changes. The codetta starts at 335 in C major, but changes at 345 so as to reach the tonic key at 349. It is unusual to be so long in reaching the tonic key, but 349 starts a coda which is entirely in the tonic. It is based on the first subject and a descending scale in minims in the bass, and it gets louder and quicker until the opening bars are reached at 386. They make a grand plagal cadence, with the drum very much to the fore.

Carnival Romaine: Berlioz

This overture is based on a *saltarello* from an unsuccessful opera, "Benvenuto Cellini", written some years earlier. It is full of the exciting orchestral colour usually associated with Berlioz, and was written in 1844.

It is scored for piccolo, cor anglais, two cornets and an unusual amount of percussion, in addition to the instruments usually found in a classical orchestra. Notice the use of two pairs of horns in different keys, as was fairly common in this period; and notice also the composer's instructions about the number of strings he requires. This was far more than was used in the normal orchestra of his day, and more than many a British orchestra can afford today. "Tamburi piccoli" are side drums.

The overture starts with a long introduction, in which two contrasted themes appear. The first (bar 1) makes use of the *saltarello* rhythm, and reveals itself in full, later, as the second subject in the exposition. The second (bar 21) is a main theme in the development section. The two themes are contrasted in every conceivable way. The first is a *tutti allegro* in $\frac{6}{8}$ time and the key of A major, while the second is an *andante* cor anglais solo, in $\frac{3}{4}$ time and the key of C major. This second theme is transferred to the viola in bar 37 and to the key of E major. By bar 53 it is in the tonic key, with a canon between the upper and lower strings. Bars 75–8, in which piccolo scales figure prominently, lead into the exposition.

The exposition begins at 78 with a return to the opening $\frac{6}{8}$ *saltarello* rhythm but with a different theme, which must be considered as the first subject in the tonic. Notice the clever scoring, with the muted *staccato* violins and the *p* drum roll effect in the lower strings. It is a subdued, rhythmical anticipation of the excitement which is to come later. Strings and woodwind alternate for some time. Notice the effective *ppp* passage beginning at 102, with its sudden change to C major at 112. A rapid *crescendo* at 126 leads to the *tutti* entrance of the second subject in the dominant at 128, a complete version of the theme first heard in bar 1. This section is punctuated by *fff* bangs on the percussion. It moves back to the tonic for a repetition of the exposition starting at 168. The repetition is written out because the scoring is quite different. The first subject is now *ff tutti*, and it goes to C sharp minor instead of C major at 203. The second subject (225) is the same as before until it reaches bar 255, where it stays in the dominant key.

Two bars in $\frac{2}{4}$ time lead into the development section at 276. It begins by developing the part of the second subject which first occurred at 132–3, *pp*, in F major, then in D flat major. A tonic pedal starts at 300, beginning quietly in the violins, but gaining in intensity until the end of the development section. Over it is heard the cor anglais theme from bar 21, played first by the bassoon in F major, then by the trombones with imitations in the woodwind.

The recapitulation starts at 344 with the *second* subject in the tonic. It is a noisy *tutti*, with the side drum and triangle adding to the excitement. But the tone-level drops abruptly at 356, when quiet *fugato* entries of the second subject appear. Bar 367 brings in a brief hint of the first subject, the only reference to it in the short recapitulation. Having had such a long introduction and a repeated exposition, Berlioz probably felt the need to shorten the recapitulation, which ends with the trombones bringing in the theme from bar 21 once more.

A perfect cadence in the tonic key is reached at 387, where the coda starts, and from here the excitement mounts to the end. Wind and strings alternate in D flat and A major to the accompaniment of the side drum. A *tutti* starts at bar 397, which quickens into $\frac{2}{4}$ time at 403, and leads into a final reference of the second subject at 413, bringing the overture to an end in a blaze of brilliant excitement. (Some readers may have a Eulenberg score in which the bar numbers from 380 onwards are printed six bars later than they should be.)

Overture to the Bartered Bride: Smetana

The themes from this overture are taken entirely from the orchestral part of the finale of Act II, instead of from important vocal themes, as is more usual. Its setting is that of a village festival, with a fussy marriage broker holding the limelight. The opera was written between 1863 and 1866.

The overture is in sonata form, but the balance is unusual, because it contains a very short middle section, which is largely episodic; a recapitulation, containing a good deal of development; and a very long coda.

The first subject gives an impression of excited bustling. After a noisy opening it continues with *fugato* entries in the strings which sound rather like a dog running after its own tail! The second subject, in the dominant, starts with a noisy *tutti* at bar 100, and is very syncopated.

The middle section starts at bar 175, and is largely new matter. The recapitulation starts at 221, but the woodwind now shares in the *fugato*: it is much more elaborate than in the exposition, and modulates freely. There is a development of the second subject at 274, with the first two bars combined with the second two bars. The second subject then appears normally in the tonic at 297. By about 320 we think we are nearing the end—but no—there is a change, and a long extension. The same thing happens round about 360; but now, at 362, it runs into the coda, with the first subject in the tonic key again. A dominant pedal starts, *pp*, at 394, and an enormous *crescendo* is built over it. This is surely *now* the end. But again—no! The second subject reappears at 422, the opening figure at 442, and at last the end is in sight. One had begun to think the music was in perpetual motion, and would *never* run down!

Overture to The Mastersingers: Wagner

The overture is scored for a piccolo, in addition the usual woodwind; a heavy brass section, consisting of four horns, three trumpets, three trombones and a tuba; tympani, triangle, cymbals and harp; and the usual strings. It is an extraordinarily sonorous work, and brings a feeling of exaltation to both performers and listeners.

The opera (or, as Wagner preferred to call it, the music drama) "The Mastersingers" was written between 1862 and 1867. But Wagner must have had his main themes planned from the beginning, because he finished the overture, which includes many of these themes, long before the rest of the work, and it was performed by itself at concerts.

Wagner used short, significant themes to represent persons or ideas throughout his music dramas, and called them *leitmotive*. He used many of them in "The Mastersingers", in addition to longer themes such as Walther's "Prize Song", which we see developed in stages in the opera. They are combined in the most exciting way in this overture, or as Wagner preferred to call it, *vorspiel*, prelude.

The overture opens with a magnificently sonorous statement of the "Mastersingers" main theme in C major. This is the first section of the first subject in a free example of sonata form, and it is extended by sequence piling on sequence into a sentence of twenty-seven bars. In the opera it is used when David is preparing for the entry of the Mastersingers; when they enter in the last act; and also it accompanies Beckmesser in Act III, in diminution, a form in which it appears later in the overture. It is a symbol of conservative power.

A second theme, called the Lyric motive, appears at 27. This is much more free rhythmically than the first theme, its variety of subdivision of the beat providing a study in contrasts between conservatism and freedom. But this, too, is another long sentence, full of extensions. It first appears in the opera in the church scene, when Walther is trying to communicate with Eva; then a parody of it is used in Beckmesser's serenade to Eva; and finally we hear Walther using fragments of it, as he builds up his prize song in Sach's shop.

But this free, lyric motive is interrupted at 41 by the Mastersingers' March. This is based on one of the "Prize Master Tones", printed in Nuremberg in 1697, in a book by Wagenseil. It leads to the "Art Brotherhood", another Prize Master Tone, at 59. This grand march is used in Act III when the Mastersingers enter, and it is also parodied by the apprentices, in diminution. In the overture this section is full of sequential development and counter-melodies, and produces a magnificent thirty-one-bar peroration.

All these themes are centred on key C and may therefore be considered as being in the first subject group. But the next *leitmotive* "Longing", which appears at 89, begins to modulate and may be thought of as a short transition leading to the second subject. In the opera it is used in conversation between Eva and Walther.

The second subject, when it appears at 97, is in the surprising key of E major. It is the main "Prize Song" theme, and its flowing style and irregular subdivisions of the beat give it an affinity with the "Lyric" theme. The two are combined to produce the prize song in the final scene. The subsidiary theme, which starts at 103, is called "Spring". This second subject is quicker and lighter here than when it appears in its final form in the opera.

A short dominant pedal in C major, over which "Spring" continues, leads to the development section.

This starts at 122 in E flat major, with the Mastersingers theme in diminution. It is parodied thus by the apprentices in the opera, and in starts in woodwind only, which is an effective contrast after so many soaring violin themes. It is later combined with "Spring", and with "Art Brotherhood". The theme "Ridicule" also appears in the 'cellos at 138, and is developed imitatively in conjunction with the other themes.

The return to the tonic key at 151 heralds the recapitulation, with the "Mastersingers" theme in trombones over a dominant pedal. But the woodwind and violins are continuing with their own, quicker themes at the same time, so the sections are beautifully welded together.

Then, at 158, comes that marvellous moment when the "Prize Song", "The Mastersingers" and the "March" in diminution all occur together, in a wonderfully light, springy texture that quite hides the contrapuntal skill. Further combinations of themes follow, with "Art Brotherhood" well to the fore at 174, and diminutions of it at 179. Then the trumpets and trombones enter with the march in C major, *marcato*, at 188. This builds up to a big climax, and finally the first "Mastersingers" theme enters at 211, and brings the overture to a magnificent conclusion.

Siegfried Idyll: Wagner

This delightful miniature was written to celebrate the birth of Wagner's son, "Siegfried", and it was first performed at Triebschen, on the staircase outside his wife's bedroom as a Christmas present to Cosima, in 1870. The Villa "Triebschen" a mile or two outside Lucerne, is now on view to visitors, who can see for themselves the conditions under which the work was performed.

The small orchestra consisted mainly of Wagner's friends. Notice that it is scored for only one flute, one oboe, one bassoon and one trumpet, although there are two clarinets and two horns. In fact, it approximates more to chamber than to orchestral music.

Siegfried, the subject of this idyll, was (at the time) a baby, hence the introduction of the old German cradle song at bar 91. He lived to produce his father's operas in Bayreuth, and died in 1930. He was named after the hero, Siegfried, in Wagner's cycle of four music dramas, "The Ring"; and apart from the cradle song, all the themes are *leitmotive* from these operas, most of them coming from "Siegfried" itself. Anyone who is familiar with these operas will recognize the themes; and the student who is able to relate them to their place in the operas will find the Idyll much more interesting. The *leitmotive* have been given various names by different commentators and translators, but the following titles should be recognizable.

There is a short introduction, which hints at "slumber" in bar 1 in violas and 'cellos, and uses "love's peace" in the violins in bar 4. An imperfect cadence at 28 leads into the exposition of the work, which is in a free sonata form. The first subject, "love's peace" enters in the violin at 29, and has as its ancillary, "slumber", introduced by the flute at 37. The two themes move from one instrument to another in free imitative counterpoint for some time, until the music reaches a new figure of a drooping sixth at bar 50, with punctuating triplets in the wind. This leads into the second subject in the dominant at 55. The first theme in the clarinets comes from "Siegfried", and it is combined with the falling sixth and with hints of "love's peace", as at 64 in the bassoon. The second section is the cradle song, played by the oboe, starting at 91. A codetta rounds off the exposition from 106 to 114.

The development section, in which all the themes are cleverly combined, starts at 116 in the tonic key. For example, you will find "love's peace" in the violin at 116; the cradle song in the horn at 117, and again in clarinet and bassoon at 119; the falling sixth (now become a seventh) in the violin at 120–1, with the triplet accompaniment in the horn at 121; bars 5 and 6 of the cradle song at 125; and so on.

Some trills and sweeping string arpeggios lead to a new theme at 148 in the clarinet, "Siegfried the protector" from the last scene of the opera "Siegfried". Notice that it is in the remote key of A flat major, and that there is quite a long section for wind alone. The strings re-enter effectively in 181, and now they have a section to themselves, until the oboe enters with "love's peace" at 201. The themes continue to combine, with frequent changes of key, and work up to a climax at 255.

Yet another theme appears at 259. This is "Siegfried the impetuous", from the last scene of "Siegfried", played by the first horn, with the clarinet chirping in with "the forest bird" at 262.

The recapitulation starts at 286, with the return of the first subject in the tonic key. It is much shortened, and contains many further combinations of themes and changes of key. The first section of the second subject appears in the tonic at bar 315, though the cradle song does not return.

The coda begins at 351, and is built mainly on a tonic pedal. Most of the *leitmotive* appear in some form in this coda, and the student should be able to recognize them. "Siegfried the protector" appears *pp* in the violins in augmentation at 396, then the 'cellos make a last reference to "love's peace" in 398, and end with the augmentation of "Siegfried the protector". All the last part is quiet and peaceful, so that the idyll ends with the mood in which it began.

Academic Festival Overture: Brahms

This work is not in the least "academic" in the accepted sense of the term. It is based on a string of well-known students' songs, and is a jolly work that makes an excellent introduction to Brahms' orchestral music. It was written for the University of Breslau in 1880 because they had made him an honorary doctor of philosophy the previous year.

It is scored for an unusually large orchestra, including a piccolo, a double bassoon, four horns, bass drum, cymbals and triangle. The piccolo and the extra percussion certainly add to the feeling of festivity.

It is in modified sonata form, which is quite usual for overtures; and it contains many more themes in the first subject group than in the second, which is not so common. The first subject has almost a rondo-like construction. Its themes are as follows: first theme, bar 1, C minor, strings, *pp*; second theme, 25, F major and D flat major, strings and horns, followed by a reference to the first theme again; third theme, 46, E minor, *tutti*; fourth theme, 64, C major, trumpets over a continuous drum roll. Then follows a return to the first theme at 88, now in C major, *tutti*. Other references follow: 92, fourth theme in diminution; 96, first theme in E minor; 100, second half of the fourth theme in G major; 106, first theme in G major; and at 113 the first theme reappears quietly in the tonic, thus rounding off this unusually long and tuneful first subject.

The theme which follows at 127 may be regarded as a transition or as the beginning of the second subject. It begins in E major, with the second half in the dominant at 139, and it reappears in the tonic in the recapitulation, so it is logical to regard it as the second subject.

Also it is unusually tuneful for a mere transition. But the theme which follows at 157 in the bassoon is a very assertive tune in the dominant, and the analysis given with the Boosey and Hawkes score refers to it as the second subject.

Notice that this new theme appears in the bass at 175 against an inversion of it in the treble, and that a counter-theme appears against it at 188. This quieter section is followed by a return of the theme *ff tutti* at 231, which brings the exposition to the end.

The recapitulation starts with the return to the tonic at 241, and contains a number of changes. It begins with a variation of the first theme; omits the second theme; goes on to the third, in F minor, at 255; returns to the first theme at 269 as before, but now extends it; and gets to the fourth theme at 290.

The theme which can be called transition or second subject starts in the tonic at 314, swinging along in fine style, and moving into E flat major. There is no equivalent of 157–210, but 346 corresponds to 211 and the final theme appears *ff tutti* in the brass at 367.

This is followed by a *maestoso* coda which brings in, for the first time, the well-known student's song "Gaudeamus igitur", played mainly by the brass against sweeping scales in the strings.

Carnival Overture: Dvořák

"Carnival" is a concert overture, and is one of a set of three programmatic works. The first is "Amid Nature", the second "Carnival" and the third "Otello". All three show some aspect of nature and man's reaction to it, and there is a common "motto-theme" which is shown in "Carnival" in the opening theme and again in the clarinet solo in the *andantino* episode in the development section.

The overture is in sonata form, and is a noisy, joyful work, containing a large number of tuneful themes. It was written in 1891. It is scored for piccolo, cor anglais, cymbals, tambourine, triangle and harp, in addition to the standard symphony orchestra. The percussion instruments come through, even on records.

The first subject is a complete theme in ternary form (1–8; 9–25; 25–43). The transition contains three distinct themes, at bars 43, 60 (an augmentation of the previous few notes) and 86. It leads to the second subject in the dominant *minor* at bar 102. There is a second section in G major at 132; a third section in the dominant major at 176; and a fourth section or codetta in the same key at 184.

The development starts at 192, with most peculiar harmonies and orchestration of the first subject; and it leads into a quieter *andantino* episode in the remote key of G major. The scoring of the whole of this section is worthy of note, particularly the plaintive figure first heard in the cor anglais. The main theme occurs three times, in the flute, a solo violin, and violins *pp tutti*. A return to the *allegro* at bar 262 develops three figures from the first subject and the transition, until the first transition theme comes back in full at 345, and a *crescendo* leads to the recapitulation at 386.

In the recapitulation the first subject begins as before, but its middle section is now in the wind alone. The first two themes of the transition are omitted, and the second subject, which begins at 457, omits the first three sections and moves straight into the fourth section or codetta, though there are references to part of the second section. The large omissions in the recapitulation are doubtless due to the length of the development section.

The coda starts at 479, and after referring to parts of the second subject, ends with a grandiloquent cadence based on the first subject.

17

Debussy and Ravel: Piano Music

Debussy and Ravel were French composers who reacted against the rich, emotional style of Germanic composers such as Wagner and Brahms who were writing at the end of the nineteenth century. They were, first and foremost, Frenchmen, concerned with clarity and moderation. Debussy (1862–1918) is known particularly for his new style of piano writing, though he also wrote one opera, "Pelléas et Mélisande", several orchestral works, including "L'Après midi d'un Faune", a little chamber music, and a number of songs. Most of his best-known works were written at the end of the nineteenth century. Ravel (1875–1937) wrote most of his best-known works at the beginning of the twentieth century. He was influenced, to a certain extent, by Debussy, and most of his works were first conceived for the piano, though he orchestrated many of them later. But he also wrote two short operas, three ballets and some chamber music.

Both of them were considerably influenced by the rise of impressionism in France. This began with a group of French painters, among whom were Manet, Monet, Renoir and Cézanne. They aimed at painting what could be seen at a glance, without recording every detail in the way that earlier painters had done. Some wonderful experiments in colour and atmosphere resulted. Although the movement started as early as 1859, it really became established with an impressionist exhibition in 1874.

The movement spread to French poets such as Mallarmé and Verlaine, who called themselves symbolists, and who tried to evoke and suggest rather than to make direct statements. Debussy met Mallarmé in 1887 and, from then onwards, began to be associated with the impressionists and to imbibe their ideas. He applied them to music in a most original way and became the first musical impressionist.

Debussy invented a new pianistic idiom. But so much impressionistic French and English piano music has been written since his day that we now accept it without surprise, though there is something so idiomatic in his writing that his style is always recognizable. He occasionally experimented with the whole tone scale, though this is not shown in the pieces analysed below. He liked to add a second or a sixth to a triad, treating the new effect as a concord, and this device is now a common feature in modern popular music. He sometimes used parallel discords, writing a series of them in the way an earlier composer would have written a single line of melody. And he experimented with the effects of the higher discordant overtones, as for example in the bell effects in the well-known "La Cathédrale Engloutie". All of these effects were very dependent upon the skilful use of the pedal, which is sometimes directed to be held on throughout a number of changing harmonies. The result of all these devices created a feeling of "atmosphere" which is closely related to the effect of an impressionistic painting.

Debussy's Arabesques, analysed below, are two of his earliest piano pieces, written in 1888, the year after he had met Mallarmé, but they are undoubtedly impressionistic in style. His "Suite Bergamasque" also analysed below, was written in 1890, two years before he started "L'Après midi d'un Faune" and "Pelléas et Mélisande". So it, too, is an early work, showing little of the characteristic idioms which were to appear in his later piano works. But "Clair de Lune" is frequently played and, like the rest of the suite, owes a good deal to the influence of Massenet.

Although Ravel showed more clarity than Debussy, and was more classical in outlook, he, too, can be called an impressionist, as can be seen in the Menuet from the Sonatine and the four numbers from "Le Tombeau de Couperin", analysed below. He was a miniaturist, who preferred to write on a small scale.

Two Arabesques: Debussy

The Arabians were very fond of delicate filigree ornamentation, particularly in their architecture, and the title "arabesque" given to a piano piece is presumably meant to indicate the same decorative style.

Debussy's *first Arabesque* largely consists of single or double strands of melody, and is full of charming delicacy. It is in ternary form.

The first six bars form an introduction, starting with IVb and a series of first inversions making a broken chord melody, and leading to the tonic chord in bar 6. This is undoubtedly a diatonic beginning in E major, but all the same it is an unusual succession of opening chords, and an unusual treatment of them.

At bar 6 a sinuous melody in triplets is heard against a swaying broken-chord bass in duplets. The two melodic lines continue in this way for some time. Bar 17 refers to the introduction again, but there is still a good deal of 3 against 2, and a rhythmic undulation that reminds one of an Arabian dancer.

Gradually the texture thickens slightly, until it leads to a perfect cadence in the tonic at 37–8, and the end of the first section.

A contrasting *tempo rubato* section starts at 39, in which the prevailing key is A major, though there are several short returns to the tonic. This section is more harmonic in style, and makes much use of syncopation. It ends in the tonic at 62, then abruptly goes to C major for a few bars. But the *f risoluto* style soon melts into a return to the opening bars.

Bar 71 returns to the opening section, but the music begins to change at 89, while keeping the same style. It sinks into a perfect cadence at 99, and the last nine bars form a coda on a tonic pedal.

The *second Arabesque* is similar in formal construction to the first, being in ternary form, with a short introduction and a middle section in the subdominant key. But its texture is different. The first section makes almost continuous use of a one-beat, dainty triplet figure over a simple chordal basis. It ends with a codetta, starting at 28.

The middle section, starting at 38 is short, but provides a contrast of style. Notice how the outside voices move outwards and then inwards at first. This idea is repeated an octave higher at 46, but it changes at 50, and the figure is built over a dominant pedal in E major. At 56 the bass slips down a semitone to B flat, then it quietly and unexpectedly leads to the return of the opening section in the tonic key at 62. The second half of this section, starting at 72 is different and shorter.

The coda starts with the *meno mosso* at 82. The triplet figure of the first section is now spread over two beats instead of one, and the augmentation thus produced has the effect of slowing down the movement. A reference to the middle section starts at 90; and then, unexpectedly, at *a tempo*, the whole of the codetta from the end of the first section is repeated exactly. It is usual for a codetta to merge into a coda, but rare to find the opposite.

Suite Bergamasque: Debussy

The term "suite" today is applied to any collection of pieces which are relatively light and not on the sonata plan. It may consist of dances from a ballet, as in Tschaikowsky's "Nutcracker" suite, or in excerpts from a play, as in Grieg's "Peer Gynt" suite, or even in pieces drawn together by a common non-musical motive, as in Holst's "Planets" suite.

Debussy's "Suite Bergamasque" is a mixture of old and new. The name "Bergamasque" comes from an old Italian dance *Bergamasca*, which takes its name from the town of *Bergamo* in North Italy. It was based on repetitions of the chords I, IV, V, I—a sequence often played today by popular guitarists—and the English Hornpipe is a variant of the same thing.

However there is nothing of the Bergamasca or Hornpipe about this suite, nor is it primitive or peasant-like. After an opening Prelude it continues with a minuet, which is a courtly, stately French dance. Then follows an atmospheric tone-picture "Clair de Lune", and the suite finishes with a Passepied, another old dance, sometimes found in eighteenth-century suites, and also French in origin. Not only are the movements in different keys but there is no attempt at linking up the tonality—the pieces are in F major, A minor, D flat major and F sharp minor. So, apart from using two eighteenth-century dances, "Suite Bergamasque" has little affinity with the classical suite, and the term "suite" is used in its free, modern sense.

Prelude contains many rhythmic figures and is in a free rhapsodic style, though it is a loose kind of ternary form.

The first section, in F major, contains two main rhythmic figures, **A** at bar 1 and **B** at bar 11. The first part, **A**, contains a repetition (7–11), corresponding to 1–4 but, though the tune is the same, the harmonies are different; and when Debussy brings this theme back at 66–9 and 72–6 he provides two more lots of harmonies.

The "**B**" figure, bar 11 onwards, also contains repetition; and notice the peculiar rhythmic grouping in bar 16. This section comes to an end with a perfect cadence in the tonic key at 19.

The second main section starts in A minor at bar 20, and contains three chief figures, **C** at 20, **D** at 26, and **E** at 30. Then **C** returns at 36, but changes at 41, and ends in A minor at 43.

Then follows a long transition, based mainly on **B**. It starts softly, with a repeated descending bass, and gradually builds up to a climax and a return of the first section in the tonic key at 66.

The return of **A** is the same as before, apart from the different harmonies already mentioned; but it adds five bars of *crescendo* (76–80). When **B** returns at 81 it starts at the tonic instead of the subdominant and works up to a *ff* ending.

Although the beat of *Menuet* is quite slow, the rhythmic pattern consists of almost continuous semiquavers, which is certainly unusual for a minuet.

The tonality of the opening is unusual too, for though the minuet is in A minor, no key is clearly established at first, and apart from one brief chord at the end of bar 2, the first unequivocal chord of A minor comes at bar 18–and even that is approached from a chromatic chord! To be sure, there is a whole bar of dominant harmony in bar 4, but it resolves on to submediant and not tonic harmony; and then it moves to F major. Dominant harmony in bar 11 again sounds as if it is going to resolve on to the tonic, but it moves on to the same curiously indeterminate harmony of bar 1, and to a repetition of the opening bars.

At last, however, we are settled in A minor with a new figure in bar 18. But two bars later it is repeated in C major, and two bars later again we find ourselves in E flat major. The shifting tonality certainly seems very different from that of the minuet of the classical period: there seems to be no point of repose. Even when we come to a dominant pedal in key B flat (26–9) it does not resolve on to the expected tonic chord but shifts away for another five bars before reaching a chord of B flat in 35.

Melodically, too, the music gives us the same feeling of insecurity. Now and again a melodic figure catches our attention, as at 26, and 30–1; but, after playing with it for another few bars, Debussy seems to forget about it, and our attention is shifted to something else. But bar 26 might be thought of as a kind of second subject, though in a very remote key, particularly as it returns again towards the end, at 82, in the tonic major.

Bar 42 returns to the opening figure, and continues with it as at bar 14; but by bar 46 we have wandered into another figure and the key of G major, though we are pulled back again at 49 with—at last—a perfect cadence in the tonic key.

Now comes the middle section of the movement. It is completely new material, with new themes at 50 and 58. Bar 50 makes use of semiquaver scales, first in F major, repeated at 52; and then, a tone lower, in E flat major at 54, repeated at 56. Bar 58 starts a theme with fewer semiquavers. It is repeated at 62, and comes an octave higher at 65.

Bar 73 unexpectedly starts a dominant pedal of key E flat, and over it, at 75, the opening figure (the first subject) returns in key E flat. It starts a kind of recapitulation, though the key is very remote. The second subject (from bar 26) returns at 82, but by now the pedal has slipped down to E, and we are in the tonic *major*.

Bars 97 to the end form a short coda which bears a resemblance to bars 18–21.

By comparison with the Minuet "*Clair de Lune*" is easy to follow, though it, too, contains some unusual features. It is a lovely atmospheric tone-picture, and is deservedly popular.

The opening theme is in D flat major and there is a modified repetition of the first part of it at bar 9. The second part starts *pp* at 15 with strings of block chords, of a kind often found in later works of Debussy. Notice the rising bass from 19 to 25, forming a *crescendo*. Then it dies down rapidly into a perfect cadence in the tonic at 26–7.

The cadence coincides with the beginning of the middle section, which surprisingly begins and ends in the tonic key, though it moves to the remote key of E major in the middle, at 37–42. When the theme returns in the tonic at 43 it is over a double tonic and dominant pedal for the first four bars.

The music merges into a repetition of the opening section, starting at 51 with a *mediant* pedal below it at first, and with a number of other harmonic changes. It omits the second part of the theme (15–27), and moves into a coda at 66, which is based on the middle section.

The *Passepied* originated among the sailors of Brittany, and, like the Minuet, was frequently placed between the Sarabande and the Gigue of the eighteenth-century suite. It was quicker than the Minuet, but was always in triple time, so it is surprising to find Debussy's Passepied in quadruple time. It was also usual for the first section or sections of a Passepied to begin in a major key and the last section or sections to be in the minor; but this Passepied begins and ends in F sharp minor, though this key alternates with A major.

This piece is really built on two figures, occurring at 3 and 59, together with variants of them, and it will be convenient to call them **A** and **B**.

A starts at bar 3, and soon repeats itself, with varied harmonies, just as all the other pieces in this suite have done. This repeat occurs at bar 11. Then, at 19, a new variant appears. It begins with the first three notes of **A**, though the third note is now only a semitone away from the second, thus making an augmented fourth with the first note. This variant is frequently used later. This section is in A major.

Bar 31 returns to the original theme in the tonic key, though with different harmonies. Bar 39 introduces yet another variant, though it starts with the three notes in the second form, that is, from bar 19, not from bar 3. But it is again in the tonic key.

Bar 59 introduces the new theme, **B**, in key A major. It is repeated a tone lower at 63 in G major, then returns to A major at 67. Bar 76 introduces a rhythmic variant of **B** in A flat major, but it returns in its original form at 88, though now starting in E major.

The recapitulation of **A** occurs at 106, though the theme is now in the middle of the texture. Bars 106–22 correspond to 3–19.

Then follows another rhythmic variant of **B**, at 126, in D major. A last reference to **A**, in its form as at bars 39–44, occurs at 138–43, and it merges into a coda in which the first three notes of **A** are heard in the bass in augmentation.

Minuet from Sonatine: Ravel

Ravel uses the rhythm of the old classical minuet, and the style is limpid and restrained, with lovely, impressionistic harmonies. The Minuet is built on little melodic figures; and the general plan is: **A**; **B**; development; **A**; **B**; coda. Bar 13, **B**, is really another version of **A** now in F minor instead of D flat major. The development section starts at 23 with yet another version of the same theme, plus a counter-theme in the tenor. It works up to a climax, and is followed by an inversion and contraction of this same theme (39). **A** returns at 53; and **B**, at 65, is similar to the first **B** at 13, but now in the tonic minor. It is possible to argue that the movement is in a miniature sonata form, but this is perhaps too grand a title. There is no real contrast between **A** and **B**; and the whole piece is largely built from three little fragments that first appear in bars 1, 3 and 30 in the tenor.

Notice the term "en dehors" at 27, which directs the pianist to make the tenor part stand out. And realize that the rest over the pause at 78 does not result in silence, as the chord from the previous bar is meant to be held on by the pedal.

Le Tombeau de Couperin, Nos. I, III, IV and VI: Ravel

"Le Tombeau de Couperin" was begun during the 1914 war, and finished in 1917 when Ravel was invalided out of the air force. In the same year he orchestrated nos. I–IV from the suite. This was the last work he wrote for the piano, and it is characterized by his usual restrained, clear-cut, classical style, even though the idiom is impressionistic. Revering the classicists as he did, it was natural that he should pay homage to Couperin, the greatest of the French keyboard classical composers. Each movement is dedicated to the memory of one of his comrades who fell in the war.

The opening bars of the *Prélude* (I), with their two strands of melody and their mordent decorations, are very much in the style of Couperin. Soon the harmonies become much more modern, however, the texture thickens, and by the last page the pitch range has gone far beyond that of the clavecin.

The movement is in binary form, as it would be if it were by Couperin. It begins in E minor, with the treble and bass parts interchanging in alternate bars. It reaches B minor bv bar 10, but continues with the same ideas. In bars 14–15 very chromatic harmonies are heard over a descending chromatic scale; and bar 18 continues in sequence a seventh higher.

The second main figure starts at 22 in C major, and much use is made of it later. The first section ends with a perfect cadence in the relative major, and it has the usual repeat.

The second section starts at 33 in C major, but with the same figure as bar 1. Five bars later the figure from 22 appears, but the first figure returns again at 44. The two figures interchange for some time, with no clearly established key. Most of the chords are sevenths or ninths. Bar 44 onwards repeats bar 33 onwards on a different series of chords. The *pp* section, starting at 57, which is based on bar 1, leads to the second figure again at 67. The mordent figure continues *crescendo* from 70 to 76 and leads to a very extended plagal cadence in the tonic key, starting at 76.

A *Forlane* is an old Italian dance in compound time. It is not unlike a Gigue, though it is not so commonly found in suites. This Forlane (III) is in the same key as the first two numbers of the suite (as it would have been in a suite by Couperin), though the key changes in nos. IV and V. Perhaps the first, very chromatic chords may not strike the student as being in any key at all; but E minor is the prevailing key, as can be felt when the E minor chord is reached in bar 5. E minor is the prevailing key throughout the movement, but it is very chromatic.

The movement is broken up into a number of short sections, and is rather rondo-like, though a coda takes the place of a return to the opening section. It can be summarized thus, in relation to bar numbers:

I. Introduction. ||: **A** 9 :||: **B** 29 :||: **C** 37(b); **B** 45 :|| **A** 53||.
II. ||: **D** 61 :||: **E** 69(b); **D** 85||.
I. Introduction, 93; **A** 101||.
III. **F** 121 ||: **G** 129 :||.
Coda, 137 to end, with reference to introduction at 153.

A *Rigaudon* is an old Provencal dance in duple time. As the phrases usually begin on the last quarter of the bar, the rhythm is not unlike that of the Bourrée. This particular Rigaudon, (V) begins on the strong beat, but later phrases often begin on the last quarter of the bar, as for example the second phrase, starting at the end of bar 2.

It is in C major, with a middle *minore* section in C minor at "*moins vif*". This is followed by a very chromatic modulatory link, leading to a return of the opening section at *tempo primo*. The repetition is exact except for slight changes in the last few bars.

A *Toccata* is a quick, brilliant keyboard composition, designed to show the executive skill of the performer.

This Toccata (VI), being the last movement of the suite, is in E minor, the same key as the first, though it ends in the major mode.

The first section is based on a series of pedals: E, bar 1; F sharp, 14; B flat, 29; F sharp, 42. After all this excitement the next section, starting at 57, is quieter and slower, and has a little tune over the continuous semiquaver rhythm. But the opening style of the movement recurs at 70, with pedals on B, G and D sharp in turn.

An inner melody, in longer notes, begins at 96, as can be seen from the arrangement of the stems. It ceases at 121, and the opening figure recurs in key C. An F sharp pedal starts again at 145, and there is again an inner melody, up to 172. The music gradually builds up to a *ff* climax at 206–16; and a brilliant coda, which starts at 217, builds up to a great *bravura* ending.

18

Elgar and Vaughan Williams

Elgar and Vaughan Williams stand out as the two greatest English composers in the first part of the twentieth century, thus holding a position similar to that of Debussy and Ravel in France. But it did not seem so thirty years ago, and it is too soon to say yet where they will stand thirty years hence.

Elgar achieved sudden fame in the first decade of the twentieth century, and for some time stood out as the musical equivalent of the Poet Laureate. But even then there were his detractors in England, and he has never been ranked as a great composer abroad. There are music lovers in England today who rank him with the immortals, while others dislike his music equally strongly. He was one of the last of the romantics, and romantic grandeur does not appeal to the young musicians of today. Perhaps the pendulum will swing again towards this kind of music in the years to come.

Thirty years ago Vaughan Williams seemed to be merely one of a group of equally important English composers which included Holst, Bax, Delius and Ireland. But Holst and Delius died in 1934 and, though they still have their admirers, their music is not heard very frequently today. Bax died in 1953, and it looks as if his music is gradually being forgotten. But Vaughan Williams lived till 1958, dying as a grand old man of eighty-six, and he was composing until the very end of his life. His stature seems to have risen steadily in in the last thirty years, so that he now ranks higher than his contemporaries mentioned above. Young students who read this book now will find it interesting to see what is the position thirty years hence.

One often reads that Elgar was self-taught; but all that "self-taught" really means in this case is that Elgar did not study composition under a famous teacher. He did not go to the Royal College of Music and learn from Parry or Stanford, as so many of his contemporaries did; he learned how to compose by making a study of the works of other composers. But, as a boy, he studied the violin, the piano, the organ, the bassoon, "theory" and harmony, by having lessons from his father or from local provincial teachers, just like anyone else.

Elgar's early works, which were mainly choral, were just like dozens of others which were turned out at the end of the nineteenth century, by composers whose names are now forgotten, for the "Three Choirs" the "Norwich" and similar festivals. Then, around 1899, something seemed to happen to Elgar, because the "Enigma" variations, produced in 1899, and "The Dream of Gerontius", produced in 1900, are inspired works of genius. Can it be that Newman's poem "Gerontius" had a catalytic effect? Until then he had not set any particularly good librettos, nor did he appear to have much sensitivity towards English poetry and the setting of it to music. Or did something happen in his private life in quiet Malvern to mature him? Perhaps he took longer to mature just because he was "self-taught". Certainly a great composer emerged suddenly, at this time. Elgar must have felt this himself because, at the end of the "Gerontius" score, he wrote "This is the best of me".

"Cockaigne" overture was composed in 1901, just after the "Enigma" variations and "The Dream of Gerontius" had been greeted with acclamation in Germany, but before the composer had become really well known in England. It was performed in June in the Queen's Hall, London, and had, as dedication "To my many friends, the members of British orchestras".

It had an immediate success and was subsequently performed at the Three Choirs Festival in the West Country, where he was born and still lived, and where most of his earlier choral works had received their first performances. It came at a time of rapidly changing fortunes; and by 1902 he had become so well known that he was asked to write the official ode in honour of Edward VII's coronation.

The best of Elgar's early works were written for strings (the Serenade, op. 20) or for small orchestra "Chanson de Matin" and "Chanson de Nuit", op. 15). In other words, he seemed to mature earlier on this side than on the vocal side, though fifteen years elapsed between the string serenade and the first symphony. Six years after the "Enigma" and four years after "Cockaigne", Elgar produced the "Introduction and Allegro for Strings", op. 47.

The "Enigma" variations, "The Dream of Gerontius", "Cockaigne" overture, and "Introduction and Allegro for Strings", four of Elgar's most popular works, are discussed below.

Although Vaughan Williams, like Elgar, was a West Countryman, he was sent to London for his musical education, after passing through Charterhouse and Cambridge. At the Royal College of Music he was a pupil of both Parry and Stanford, and so he was in the centre of English musical life while Elgar was still working quietly in the West Country.

He began to take an interest in old English music, both folk music and the music of the Tudor and Stuart composers. His well-known "Fantasia on Greensleeves" and his "Norfolk Rhapsodies" are instances of the former, and his "Fantasia on a theme of Tallis", analysed below, is an instance of the latter. But his interests ranged over every branch of music: hymns and church music; songs; symphonies; operas; ballets; and film music.

The overture to "The Wasps", which is analysed below, was written for a performance of the Aristophanes comedy at Cambridge University (Vaughan Williams' "Alma Mater") in 1909, and it uses themes heard in the play, for which he wrote the incidental music.

Enigma Variations: Elgar

This work is dedicated to "My friends pictured within", and consists of a series of portraits, all of which have a link with the opening "Enigma" theme.

It is tantalizing that no one knows what the "Enigma" is, or even if there really was one! "Dorabella", who wrote *Memories of a Variation* (publishers, Novello), thinks it was the line of the Malvern Hills, as seen from the composer's window. Others have suggested that the hidden theme is "life"; and yet others have discovered that "Auld Lang Syne" can be made to fit the theme. But Elgar had such a love of playful little jokes that it is quite possible he was just teasing, and there was no "enigma" at all.

The theme is in ternary form, in the minor key, with a middle section in the major. In the first section the short figures, starting on the second beat of the bar, and the leaping sevenths in the third and fourth bars are characteristics which are easily recognizable in the variations; and the flowing thirds in the middle section provide a good contrast.

C.A.E. (I) is a portrait of his wife, Lady Elgar, and uses the theme in different note-values. There is also a touch of the theme in the little triplet accompaniment figure, which first appears in the oboe in bar 3, and which represents the whistle Elgar gave to his wife on his return home.

H.D.S.P. (II) was an amateur pianist, who was in the habit of starting to play with a finger-loosening exercise. This is shown at the beginning of his portrait. The theme appears in the bass in bar 18, again in different note-values. This variation also changes to triple time.

R.B.T. (III) was a "character" with a didactic manner of speaking, hence the clipped, oboe version of the theme. Not only has the theme another time pattern, but it is now on a different chord scheme. The theme is in the major, though the tonic is still G. But the middle section moves to a remote key.

W.M.B. (IV) was an energetic Gloucestershire squire. The theme is back into G minor, with yet another rhythm. He was in the habit of giving orders to his guests for the day, and the sharp, vigorous ending represents the banging of the door as he went out.

R.P.A. (V) was the son of Matthew Arnold, and a "Gentleman of the old school". The key changes from G to E flat, but the theme reverts to its original time and rhythm. It is now in the 'cellos and basses, with a lovely counter-theme in the violins on the G string. When the first section returns the two themes change round.

Ysobel (*VI*) was a viola pupil of Elgar's, and this variation is based on an exercise on crossing the strings that Elgar wrote for her. The theme is, of course, in the violas, and the large intervals suggest that she was tall.

Troyte (*VII*) was nicknamed "the giddy ninepin", and the *presto* drums represent an occasion when Elgar tried to make him play the piano with one finger of each hand. The middle section of the theme is introduced in bar 5. Notice the unusual time signature—the variation is over in a flash.

After all this noise it is a pleasure to come to *W.N.* (*VIII*), a lady with a gracious old-world courtesy. The clarinet and the violin alternate in this charming variation, which has returned to the tonic key.

The end of this variation is one of the magic moments in music. There is a *pianissimo* chord of G in the strings. Then the lower strings quietly fade away, leaving a single G in the violins. Under this G the rest of the strings enter *ppp* with a chord of E flat, which is the beginning of the lovely variation "*Nimrod*" (*IX*). This represents Jaeger, a reader for Elgar's publisher, Novello, who was a close friend. He had a strong, vivid personality. But this variation is the result of a talk they had on Beethoven's slow movements. It starts in the strings only, but builds up to a wonderful climax. It has several times been used as a funeral march on important occasions, as at Elgar's own death, and the death of George VI.

It is customary to make a pause after "Nimrod". *Dorabella* (*X*), which follows is called an intermezzo, because this is not really a variation. Dorabella was a young, fairy-like girl, who was entranced to hear her portrait played by the composer just after it was composed. She had a slight stutter, which is shown in the music. In the middle of these fluttering figures appears a delicate viola solo.

(Elgar, himself, played the viola, so perhaps this theme represents him.) This variation is longer than any of the others except the finale, and it is played entirely by muted strings and woodwind.

G.R.S. (*XI*) was the organist of Hereford Cathedral, but the first part of his variation is a description of his dog rushing into the river, retrieving a stick. However, the theme is still there, and back in the tonic key.

B.C.N. (*XII*) was a 'cellist, so his variation opens with a 'cello solo, making impassioned use of the characteristic seventh. The cello *tutti* theme that follows is another lovely variant of the theme.

★★★ (*XIII*) appears to be anonymous, but it is now known that it represented a friend who was on the high seas at the time, a beautiful and charming woman. Elgar wishes her a good voyage by quoting from Mendelssohn's overture "Calm Sea and Prosperous Voyage" at bar 13. This has, as accompaniment, a quiet drum roll and a swaying figure in the violas which gives the effect of a slow-moving ship. But the main theme is also present, in yet another guise, starting at bar 4.

Elgar did not originally think of writing a finale, but he soon realized the need for a grand summing up, and this is provided in *E.D.U.* (*XIV*), which is a portrait of himself. Lady Elgar's pet name for her husband was "Edoo", hence "E.D.U.". It starts with a long tonic pedal, and contains references to the most potent influences in his life, Nimrod (at figure 68 in the bass) and Lady Elgar (at figure 73) with the whistle used to call his wife four bars before figure 73. The broad variant of the main theme at figure 79 adds a fitting peroration to the whole work.

The Dream of Gerontius, The Angel's Farewell: Elgar

When studying this work the student should know something about Cardinal Newman, as well as Elgar. Newman has been called the greatest poet of Victorian times, and his life story is told in Lytton Strachey's *Eminent Victorians*. The poem will not appeal to everyone, but the student should endeavour to get a sympathetic understanding of it. Students may not have realized that "Praise to the holiest in the Height", which is now in every hymn book, originally came from this poem.

The oratorio has a most moving overture, a fine chorus at the end of Part I, "Go forth", and a wonderful "timeless" opening to Part II. "The Angel's Farewell" at the end of the oratorio is briefly analysed in the following paragraphs.

"The Dream of Gerontius" owes a good deal to the influence of Wagner, and it uses the Wagnerian idea of *leitmotive* throughout the work. As "The Angel's Farewell" comes at the end of the work, it is natural that it should refer to many of these *leitmotive.*

The theme "Judgment" comes at figure 118 in the vocal score; and it works up rapidly to figure 120, where Elgar writes, in the full score "For one moment must every instrument exert its fullest force", as the Soul is "consumed, yet quickened by the glance of God". The Soul then sings "Take me away" to the theme "Novissima hora est"; and there are references in the next few pages to the themes "Sanctus", "Miserere", "Pace mihi", and "Presage" before the souls in Purgatory sing "Lord, Thou hast been our Refuge".

This leads into the "Angel's Farewell" section, which is the coda to the whole work. It begins with the lovely theme which has been called "Quiet, holy Rapture". At figure 129 the souls repeat "Lord thou hast been our Refuge", from figure 125; and figure 130 is derived from this also. At figure 131 the Angel sings the "Angel" theme; and at figure 132 there is a distant sound of the chorus of angels singing "Praise to the Holiest". The harp gradually comes into prominence; and, although the music is so quiet, it is scored for the Angel, semichorus, double chorus and full orchestra. The "Angel" and "Praise to the Holiest" theme alternate until the last few bars; and the work ends with a sevenfold Amen.

Cockaigne Overture: Elgar

The dictionary says that Cockaigne is "an imaginary land of idleness and luxury"; and also "(punningly, with reference to cockney) London". Fowler says it is "properly the name of a luxurious Utopia"; the name of it for London as the home of the cockneys is a mistake or a pun. However it is quite obvious here, from Elgar's sub-title "In London Town", which meaning is intended.

Elgar's picture of London is rather hard for us to imagine today. It was at the beginning of the gay, care-free Edwardian period, when London seemed to be the centre of the world. He shows us the grand, dignified side of London, the beauty of the parks with lovers strolling through them, cockney youngsters, and a military band marching down the street. Professor Tovey says that Elgar expressed his love of London in an overture neither more nor less vulgar than Dickens. It is as evocative of Edwardian London as the "Mastersingers" is of mediaeval Nuremberg; and it even has a diminution of a solemn theme by a cheeky cockney street boy, just as Wagner's apprentices parody the theme of the Mastersingers.

Elgar, like his contemporary Strauss, usually wrote for a very large orchestra. It was in the days when the cost did not need to be considered—a generation later composers tended to write for smaller orchestras, partly perhaps because they preferred to do so, but also because they realized that, by so doing, their work had more chance of performance.

"Cockaigne" is scored for the following woodwind: two flutes, two oboes, two clarinets, two bassoons and one double bassoon; that is, double, not triple woodwind, except for the double bassoon, though the second flute sometimes changes to the piccolo. But the brass is unusually heavy, so that the work sounds very noisy in performance. He requires four horns, two trumpets, two cornets, three trombones and a tuba; and he suggests that two extra trombones may be employed, doubling the parts of the other two tenor trombones, at frequent places in the score, notably when the military band is blaring out its theme. It is rare to use cornets in a symphony orchestra, but they add to the brassy climaxes here.

He also uses quite a lot of percussion, in addition to the usual timpani: bass drum, cymbals, side drum, triangle, sleigh bells, and a tambourine. They all add colour at appropriate moments, as for example the use of the bass drum and tambourine when the Salvation Army band approaches.

Finally, in addition to the strings, Elgar uses an organ at the end of the work. The music has reached a great climax, and one would say that no more noise was possible, when the organ enters, adding a noble splendour to the citizen theme.

The Boosey and Hawkes score contains a good and unusually full analysis of Edwin Evans, and use is made of this in the following paragraphs.

The overture is in sonata form and starts with a *scherzando* first subject in the violin, which swaggers along till it reaches a pause in the third bar, and reminds one of the style of a popular song of the period. It contains three themes, which appear in the violins: (*a*) in the opening bars and again at bars 7 and 8; (*b*) in bars 5 and 6; and (*c*) in bars 12 and 13. The *tutti* repetition of this section starts at 18, with a clash of cymbals and a roll on the side drum.

The second section of the first subject occurs at bar 27, and is marked "*nobilmente*", a musical term of which Elgar was very fond. It has become known as the "citizen" theme, and starts in the second violins and violas.

The transition begins at 37, and refers to the (*a*) theme of the first subject. It brings in the two extra trombones, but gradually quietens down and modulates to E flat major—notice the woodwind figure at 44, because it is used later.

The first section of the second subject starts in the strings in E flat major at 49 and represents a pair of lovers in a London park. Its continuation in the violin at 56 is also made use of later. Then the beginning of the theme returns at 64, an octave higher. Bar 56 reappears briefly at 75 and leads into the second section of the second subject at 79.

This consists of the second *nobilmente* section of the first subject from 27, now played *scherzando* in diminution, and is undoubtedly meant to be a perky youthful version of the sedate citizen theme. It starts on the clarinet and is later transferred to the violin, then to the oboe, then to the violin again. By 92 the semiquavers of the theme are developed alone, and lead to the (*b*) theme of the first section of the first subject at 95, played *ff*, and sounding much more assertive than it did before.

It is followed by the (*c*) theme at 99, and then (at 102) by a reference to the opening of the second subject. Bars 99–109 are based on a tonic pedal, and can be thought of as codetta. But the diminution at 79, in spite of being derived from part of the first subject, is important enough to be considered as a section of the second subject in its own right.

The development starts at 111 with the citizen theme in B flat major in strings alone. Its middle section (from 56) appears at 126, and is used in imitation. Then an episode starts at 134 with a new theme in the solo clarinet, which heralds the arrival of the military band. It alternates with snatches of the second subject for some time, but the cymbals and the side drum enter at 146 and the excitement grows as the band approaches, so that the other themes are ousted. Notice the quick scalic figure starting in 149, and the figure starting in trumpets and cornets at 152, both of which are used to whip up excitement for the entry of the band at 159.

The band theme enters on cornets and trombones, with cymbals, sleigh bells, triangle, bass drum and side drum as accompaniment. This section is blatantly noisy, though it probably gives a true picture of the excitement in the streets. It quietens down a little at 167, when the theme passes to the strings, but everyone plays *grandioso* again at 173.

At 178 the first three notes of the band theme are tossed about in the orchestra, and one realizes at 182 that they are also the beginning of the citizen theme in its diminuted form. There seems little doubt that this is meant to represent the street urchins following the band.

As the band dies away there is a hint of the first subject heard in the oboe at 189; and then the bass drum and the tambourine (196) herald the approach of a Salvation Army band. The clarinets and bassoons enter at 197 with a typical Salvation Army tune, starting in G flat major, which sounds horribly out of tune with the pedal bass on F. The pedal changes to F sharp and then G in an effort to fit with the clarinets, but now they have moved too; to A flat major!

But the episode is short. The lovers, at 212, reach a church and go inside, to take refuge from the noise of the outside world, and listen to a typical piece of organ improvization—two strands of meandering themes in invertible two-part counterpoint. Here Elgar makes use of woodwind instruments against strings, and they can easily be imagined as characteristic organ stops. It may seem strange that he should not use an organ, when one is down in the score. But he probably preferred to hold it in reserve for the climax in the coda. Quiet references to the lovers' theme (228, 230, 231) and the diminuted citizen's theme (233), mingling with the organ theme, bring a rapid return to the first subject in the tonic key and the recapitulation at 235.

The recapitulation starts with (*a*) of the first subject alternating with a development of (*b*). The theme (*a*) is played first by trombones (235), then by horns (237) then by trumpets and cornets (240), and then by upper woodwind (243), thus getting progressively lighter. The theme (*b*) is played by strings each time, and begins to work up to a climax at 237. Then (*c*) appears at 251, and builds up to a repetition of the first section, *tutti*, as at 18. But the second section of the first subject is not used here—Elgar was probably reserving it for the climax in the coda.

Rushing semiquavers (267–74), acting as a brief transition, lead to the first section of the second subject in the tonic key at 275, played *ff* by violins and horns. It quietens down for its continuation, still in violins and horns, starting at 282. Then it returns to its beginning as before, at 290, but now it is *pp*.

The second section of the second subject, the citizen theme in diminution, returns, also in C major, at 305, but it quietens down suddenly at 320, thus giving a chance for a quiet hint of the returning military band, starting at 323. The last section of the exposition, the codetta, is not repeated, and it could be considered that the return of the band episode marks the beginning of the coda, at 323. But it is still in C major, and Edwin Evans suggests that the coda starts at 342 with the modulation to E flat major and the entry of the organ with the citizen theme. Either interpretation is possible. The band returns in full at 330, and builds up to a noisy climax.

But with the entry of the organ and the *nobilmente* citizen theme the music takes on a new grandeur. Notice the footnote to bar 342, stating that the cornets must not be too prominent. Elgar probably thought that they might sound too trivial and cheap at this thrilling moment.

However, after broadening out to *allargando*, there is a last, sprightly reference to the first subject, with the piccolo, the side drum and the cymbals adding to the brilliance. A final bang on the bass drum brings the colourful overture to an abrupt end.

Introduction and Allegro for Strings: Elgar

This work is for string quartet combined and contrasted with string orchestra, in the style of the old *concerto grosso*. The opening provides one of the grandest and most sonorous effects that can be heard in the concert hall—it hardly seems possible that strings can produce so much tone.

After four bars of this sonority the quartet introduces a figure which is imitated by the *tutti* in bar 6. A third idea is introduced at bar 16, when the viola solo starts a melody which Elgar says was suggested by hearing some Welsh singers on a cliff in Cardigan Bay. Later he heard a similar melody containing drooping thirds in the Wye Valley; and this "Welsh" melody was inspired by these two occasions.

The *Allegro* starts at figure 7, and is in a loose kind of sonata form. The first subject is a major version of bar 5. The second subject starts at figure 10, with *staccato* semiquavers in the woodwind. After a reference to the opening bars at figure 12, a new theme appears in the violins and violas. It is again very sonorous, and makes much use of a rising seventh. The Welsh tune brings the exposition to a close.

The middle section consists of new material, and starts thirteen bars after figure 15, with a reversion to the signature of G minor. It is a *fugato* based on a peculiarly angular theme.

The recapitulation starts at figure 22, and the second subject returns in the tonic at figure 25. There is a *nobilmente* version of the opening bars at figure 27, followed by the sonorous theme containing rising sevenths, as before; and, after a *ff* climax, quartet and orchestra triumphantly play the Welsh theme in full. A *decrescendo* leads to a return of the theme from bar 5, but this rapidly rises to a climax, and ends with a unison G and a *pizzicato* chord.

Overture to The Wasps: Vaughan Williams

For a modern work this overture uses quite a small orchestra. It can be played with only one oboe, one bassoon, and one trumpet, instead of two of each, and with two horns instead of four, an indication that it was first performed by an amateur orchestra of limited numbers. The "battery" consists of bass drum, triangle and cymbals, and is much used to aid the spirit of jollification. The harp also plays an important part.

The overture divides itself into three main sections: bars 1–169, which contain two main tunes, in addition to the introductory buzz; bars 170–328, which contains a short figure, tossed about from one solo instrument to another, and a broad theme in E flat major, in addition to a certain amount of development of earlier themes;

and a third, recapitulatory section, bars 329–end, which uses the themes of the first section, and ends with a coda in which the first main theme is combined with the E flat theme of the middle section. It cannot be said to be in sonata form or another recognized form, but the three sections are clearly defined.

The first section starts with the buzzing of the wasps in the woodwind and string instruments in turn, with muted horns, occasional harp chords and soft booms on the bass drum adding to the effect. Cymbals enter *pp* at bar 49, and a rapid *crescendo* leads into the first main theme, **A**, at bar 58.

This is a rumbustious modal tune, played first by clarinet and bassoon in octaves, and immediately repeated by the violins. It is followed by an equally hearty second theme, **B**, in the violins in D major at bar 84. It begins *marcato* on the G string, and is combined with theme **A** in the 'cellos and basses. For most of the rest of this section these two themes are heard separately and combined, in D or F major. In addition, the buzzing recurs at 123, in rising and falling semitones.

The middle section begins at 170 with a change of key and rhythm, over which hints of theme **A** occur. Notice also a short figure beginning with a triplet which first occurs in the horn at 182. After a repetition of it in a solo violin at 186, the broad main theme, **C**, starts in E flat major at 191. It is heard first in horn and viola, then it is repeated by strings and upper woodwind at 199.

The buzz recurs at 212, and the little figure beginning with a triplet recurs, first in the oboe, then in the flute. This moves from one solo instrument to another for some time, until the buzz recurs at 237, combined with hints of **B** (245) and **A** (246, 259, etc.). Notice also the theme which first appears at 284. A big climax is worked up, in which harp *glissandos* are a feature.

Bars 327–9 change from *fff* to *ppp*, and the recapitulatory section starts with a return to theme **A** at 329, now in the oboe and bassoon. Theme **B** recurs at 355. The figure starting with a triplet is heard again at 393. Then **A** is combined with **C** at 403. **B** recurs at 413, followed immediately by **A** at 417, and the two alternate to the end.

Fantasia on a Theme by Tallis: Vaughan Williams

Vaughan Williams was very interested in hymns, and he edited the *English Hymnal*. He chose this theme by Tallis for inclusion as one of the hymns. Tallis was a member of the Chapel Royal from about the year 1542 until at least 1577. In 1567 he contributed nine tunes to Archbishop Parker's psalter, including the famous "Tallis's Canon". The tune which Vaughan Williams used for this work is one of this set.

The fantasia was written for the Gloucester Festival in 1910, and is scored for a large string orchestra, in which the leaders play as a separate string quartet, and the rest are divided into two orchestras, as instructed on the preliminary page of the score. The result is a wonderfully rich, polyphonic texture, just as sonorous and satisfying as Elgar's "Introduction and Allegro for Strings", though the style is very different.

The music is not based on the modern tonalities of major and minor keys, but goes back to the older modes. The theme itself is in the Phrygian mode: white notes of the piano E to E′, transposed to G. However the fantasia does not keep to this scale, but is full of "false relations". Look, for example, at the first five chords. The first is a major chord on G (G, B *natural*, D), but the third contains a minor triad of B *flat*, and it is followed by major triads of A flat and G flat, and then by a single D *natural*. This is neither modal nor in a major or minor key, though it is diatonic in the sense that G feels like the tonic throughout the fantasia. The false relations surely owe something to Purcell, though they are more stringent than his would be.

The rhythmic freedom of the fantasia has a Tudor flavour, and the parallel triads, involving consecutive fifths and octaves, as in bars 6–8, go back to an even earlier tradition, that of *organum*. Vaughan Williams' Mass in G minor is based on this idiom.

After hints of the theme in the opening bars it is heard in full, starting at bar 15. It contains three subsidiary motives: (*a*) bars 15–17; (*b*) bars 18–19 (syncopation); (*c*) bars 24, 28 and 29 ($\frac{6}{8}$ time); and all are made use of later. The theme is in unison in second violins, violas and 'cellos, with a bass below it and *tremolo* harmonies in the first violins above it. (Note the B flats and B naturals, as in bar 19.)

The theme is then repeated in full at 32, *appassionato*. The first violins now join the theme, while the second violins decorate in semiquavers. At bar 51 the two orchestras divide for the first time, using motives (*a*) and (*b*) antiphonally.

A viola solo at 79 introduces a middle section, in which the (*c*) $\frac{6}{8}$ figure appears *piu animato* in a decorated form. The first violin solo then takes it up, and soon the whole solo quartet is playing antiphonally to the orchestras. The texture for the next few pages is very complicated, with the twelve parts making ever-new combinations.

By 149 however they have all merged into one grand stream of sound, which builds up to a magnificent *largamente* climax at 173. Gradually it quietens down, and a few bars *molto adagio* lead to the return to *tempo del principio* at 194.

A violin solo now has the original theme in its entirety, with the solo viola weaving a counterpoint below it and the orchestras accompanying *tremolo, sur la touche*. Bar 211 starts a coda in which, after further references to the theme, the first violin solo soars to a *ppp* ending.

19

English Vocal Music

In the past, England has been more interested in vocal than in instrumental music. The singing of Handel's oratorios started a great choral tradition, which was later nourished on the oratorios of Mendelssohn—"Elijah" was written for Birmingham. Native composers of lesser importance continued to supply similar works; and at the end of the nineteenth century English composers were providing oratorios and cantatas for the many amateur choirs throughout the country. Parry and Stanford were the greatest of these composers, but their works are rarely performed today.

Elgar continued this tradition, writing for the Three Choirs' Festival of Gloucester, Hereford and Worcester in his native West Country. His early cantatas are rarely heard today, but his oratorios "The Dream of Gerontius" (referred to in the last chapter), "The Apostles" and "The Kingdom" are still regularly performed.

A generation later Walton continued the tradition, though his exciting work "Belshazzar's Feast" was considered unsuitable for performance at the Worcester Festival. It was certainly very different from "Messiah" and "Elijah".

Walton has also written one opera "Troilus and Cressida". But the first English composer of stature to write a number of operatic works was Britten. "Peter Grimes" was his first opera and was a great success.

Britten seems to be more interested in the setting of words than in purely orchestral music. In addition to his operas he has written many choral works, both sacred and secular. He has set words by older classical poets, such as Michelangelo and John Donne, but he also often seeks out poems by obscure or unusual poets, sometimes of a kind that one would not expect to be set to music. The first six numbers of his "Ceremony of Carols" are analysed below.

The British Isles, like every other country, has a rich store of traditional folk songs. Many were collected and written down at the beginning of the twentieth century, when they were nearly dying out in the country villages. Cecil Sharp was the first great folk song collector, but both Vaughan Williams and Britten, among others, continued to collect and arrange folk music of all kinds. Britten's modern accompaniments to traditional folk songs are well known.

The solo "art" song dates back to Elizabethan days, and Dowland wrote some lovely "ayres" with lute accompaniment. Thereafter there was a steady stream of airs and ballads, with Playford, Blow, Purcell, Arne, Boyce, Dibdin, Shield, Bishop and Horn carrying on the tradition. Arne's "When daisies pied" and "Rule Britannia" and Horn's "Cherry Ripe" are well-known examples of solo songs written in the eighteenth and early nineteenth centuries.

The works of the romantic German *lieder* writers, Schubert, Schumann, Mendelssohn and Brahms became known in England in the nineteenth century. Sterndale Bennett, who wrote "Maydew" was a friend and disciple of Mendelssohn. But it is Parry and Stanford, at the end of the century, who brought the art song to fruition in England. Stanford's "Songs of the Sea" are discussed below.

In the twentieth century England has produced many fine song writers, including Bax, Ireland, Delius, Vaughan Williams, Frank Bridge, Peter Warlock, Armstrong Gibbs, Gerald Finzi and Britten. Three songs by Delius and four by Warlock (the latter from *A Book of Songs*, published by Oxford University Press) are discussed below.

Songs of the Sea: Stanford

"Songs of the Sea" is a cycle of five songs, with words by Newbolt, written for baritone solo, male voice chorus and orchestra. It was composed in 1904. In this group of songs the words are as important as the music, and the student should know something about both Newbolt and Stanford.

British music owes more to Stanford today that is perhaps generally realized. He was not only a prolific composer, who contributed to the re-birth of British music at the end of last century, but he was also a great teacher, both at Cambridge and at the Royal College of Music, London. Holst, Vaughan Williams and John Ireland were all pupils of his. Perhaps, if he had been less prolific, his music would be better known today. But his Irish rhapsodies, and some of his choral works and songs are performed occasionally.

"*Drake's Drum*", I, is well known. Although the piano accompaniment is simple, the steady, tramping crotchets and the muted drum roll are most effective. The song is strophic; but the last verse is in the tonic major, *largamente*, and with many of the note-values in augmentation. (For example, the first phrase is spread over four bars instead of two.) It also modulates much more freely in the second half of the verse.

The optional male voice chorus takes a more important part in the second song "*Outward Bound*", II. The words are full of nostalgia for the land, while the swinging triplets of the accompaniment in $\frac{9}{8}$ give an impression of the moving sea. The time signature, $\frac{3}{4}$, given in brackets in the voice part, may create some confusion. In reality there are only two bars (bars 5 and 11) where Stanford has actually *written* in $\frac{3}{4}$ time, though there are a number of other places in both solo voice and chorus where he has used duplets. It would have been more consistent to have used the duplet sign whenever the division of the beat into two occurred. There are slight differences in rhythm between the two verses, and the chorus is made use of in the short coda.

Drake is the subject again in "*Devon, O Devon*", III. The continuous quavers in the bass in the first two verses give the impression of Drake pacing the deck, waiting for action. The last verse becomes more exciting, with its off-beat chords in the right hand, its augmentation of the tune at "all day tight'ning" and "twilight grey", and its extension on "wind and rain" at the end.

"*Homeward Bound*", IV, gives a picture of a great ship gliding home, and of seeing the chalk cliffs of England through the mist. The swaying $\frac{6}{4}$ rhythm aptly suggests the movement of the ship.

The introductory six bars are a voyage in themselves, because they start in D flat major, modulate abruptly to A major, and pass through F major before returning to the tonic. Stanford frequently goes to A major in this song, and it is the most remote key it is possible to reach from D flat major. Was it a demonstration to his pupils of how it could be done, or is it an attempt to provide the contrast to the homecoming? The remoteness of the key is certainly significant.

The voice enters at bar 7 with two three-bar phrases, which start in the tonic but again reach A major at bar 12. The orchestral parts make an enharmonic change, from flats to sharps, in order to reach this key, but the voice does not do so, and is therefore written in B double-flat major. However another two-bar phrase brings the music home to the tonic key again at 15.

The orchestra then starts a gliding figure over a tonic pedal and repeats it six times, while baritone and chorus move quietly over the top. At 21–2 the voices imitate each other at "Northward she glides"; and "enchanted haze" (23–5) is on an inverted dominant seventh which seems about to resolve into key C. But, after a pause, F major is established at 28 instead; and "faint on the verge" moves to E flat minor at 30 and to F flat major at 32 before returning to the tonic key for the end of the verse.

In the second verse the orchestral accompaniment starts an octave higher than in the first verse, and the first bar of the baritone solo (40) is different. Otherwise there is little difference between the verses until 56, when the music goes to A major instead of suggesting C major as in the first verse. But after a pause at the end of 59 the final *piu lento* section moves home to the tonic key for the words "there lies the home". The orchestra ends with the gliding figure over the tonic pedal that first occurred in bar 15.

"*The Old Superb*", V, is the story of the "lame duck" of Nelson's fleet. It is a simple three-verse strophic song; but notice how Stanford changes the quaver rhythm to crotchets at "Old Superb is old and foul and slow", and also at "lame duck lagging, lagging all the way". This is similarly changed and suited to the words in verses 2 and 3 also.

Songs: Delius

Delius, the English composer with German-Dutch parents, was intended for a business career, and in his youth he made business visits to Scandinavia, where he came in touch with Norwegian music. As he would not settle in business he was sent to Florida as an orange planter; but eventually, through the intervention of Grieg, was allowed to go to Leipzig to study music. Grieg was living at Leipzig at that time, and Delius was more influenced by him than by his teachers at the conservatory. His earliest works, and particularly his songs, show this Grieg influence clearly.

His first published song was "Two Brown Eyes", with words by the Dane, Hans Anderson. Then followed five songs from the Norwegian, including "Sunset" with words by A. Munck; and seven songs from the Norwegian, including "Cradle Song" with words by Ibsen, and "Venevil" with words by Björnson. Both sets were dedicated to Nina, wife of Grieg, who was a famous singer. They were written between 1888 and 1890.

Sunset

This song gets its atmosphere with the quiet *tremolo* chords of the accompaniment and the simple rhythmic rise and fall of the melody. The three verses have the same melody, which is in a simple binary form, with the first half ending in the dominant key and the second half returning to the tonic. The last line of the verse ends on a discord and the piano then carries on for three bars, leading to a repetition of the last line of words, now ending with a perfect cadence. The piano ends the song with a *ppp* coda of three bars.

Grieg also set this poem by Munck (or Munch), and students may like to compare the two settings. It is op. 9, no. 3.

Cradle Song

The words of "Cradle Song" are by Ibsen, the great Norwegian dramatist. Students will know of "Peer Gynt", and may have heard of other plays, such as "The Doll's House". Grieg set seven of Ibsen's songs besides writing incidental music to "Peer Gynt".

This is another short and simple song. But, although the style of the accompaniment is so simple, the harmonies are quite modern and chromatic, and the tonality has some surprising shifts. The syncopation in the first bar is a feature throughout the song.

The first verse starts quietly in D flat major over a double tonic and dominant pedal. But bar 6 introduces an augmented triad, which leads unexpectedly into F major, though the tonality is not confirmed until the first bar of the second verse. Then it immediately shifts away again, and two bars later a tonic and dominant pedal in key A flat establishes itself for the rest of the verse.

The third verse returns to the key and theme of the first verse, but changes after five bars, so as to stay in the tonic key. However, like the previous song, the last line of words ends with a discord and the piano carries on, leading to a repetition of the line, now ending with a perfect cadence.

Sweet Venevil

Björnson, who wrote the words of this song is perhaps Norway's greatest poet, and his statue, like Grieg's, is in a prominent position in Bergen.

The original words are, of course, Norwegian, so both German and English words are translations, and the meaning has become a little obscure in translation. But there is no doubt that the girl weaves a garland for a fickle lover, who throws it away, and goes off to enjoy the Midsummer Eve festivities. The last words in German are "guard thy wreath", and there is no reference to being his bride, as there is in the English words.

This song, like the other two, could almost be by Grieg. The two verses are exactly alike, and the style is simple, almost folk-song-like. The melody begins in C major, moves into A minor, and then returns to C major. The lilting $\frac{6}{8}$ rhythm has a dancing effect, and the leaps in the tune, particularly at the cadences, add to the carefree mood.

Songs: Warlock

Philip Heseltine, whose tragic death in 1930 was a great loss to British music, was a writer and music critic of distinction, who made a particular study of old English music, and transcribed and edited many old works, including six volumes of *English Ayres.*

But he was conscious of a dual personality, and he adopted the pen-name "Peter Warlock" for his own compositions. He was a friend and admirer of Delius and Van Dieren, both of whom influenced him as a composer. He is known chiefly as a composer of songs which, although very varied in style, all show a feeling for the poetry of the words, and beautiful, often unusual harmonic colouring. Many of them make use of early English poets, and they have an Elizabethan or folk-song atmosphere. He also wrote an unusually large number of carols.

Sleep

"Sleep", as befits a poem by Fletcher, has an Elizabethan feeling about it, though the harmonies are twentieth century. Its rhythm is very free, with the quaver as the unit, and the bar lines acting as guiders rather than denoting a strong beat. Compare the first and second verses, to see how the differences are dictated solely by the rhythm of the words.

Pretty Ring Time

All the above comments apply equally to the song "Pretty Ring Time". Here there are four verses with subtle differences in both tune and accompaniment between each. Notice the bell-like effect in the piano at the beginning of verse 3, and also how the accompaniment gets fuller and more exciting for each verse. Do not try to look for modulations. E flat is the key centre throughout, though a fair number of chromatic chords are used, and the frequent D flats give a modal flavour. Students may be able to compare this with Morley's setting of the same words.

The Lover's Maze

Although the words of "The Lover's Maze" are again Elizabethan, and the melodic line and the cadences have an Elizabethan flavour, this song is much more modern in conception. The tune itself is quite diatonic, and begins and ends in F minor, with obvious modulations to A flat major, C minor and B flat minor. The minor key cadences end with major tonic chords, as is customary with older music; and the falling quaver figure, which is used sequentially in the third and fourth bars of the melody and again at the last two cadences, is Elizabethan in style. But, in contrast to the tune, the harmonies are very modern and discordant. They seem to take their clue from the title, and create the effect of a maze. Not only are there frequent "false relations", and effects such as the chord of A flat major followed by the chord of D major at the end of bar 1, but there are many very discordant passages, such as that at the words "delight not yourselves for to stand and gaze". Warlock seems to be revelling in getting as many different clashes against the tune as possible, for his harmonization of each of the three verses is different.

Cradle Song

"Cradle Song", is the most discordant of these four songs, so it is perhaps not surprising that, as the preface says, it fell on deaf ears at first. Even the tune contains quite difficult intervals, and at times the conflicting harmonies make it very difficult to hold the vocal part. It is a modern version of the dorian mode, with G as a clearly-felt tonic, but with very chromatic harmonies. There are few "full closes" that are quite as unusual as that made by the final two chords. Yet, in spite of the harmonic dissonance, the soothing lilt of the cradle song is clearly felt throughout and after the augmentation in the last two bars of the voice part, the accompaniment slows down into silence.

A Ceremony of Carols: Britten

"A Ceremony of Carols" was written in 1942, when Britten was 29. This was before he had written any of his operas, and in the same year that he wrote his "Hymn to St. Cecilia". These two works and four British folk songs appear to be the only works that he composed that year; and the words perhaps provided an escape from the horrors of war.

"A Ceremony of Carols" is for three-part treble choir and harp, but the harp part can be played on the piano. There are eleven numbers and the first six of them are analysed here.

"*Procession*" forms a lovely opening to the work. It uses the plainsong melody which is the Gregorian antiphon sung for vespers on Christmas day in the Roman Catholic Church. It is therefore in a free rhythm and the words are in Latin. It was usual for the opening line of a plainsong melody to be sung as a solo, before the entry of the main body of singers; also the singers went a little slower at the end of every line. Several notes to one syllable were called a "neum", and the first note of the group was given a slight emphasis. Otherwise the rhythm was as much like speech rhythm as possible. Strings of quavers in a plainsong melody, like the quavers in "Procession", are not meant to be sung as *equal* quavers; they are varied according to the importance of the syllable.

"Procession" is deliberately monotonous. The voice rises and falls according to the significance of the words, and there is no "tune" in the ordinary sense of the word. The whole of the first page lies within the compass of four notes. The voice rises higher and higher and becomes more exultant at the top of the second page and then falls in pitch towards the end.

Having started in Latin, the words now change to mediaeval English. It might be as well to translate the words of "*Wolcum Yole*!" into modern English in case the meaning has not been realized. Notice that, in the middle section starting at bar 22, the three voice parts have independent words for a time, each referring to a different saint's day that occurs in the Christmas period: Thomas the martyr before Christmas; St. Steven, 26 December; St. John, 27 December; and Innocents' day, 28 December.

The first section is a chordal welcome in A major. Then comes the more contrapuntal middle section, starting with imitative entries in bar 22. It moves away from A major at 33 and changes to *pp* at 38, with delicate quavers in the harp accompanying the dotted minim vocal welcome to the Queen of Bliss, the Virgin Mary, at Candlemas on 2 February.

The return to the opening key and theme occurs at 55 but now it is marked *ppp* and *pppp*. However it gradually gets louder until it ends *ff*. Notice the unexpected chord at 77, making a very unusual final cadence.

The accompaniment of "*There is no rose*" is very slight. Except for a few bars (46–50) it is built entirely on an *ostinato* bass of C and F. But the harmonies in both harp and voice move very freely over it, as, for example in bar 29 where C sharp and F sharp are heard against it. However the song begins and ends in concordance, and in F major.

English and Latin words alternate. The English words have the tune, with a return to the opening at "Leave we all this werldly mirth" at 36, after the modulatory section on the previous page. The Latin words act as a kind of refrain, on one note, C, until 28 when "Gloria in Excelsis" rises to a magnificent climax. "Transeamus" also moves freely at 42–50, but 57 returns to the repeated Cs again. The three voice parts sing in unison from 42 to the end. Apart from the *basso ostinato* the harp plays only when the voices are singing in Latin.

"*That Yonge Child*" is a solo, in the style of a *recitative*, and again the words are mediaeval English. The first verse refers to the Virgin, and it is centred on C. The second verse refers to the nightingale, and changes to A, but becomes very chromatic and almost atonal when the songs of the two are compared.

The harp alternative to the first three notes may puzzle some students. The sounds are the same as the version in large print, but by being written in this way they can be played on three different strings, which is easier than plucking the same string twice.

Notice that this figure occurs throughout the song, whether the key is centred on C or A. The voice ends on F sharp C sharp, but the little three-note figure continues as before, and ends the song, *pp*, with a chord of C sharp major underneath it.

The well-known words of "*Balulalow*" are a translation of part of the Christmas Eve carol which Luther wrote for his son, Hans, and were first published in 1535. The brothers James, John and Robert Wedderburn translated the whole fifteen stanzas in 1567, under the title "Ane Sang of the Birth of Christ", in "Ane Compendious Buik of Godly and Spirituall Sangis".

It starts with a treble solo and is in F sharp minor. The time is $\frac{6}{4}$, but the accompaniment is slurred throughout so as to sound like $\frac{3}{2}$. The solo starts with a minim and crotchet rhythm in $\frac{6}{4}$, which gives the effect of a cross-rhythm against the accompaniment. At "I sall rock" however, the minims in the voice part are an augmentation, and join the $\frac{3}{2}$ of the accompaniment.

The three-part chorus enters with a repetition of the solo. This section is extended slightly, and then the solo enters again, forming a short coda with the chorus. Notice the mixture of major and minor thirds in the final chords.

"*As Dew in Aprille*" are well-loved words that may be known in settings by other composers. An unusual canon starts at bar 12. At first the third voice has the antecedent, with the consequent divided between the first and second voice parts. Then, at 21, the middle voice takes the antecedent, with the consequent divided between first and third voices. Then, at 30, the first voice takes its turn of having the antecedent. This is followed by a climax in three-part harmony at "Mother and Mayden was never none but she".

The harp accompaniment is specially worthy of notice in this song. At first it has *arpeggi* in octaves. Then, at bar 11, appears the direction *bisbigliando e legato*. *Bisbigliando* means "whispered", and it is a special effect on the harp caused by rapid and very soft repetitions of a figure. The alternation changes to chords at 22; then, at 40, there is a *glissando* effect which is possible only on the harp. Instructions are given for chromatic tuning of all the seven notes of the scale, and a *glissando* can then be played over all the strings. A *glissando* on black keys is suggested as an alternative, if the accompaniment is played on the piano.

"*This little Babe*" is by the sixteenth-century poet Robert Southwell. It has four verses, and the first three are alike except that verse 1 is in unison; verse 2 has a canon between the first and second voices, and the third voice; while verse 3 has all three parts in canon with each other. Verse 4 begins in three-part harmony, but is developed from the same tune. The last page is in augmentation (quaver equals crotchet), and is in unison again, until the last three chords. The song is in E flat minor until the last page, when it changes to E flat major.

The harp again has an *ostinato* effect, with the chord of E flat minor and occasional modifications of it used until the last verse. These reiterations are a harp effect that is awkward to play on the piano. The last verse has more freely-moving chords, leading to the augmented *ff* climax.